THE 452ND ANTI-AIRCRAFT ARTILLERY BATTALION

THE 452ND ANTI-AIRCRAFT ARTILLERY BATTALION

DESTROYERS OF THE LUFTWAFFE AND JIM CROW

SAMUEL DE KORTE

Pen & Sword
MILITARY
AN IMPRINT OF PEN & SWORD BOOKS LTD.
YORKSHIRE – PHILADELPHIA

First published in Great Britain in 2025 by
Pen & Sword Military
An imprint of
Pen & Sword Books Ltd
Yorkshire - Philadelphia

ISBN 978 1 39903 210 0

A CIP catalogue record for this book is available from the British Library.

Typeset in INDIA by IMPEC eSolutions
Printed and bound in England by CPI (UK) Ltd.

The Publisher's authorised representative in the EU for product safety is Authorised Rep Compliance Ltd., Ground Floor, 71 Lower Baggot Street, Dublin D02 P593, Ireland.
www.arccompliance.com

For a complete list of Pen & Sword titles please contact:

PEN & SWORD BOOKS LIMITED
George House, Units 12 & 13, Beevor Street,
Off Pontefract Road, Barnsley, S71 1HN, UK
E-mail: enquiries@pen-and-sword.co.uk
Website: www.pen-and-sword.co.uk

or

PEN AND SWORD BOOKS
1950 Lawrence Rd, Havertown, PA 19083, USA
E-mail: uspen-and-sword@casematepublishers.com
Website: www.penandswordbooks.com

MIX
Paper | Supporting responsible forestry
FSC® C013604
FSC
www.fsc.org

Contents

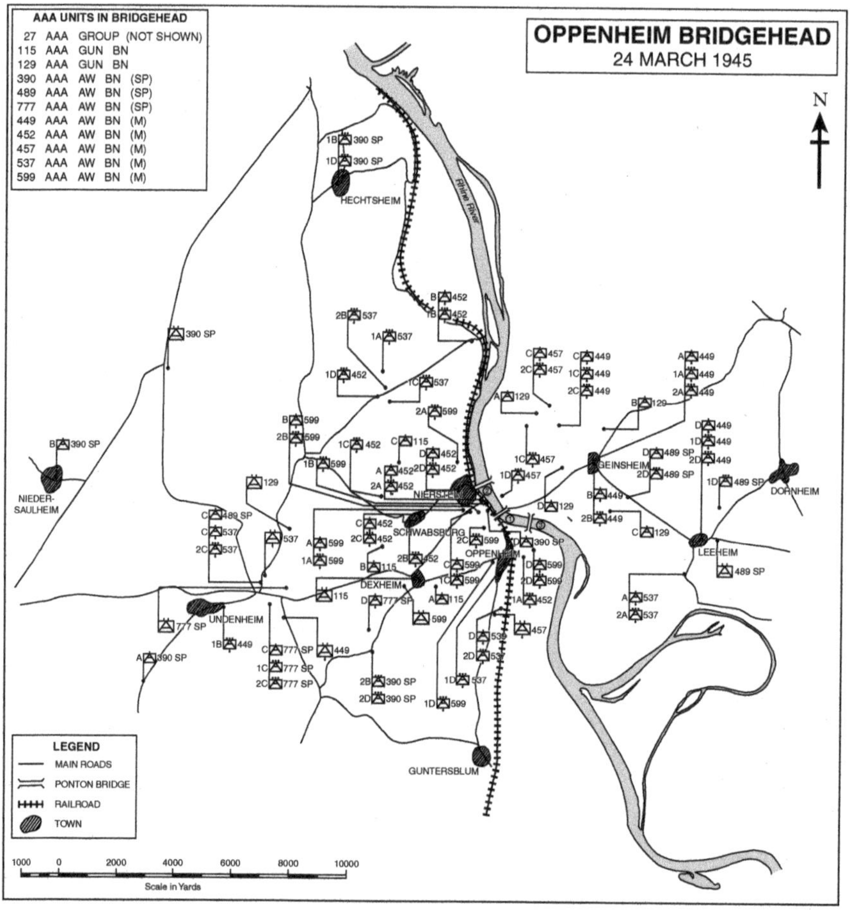

The Oppenheim Bridgehead on 24 March 1945. The positions of the 452nd AAA are marked on the map.

Foreword

African American military history is often misunderstood because many academics and historians tend to focus on well known military figures and units that have already received a fair share of coverage. The *452nd Anti-Aircraft Artillery Battalion* by Samuel de Korte sheds light on a lesser known unit that is rarely covered. Prior to 1950, most Black military history was written by Black military veterans and historians. White authors who wrote about the African American military experience often relied on military records as well as biased and racist-informed narratives written by white military officers of Black regiments, military leadership and U.S. domestic policy. De Korte, who is from the Netherlands, uses these records as one element, in addition to significant research on the lives and narratives of Black soldiers from traditional and nontraditional sources, to help craft the first publication to focus on the service of the 452nd Anti-Aircraft Artillery Battalion.

Although some authors and historians who focused on the experiences of Black soldiers during the Second World War provided new insights, more often than not they wrote about historical narratives that have already been explored. Ultimately, this leads to these narratives serving as a representation of the overall African American military experience, which contributes to misunderstanding and misinformation surrounding this subject matter. An example of this would be the Tuskegee Airmen. Over the years the majority of narratives surrounding the Tuskegee Airmen focused on the men who flew fighter aircraft in the unit. Over time, as interest grew, more research was done and more information about the pilots and their experiences emerged. However, little information about ground and support staff was included in the emerging narratives. In addition, the experiences of other African Americans in United States Army Air Forces, such as Engineer Aviation Battalions or Air Base Security Battalions, were also overlooked. As a result, this approach, combined with the limited documentation and misinformation that has been passed off as complete and truthful narratives about the African American military experience ultimately led to a disproportionate focus on African American frontline combat units rather than on the support units in which the bulk of African Americans served in the Second World War.

Despite this, the role African Americans played in military history and the legacy of their service had a broad and significant impact on how we understand this history. From detailing the connection between military service and community advocacy for African Americans in the nineteenth and twentieth centuries to how the military addressed the legal rights of soldiers, the stories of these brave men and women have been overlooked, ignored or diminished. De Korte takes a welcome departure in his approach by telling the story of the Black military experience, and in particular in detailing the impact of the 452nd Anti-Aircraft Artillery Battalion in the Second World War.

Although De Korte's book focuses largely on the soldiers and their combat experience, he offers a glimpse into the lives of Black military personnel beyond the battlefield. His retelling of how Black soldiers found allies in the people of the UK provided context for the fight back home. Unlike their experiences in America, battling Jim Crow and the efforts to deny their humanity, in the UK their humanity was not in question. The brutal clashes between the people seeking to uphold the social structures that depended on maintaining Jim Crow and Black soldiers, was a uniquely American experience. Abroad, there were more clashes between white American soldiers and UK citizens, often triggered by the latter group's defense of the injustices experienced by Black soldiers.

The *452nd Anti-Aircraft Artillery Battalion* provides a unique insight into a lesser known African American combat support unit and works towards completing the picture of the often overlooked roles that these soldiers contributed in the war effort. De Korte's contribution to the history of the 452nd and its experiences not only sheds light on the role they played in the war effort, but also highlights the importance of their service as Black soldiers in an Anti-Aircraft Artillery unit as well as the impact of Jim Crow despite their triumphant service overseas. I hope readers will come away with a new appreciation for the many roles in which African Americans served during the war, as well as inspiration to learn more about African American units like the 452nd AAA.

Cale Eric Carter II
Director of Exhibitions/Historian
Buffalo Soldiers Museum, Houston

Introduction

On 7 December 1941, the American soldiers and sailors at the Pearl Harbor Naval Base in Hawaii were rudely awakened by the sound of sirens. Imperial Japanese aircraft flew overhead, bombing and strafing the ships and the airfield. Two waves of aircraft and other vessels attacked the U.S. Navy ships and the surrounding installations. Although the Japanese suffered a few casualties in aircraft and personnel killed, the losses were nothing compared to the damage they inflicted on their enemy. Four battleships were sunk and four more were damaged. More than 3,500 soldiers and sailors were killed or wounded.

The very same day that the United States was dragged into the Second World War, Mess Attendant Second Class Doris Miller distinguished himself in combat on board the United States Navy battleship USS *West Virginia* (*BB-48*). Despite being a cook, Miller assisted the fatally wounded Captain Mervyn S. Bennion, and later manned a Browning .50 caliber anti-aircraft machine gun, firing at Japanese aircraft. After running out of ammunition, he assisted wounded sailors.

While several Americans earned medals on a day "which will live in infamy", as President Franklin Roosevelt described it,[1] Doris Miller was not among them. Captain Bennion, however, was awarded the Medal of Honor for staying at his post despite being wounded. It was only after much effort from the Black press that Miller was credited for his actions and was awarded the Navy Cross. Miller was then used in a war bond drive and he later reported for duty on the escort carrier USS *Liscome Bay* (*CVE-56*). On 24 November 1943, the carrier was torpedoed by the Japanese submarine *I-175* and sank. Miller went down with his ship and was later declared dead, although his legacy continues with the USS *Doris Miller* (*CVN-81*), an aircraft carrier due to be launched by the U.S. Navy in 2029.

From the very first day of the U.S. entry into the Second World War, Black American soldiers were active in combat. Also from the very beginning, was the participation of Black American soldiers forgotten, ignored, or actively withheld from the public. With the history of the 452nd Anti-Aircraft Artillery Battalion, that too is the case. Frequently mentioned as an example of a Black American combat unit during the Second World War, their Wikipedia page was just a paragraph with a photo. It made me curious. This unit was mentioned for their exemplary service, but details of their service were not documented. I asked my professors at university about it, because this unit had so little information, while other units had a lot of information available. That was a long time ago, but it set me down the path of Black American soldiers during the Second World War.

The contributions of Black American soldiers at the frontline or behind it, are not as well-known as they should be. This book strives to raise awareness for Black American soldiers during the Second World War, focusing on the 452nd AAA to give the unit the credit that it deserves.

The anti-aircraft artillery is different from other services in that it is in essence largely defensive. The anti-aircraft gunners wait for the enemy to approach them and then engage them. As such, there are many days or hours of waiting, and minutes or seconds of combat. As such, the history of anti-aircraft artillery battalions is less the stuff of epics than, for example, armored units.

The "primary mission" of this book, to use the terminology of the Anti-Aircraft Artillery Command, is to share the history of the 452nd Anti-Aircraft Artillery Battalion during the Second World War. The "secondary mission" is to describe the experiences of Black American soldiers during the Second World War, using this battalion as a vehicle for it. Lastly, the goal is to explain the development and employment of anti-aircraft artillery automatic weapon battalions in Europe.

In this book, there will be encounters with (verbal) abuse. This might offend contemporary readers. The decision is made to maintain these instances, offensive as they might be, because they give a glimpse into the past as it were. The past as a whole should be examined, both the good and the bad, to understand and appreciate the service of Black American soldiers during the Second World War. There will be occurrences of racial prejudice and invective. Removing them from this research could potentially give the impression that several issues did not exist or were not such a big deal at that time, neither of which is true. Thus, uncomfortable as it might be, the decision is made to keep everything.

Race and ethnicity are oft-debated topics in the United States. In this book, the decision is made to capitalize Black as an acknowledgment of shared history and cultural background, while white is not capitalized. The reason is that capitalizing white would lend credibility to the ideas of white supremacists, which is the opposite of what this book wants to achieve.

The soldiers of the 452nd AAA seem to have left few written sources. Most information is derived from the reports after action, produced by the battalion, or their unit reports. These reports were sometimes written far from the events they described and as such might contain errors. I tried to weed out as many of them as possible. If any remain, I am to blame for this. Additional information is derived from other documents, such as general orders, and from white soldiers who wrote about their experiences alongside the 452nd AAA.

This book has been several years in the making. From the time I first read about their history online, which was just a single paragraph, to the creation of this book that narrates the history of the 452nd AAA.

I didn't do this alone and I've received help from many people. This project was made possible through a subsidy from the Dutch Ministry of Education, Culture and Science, and the Stichting Lira Fonds. I'd like to thank Catharine Giordano, archivist at the *Stars and Stripes* Central Office – Archives and Library, Lisa Newman of the United States Army Heritage and Education Center. Bill Cosgrove, who wrote a book about the 945th Field Artillery Battalion, and Dr Bryon Greenwald, an expert on anti-aircraft artillery. On a personal level, I would like to thank my parents Clemens and Helma, as well as my siblings Marilou and Valentijn. Also, I want to thank Marijn Neefjes, Joris Moens, Jasper Heuer, Jonathan Mafaabi. Thank you for your friendship, wanted (and unwanted) advice, and for making my life better just by being in it. Likewise, I wanted to thank several people who inspired me during my pursuit of history: Dr Laura Jarnagin Pang, Jim Lankford, Joe Wilson Jr, Dr Judith Brouwer. You've all made this directly and indirectly possible.

Lastly, I want to thank you the reader, for taking the time to read this book. In doing so, you're keeping the memory of the 452nd Anti-Aircraft Artillery alive and ensuring that their deeds are not forgotten.

Chapter 1

Higher, Faster, Stronger

Ever since the days of the first hot air balloons, people have been thinking about ways to weaponize them. As early as 1794 anti-aircraft defenses were tested. During the American Civil War (1861–1865), the Union Army Balloon Corps was established, where the balloons served as aerial reconnaissance. When Paris, France, was besieged in 1870 by Prussian troops, hot air balloons were used to carry messages and people out of the city.

On 17 December 1903, the Wright Flyer, made by the brothers Orville and Wilbur Wright, had its first flight. Although it flew for just twelve seconds, it marked the beginning of aviation. In less than a decade, aircraft and ways to counter them had been weaponized:

> The first aerial bombing in World War I occurred on 30 August 1914 when a single German plane dropped several bombs on Paris, but there are also authentic accounts of bombing from airplanes in the Italian Campaign (1911) and in the war between Spain and Morocco in 1913. Zeppelin raids on London followed the Paris bombing and by October 1914, development of defense from the ground became imperative. The first anti-aircraft weapons were crude improvisations – guns taken from field artillery batteries, placed on temporary mounts, and fired in a skyward direction. Fire-control and technical developments were rudimentary but since planes were slow and bombing techniques were still undeveloped, this earliest anti-aircraft artillery served a purpose somewhat commensurate with the limited needs of the time. As the war progressed, improved

> pursuit planes and increasing effectiveness of anti-aircraft artillery forced the inauguration of night bombing. As a result, searchlights and sound location instruments were brought into use as auxiliaries to increase the effectiveness of night firing.[1]

The airplane had become a fierce weapon of war. Initially, its primary use was reconnaissance, although later it took on an offensive role as well. Aircraft were used to strafe or bomb enemy positions or to patrol the skies against hostile aircraft. In the static ground war, the skies provided the only opportunity to reconnoiter enemy positions.

The advent of bombers, such as the German Gotha G.V., or the British Handley Page, forced an increase in anti-aircraft measures. Not only were aircraft needed to defend different areas, but also anti-aircraft tactics were developed. Anti-aircraft matured and so did the weapons and the technology. The best way to stop hostile aircraft was by employing aircraft to seek out the enemy and engage them. However, this was not always an option. Another way to counter aircraft was to fire upon them from the ground, although this depended on the skill of the gunner, the wind, the weather, and other factors.

The American Expeditionary Force

On 6 April 1917, the United States declared war on the German Empire. White and Black Americans were drafted, although the majority of the Black Americans served in labor battalions. An exception were the 92nd and 93rd Divisions, although it was not immediately obvious how to use them because the American leadership objected to Black soldiers at the front. A solution was found in assigning the 93rd Division to the French Army, where it continued to fight alongside the French soldiers, wearing French helmets. Alongside the French, the 93rd Division fought gallantly and returned home with several decorations. The 92nd Division continued to operate under American command.

Meanwhile, the American Anti-Aircraft arm likewise developed. The task of the anti-aircraft is to deny the enemy the use of friendly airspace. When America entered the First World War, it had neither anti-aircraft guns nor the crews to serve them. A solution was found in adopting the French anti-aircraft guns, which were loaned from the French army. This went to the extent that all but two of the guns used were property of the French army. The crews were found in the Coast Artillery, whose gunners had less to do after the threat of the Imperial German fleet was diminished by blockades in the Atlantic. The chances of an attack by the Imperial German fleet were small.[2] Thus, the Coast Artillery gunners could be used as gunners for heavy artillery, trench mortars, and anti-aircraft artillery. These men were equipped with a variety of materials that they needed to counter the German airplanes, including, but not limited to, anti-aircraft artillery guns, machine guns, and searchlights.

For the anti-aircraft service, the problem was that there was no logical place to which its mission could be assigned. Colonel Jay P. Hopkins summarized this problem in December 1918:

> In our Army, the troops for this service were taken from those who were thought to be the best prepared to take up the new work with the least delay. The artillery troops were taken from the Coast Artillery Corps. The artillery materiel used is nearly that used by field artillery, but the methods of fire control more nearly approximate those of Coast Artillery. Machine gun troops were taken from the Infantry, while the Director of the Machine Gun School is from the Marine Corps. Searchlight troops were taken from Engineers, probably because Engineer troops were the field searchlight troops; but the searchlights used were nearer those used by Coast Artillery. This mixture of troops into one service that

> requires a single tactical control has not prevented effective work, but the efficiency developed has been reached in spite of, rather than because of, this complication.[3]

The new service was challenged by several technological difficulties. While the airplanes were relatively new weapons of war, they were advanced enough that they were difficult to counter from the ground. Fire control was difficult and the evasive planes could be hard to track in flight. It was aptly summarized by an American as "guess-point-shoot-and-pray".[4] In mathematical terms, the problem was easy to describe, but the equipment they worked with did not enable them to put their theories into practice. The Coast Artillery Corps had overcome this issue, fighting against ships that moved, being capable of engaging moving targets with reasonable precision. However, even for them, the airplanes posed a challenge, being capable of moving in three dimensions rather than the two in which ships moved.[5] Distance, height, and depth all played a role in hitting the target.

Although the assumption of shooting down hostile planes as the mission of the AAA is easy to make, it was not the primary directive of the anti-aircraft service. As Colonel Hopkins wrote to General Pershing,

> The principal function of anti-aircraft artillery is to prevent hostile planes from accomplishing their mission; preventing the bombing planes from reaching their objectives; preventing the artillery observation planes from remaining in the vicinity of the target; driving off photographing planes; breaking up battle-plane formation, etc.[6]

As Colonel Hopkins explained elsewhere in the same report:

> The aeroplane represents a most difficult target and the results which are accomplished by the Anti-Aircraft Service,

> are largely in keeping enemy planes at such a distance that they can accomplish their mission only with difficulty. Actually hitting planes is known to be fairly common, but to bring them down can be regarded only as a fortunate incident.[7]

Initially, anti-aircraft artillery was hardly effective, not being up to the task. Throughout the First World War, the equipment improved, such as tactical range-finders, sound-detection systems, mechanical fuses, and searchlights. This improvement is visible in the reductions of ammunition expended for each downed aircraft:

> The number of German anti-aircraft rounds for each claim fell from 11,600 in 1915 to 5,000 in 1918; French rounds per claim decreased from 11,000 (1916) to 7,000 (1918); Russian from 11,000 (1916) to 3,000 (1917); and British from 8,000 (1917) to 4,550 (1918). American anti-aircraft artillery (AAA) downed 17 German aircraft in three months, averaging 605 rounds per kill.[8]

The struggle between the destruction of hostile planes and preventing them from accomplishing their mission is also present in the ammunition that was to be used against enemy aircraft. Shrapnel shells and high explosive shells had different effects. Upon exploding, a shrapnel shell would hurl bits of metal in all directions, inflicting injuries on the airmen and wreaking havoc on the planes, although they also posed a risk to troops in the area as well. The shrapnel shells were therefore only used at the front.

A high explosive shell would burst and rely upon the concussion effect to achieve its goal. The lethality of the high explosive shells against aircraft was lower than the shrapnel shells. However, the burst of the high explosive shell was much more nerve-wracking for the aircrew. The explosions seemed much more dangerous than the relatively weak explosions of the shrapnel shells. Thus a decision needed to be made regarding which shell to use; consequently, the effect on morale was deemed so important that the high explosive shell was often preferred over the more effective shrapnel shell.[9]

Although the Germans continued to fight until the Armistice, the American Expeditionary Force started to demobilize when it became apparent that the hostilities would not resume. The Anti-Aircraft (AA) Service headquarters was demobilized first and the AA battalions were left without leadership, resulting in a disorderly administrative situation. Meanwhile, the French withdrew their bolstering of the AA Service.

The AA Service also operated under the assumption that "no American Anti-Aircraft Artillery units will be required with our 3rd Army."[10] Left without any support from the French or Third Army, the AA Service seemingly vanished. The remaining equipment, except for the two 75mm guns, was turned over to the French. The units filled the gun pits and sold the mount off their guns for scrap.

The Central Powers were barred from having an air force in the Armistice agreements and thus, because airplanes didn't have the reach to attack the United States, there was no apparent threat to oppose and the AA Service simply melted away. By 1919 the AA units had returned to Coast Artillery units and no traces of the AA service's existence remained – only to be reignited by the bombing of the former Imperial German battleship *Ostfriesland*.

The discussion about anti-aircraft defense

In 1921 the battleship *Ostfriesland* was sunk by an experiment in which Brigade General William "Billy" Mitchell demonstrated that battleships could be sunk by airplanes. It sparked an ongoing discussion between bombers and battleships that lasted until the Second World War, and the attack on Pearl Harbor by the Imperial Japanese Navy on 7 December.

During the First World War, the U.S. Coast Artillery served as anti-aircraft soldiers. Once the war was over, the U.S. Coast Artillery continued its service, protecting the country against sea attacks. They believed that objectives to the rear or vital objects needed to be protected.

After the First World War, while airplanes made many developments, the air defenders stalled in their progress. Improvements in commercial aircraft influenced the military airplanes, the anti-aircraft artillery did not have this benefit. The Coast Artillery Corps was further constrained by budgetary limits and other economic effects. During an anti-aircraft artillery demonstration in 1925 at Fort Monroe, not a single hit was scored on a towed sleeve.

The three-inch M3 gun became the standard anti-aircraft artillery gun, being capable of firing a little higher than the operational ceiling of the aircraft they needed to engage, at 21,000 ft [6,400 meters]. The guns improved with automatic breach mechanisms, as well as removable barrel liners, while continuous fuse setters improved the ammunition. However, the aircraft themselves were being improved much more and these planes flew faster and higher than their predecessors. By 1933 this anti-aircraft gun was considered obsolete, and from the middle of the 1930s airplanes held the initiative over the anti-aircraft guns.

Inaccurately assessing the threat, the Coast Artillery continued to develop inadequate countermeasures:

> In 1923, the Coast Artillery organized the anti-aircraft artillery battalions into two battalion regiments to provide a complete capability against both low- and high-altitude attacks. The first battalion had the somewhat immobile 3-inch AAA gun, developed in the United States during World War I, but never shipped overseas. The anti-aircraft gun battalion had three batteries of four guns each and a

> battery of searchlights. The second battalion (four batteries with 12 machine guns each) was termed the automatic weapons battalion, even though it was equipped with the single-barreled .30 or .50 caliber machine gun with the AAA pedestal.[11]

The Coast Artillery Corps identified two types of targets that needed to be defended. Facilities in the rear, like logistical centers or transportation hubs and forward combat units. These two had their own threat. In the case of vulnerable infrastructure, the threat came from hostile bombers, which warranted the use of the gun battalion. The automatic weapons battalion could be employed at the most critical spots. Individual accuracy was deemed of lesser importance. Preference was given to preventing hostile aircraft from completing its mission, while the secondary mission was killing the aircraft.

At the Army War College between 1929 and 1931, the students engaged in discussions about the air defense of the division. They were under the impression that in an infantry division, a soldier needed to aggressively use his weapon against enemy aircraft. In 1933 the Infantry School stated that frontline units had a major part of the anti-aircraft protection already.

The perceived threat came from enemy bombers instead, which could fly over the frontline and engage targets further to the rear. Between 1925 and 1932 three separate chiefs of Coast Artillery recommended that anti-aircraft artillery should be part of the division, because of the vulnerabilities currently exposed. After all, hostile fighters could still attack infantry soldiers. However, this was not listened to, since the U.S. Army wanted to keep the division as small as possible, and adding a host of anti-aircraft artillery guns was not acceptable. Anti-aircraft artillery would not become an organic part of the division.

Part of the friction between the Coast Artillery Corps and the other services stemmed from the fact that the Coast Artillery Corps manned comfortable fortresses, or had stations in interesting locations like Hawaii, Panama, or the Philippines, while the infantry had camps in remote locations. Furthermore, even within the Coast Artillery Corps, there was tension, because young officers believed that anti-aircraft artillery was the future of the branch, even though older officers insisted on the seacoast defense mission.

The underlying discussion was between area defense and point defense. The discussion took a more theoretical approach when the effective range of the guns and the speed of the enemy aircraft were calculated. Area defense required accuracy and control, which was not always the case with the anti-aircraft artillery gunners.

One way to achieve more control over the fire was to use special directors. In 1930 the Coast Artillery started to use the American-designed director, the Sperry M2. This director computed the data mechanically and it showed where the round needed to be to intercept the enemy aircraft. The crew could then implement the necessary changes and open fire. While it improved accuracy, it came at the cost of mobility.

Meanwhile, aircraft were steadily improving and the AAA was unable to keep pace. Aircraft would fly higher and faster than previously possible. Although airplanes had been around for several decades, it was during the Second World War that their employment became unavoidable. While aircraft during the First World War had merely been a factor, during the Second World War faster aircraft with a bigger radius, and capable of carrying a bigger load than before, meant they became a veritable weapon of war.

It too dawned on the Coast Artillery Corps that the AAA needed to improve. For example, on 30 June 1941, the following active Coast Artillery anti-aircraft units were established: forty-three mobile regiments, six semi-mobile regiments, thirteen separate mobile battalions, and one barrage balloon battalion. To put it in perspective, "the relative importance of anti-aircraft within the Coast Artillery Corps can be gained from the fact that as of this same date, there were only thirty-four harbor defense regiments, two railway artillery regiments, and seven 155mm gun regiments, plus a few submarine mine units."[12]

The Luftwaffe and anti-aircraft artillery guns

In the years leading up to the Second World War, Nazi Germany envisioned a new world order. In this world order, there would be no place for Jews, gypsies, or other people they regarded as "subhuman". To prepare for this conflict, it started to build up its army. At first, underground, but later it did openly. In secrecy, Germany had also been building up its air force. Since 1924 the Lipetsk Air Base in the Soviet Union served as a training location. Later, in 1933, training was conducted under the cover of the German Air Sports Association. The Luftwaffe, the military arm of the air force, got its first taste of combat in November 1936 when the Condor Legion served on the side of the Nationalists during the Spanish Civil War. It continued to operate until March 1939.

So when Germany invaded Poland on 1 September 1939 the Luftwaffe was ready. Its pilots had experienced combat and it had a chance to practice its tactics. In aggressive operations, dubbed *Blitzkrieg* by the Allied press, large parts of Europe were conquered. The Luftwaffe formed an essential element in these campaigns. In surprise attacks, early in the campaign, the Luftwaffe neutralized the enemy air force on the ground and then performed close air support or interdiction missions for the German ground troops to disrupt enemy supply lines or force a breach in the frontline. Meanwhile, the Germans employed 88mm guns, which could be used in an anti-aircraft and anti-tank role. It had made an impressive showing during the Spanish Civil War between 1936 and 1939 where the gun was also used to support the infantry.

Weapons for the AAA battalions and soldiers to wield them

Although officially neutral, the U.S. was preparing for war. The swift victories of the German armies in Europe forced the American military to react. In April 1941, General George C. Marshall, the Chief of Staff of the United States Army, sent a memo to the Operations Division of the Army Staff to have them find an effective way to counter the German "Blitzkrieg". Marshall wanted a combined arms force, capable of rapid movement which used aggressive offensive tactics.

The man to carry out this assignment was Lieutenant General Lesley McNair, who thought that the Anti-Aircraft Artillery (AAA) doctrine was "to protect ground troops" and to do so it "is needed in a mobile mass sufficient to meet concentrated aerial attacks."[13] McNair believed that anti-aircraft artillery was not always needed, so it would be added to a corps instead of being a component of the division.

The threat of the victorious German army also shook the Coast Artillery Corps awake. The Coast Artillery did develop and standardize a new gun. The 90mm M1 was approved on 21 March 1940 and was better than the previously used 3-inch gun. It had a range of 39,500 ft [12,000 meters] and it could use a radar. The weapon had two road-wheels as a carriage which had to be folded back, and before firing the outriggers needed to be placed. The weapon could not be depressed below zero degrees elevation and was ill-suited as an anti-tank weapon. Its successor, the M2, had a four-wheel carriage and could be fired from its travel configuration.

To protect against low-flying aircraft, automatic weapon (AW) battalions were established. In 1939 the War Department directed that the Coast Artillery should create separate anti-aircraft artillery battalions. These could operate without regimental support and could be used to protect against low-flying enemy aircraft. The Coast Artillery objected to this since the regimental structure allowed the organization to defend against both low and high-altitude enemy aircraft. The Army agreed, "but argued that the management of Coast Artillery regiments during mobilization was onerous due to the broad variety of weapons and personnel specialties found in the organization. Finding one location for a regiment to train was difficult."[14]

A study conducted by Coast Artillerymen concluded that one AAA regiment could provide protection for the corps and use the automatic weapon battalion to protect the division's rear. It was presented to General Malin Craig, the Chief of Staff of the Army, who "approved the result of the study, and directed that one two-battalion AAA regiment be allocated to each corps. He also directed the creation of the separate battalions."[15]

The Coast Artillery did so and sought a new weapon to use for its automatic weapons battalion. The Browning 37mm gun was selected, despite several shortcomings. The weapon was prone to jamming and had a range of around 1,000 yards [915 meters]. It did not have an explosive round and also didn't have fire control either. Yet the Coast Artillery was desperate to have a gun in production, and in the autumn of 1939 this gun was selected despite the shortcomings.

However, the Coast Artillery Corps was not yet satisfied with the current weapon. In September 1940, General Marshall asked the British for the loan of four Bofors 40mm guns with their fire predictor for testing. This gun was reliable and it had a range of over 1,500 yards [1,370 meters]. In addition, the British had a technological lead in the field of radar, allowing an early warning to anti-aircraft artillery guns. Later it would help with aircraft interception (both from the ground and in the air), and finally, it would help with aiming anti-aircraft guns.

A few months later the Ordnance Department standardized the Kerrison Predictor for use with the 37mm guns, and in February 1941 the Navy adopted the Bofors for use on their ships. Reluctantly the Army also agreed to standardize the 40mm gun to prevent production problems. To complement the Bofors guns, thirty-two AAA machine guns were assigned to the separate weapon battalions. These weapons could be used against aircraft that flew within 656 yards [600 meters] of the gun and thus protected the dead zone of the Bofors gun.

The Bofors 40mm gun was widely used as an anti-aircraft gun. The Swedish company started development in 1928 and fielded their first units at the start of the 1930s. In 1937 the British ordered this gun and in 1939 the Bofors was delivered to eighteen countries and used by both sides during the war. The gun fired a two-pound shell at an effective range of 1,500 yards [1,370 meters] and with a rate of 120 shells per minute.

The Bofors 40mm gun was better than the three-inch gun that was being deployed, and in June 1941 the U.S. government signed a contract with the company. This was not without problems, because the Swedes used the metric system and the conversion of these measurements caused problems when two American manufacturers used different conversion rates. Initially, 200 parts were not interchangeable, but this was reduced to only ten later in the war.[16]

Meanwhile, the separate automatic weapons battalion would be attached to a division, but they would not become an organic part of the division. Thus the division was kept small, while the division did have anti-aircraft protection.[17]

In April 1940 Major General Joseph A. Green became the Chief of Coast Artillery. He had graduated from West Point in 1906 and was commissioned as a Second Lieutenant in artillery. He transferred,

> to the Coast Artillery as a Captain in 1916, and served overseas for fifteen months in World War I with the Railway

> Artillery with the attained rank of temporary Lieutenant Colonel. He graduated from the Field Officers Course at the Coast Artillery School, Fort Monroe, Va., in 1922, the Command and General Staff Course at Fort Leavenworth, Kansas, in 1923, and the Army War College in 1926. In the years 1926–1927, he served with the 62nd Coast Artillery Regiment, an anti-aircraft unit, and followed this assignment with a four-year detail to the War Department General Staff from 1927–1931. During a subsequent two-year period from 1931–1933, he commanded the 61st Coast Artillery Regiment, another anti-aircraft artillery unit. This was followed by a two-year assignment as a member of the General Staff Corps of the Eighth Corps Area at Fort Sam Houston, Texas. In 1937, he was again transferred to Washington, D.C., and that same year became the Executive to the Chief of Coast Artillery, serving in that position until he was appointed Chief of Coast Artillery, effective 1 April 1940, Major General Green became Commanding General of the Anti-Aircraft Command on its activation, 9 March 1942. General Green remained in command of Anti-Aircraft Command until 27 October 1944.[18]

He was replaced by Brigadier General McConnell, who assumed command on 28 October 1944, and was replaced in turn by Major General Meyer, who took command on 11 February 1945 and would remain in that position for the rest of the Second World War.

There were ambitious plans for the Coast Artillery Corps. It became obvious that a separate command was needed to handle the threat of hostile aircraft. Green submitted his plans for the Anti-Aircraft Force on 28 February 1942. The Anti-Aircraft Command was activated on 9 March 1942 with Major General Green as its commanding officer. The plans also outlined the training centers and plans for establishing an Anti-Aircraft Artillery School.

> In his letter of announcement to all anti-aircraft and barrage balloon installations, General Green described the primary mission of the Command as follows: "To instruct and train officers and enlisted men for duty with anti-aircraft artillery and barrage balloon units, and to activate, organize, equip and efficiently train such units for combat service."[19]

Separate facilities were needed to train all of these units, weapons to equip these hundreds of soldiers, and find adequate officers to lead these men. Several new camps were opened by the Coast Artillery Corps: Camp Stewart, near Savannah, Georgia; Camp Hulen, near Houston, Texas; Camp Haan, near Riverside, California. Additionally, Fort Bliss, Texas, Fort Sheridan, Illinois, and Camp Davis, North Carolina, were to be used by the Coast Artillery Corps. Later, in March 1942, Camp Edwards, near Massachusetts, became an anti-aircraft artillery post.

All training was done with a single purpose in mind, as stated by the first Training Directive released by the Anti-Aircraft Command: "The principal objective of anti-aircraft artillery training is the attainment and maintenance of a complete state of readiness for combat of both individuals and units."[20] It was clarified further in a Training Directive released in December 1942:

> The attainment and maintenance of a complete state of readiness for field service and for combat of individuals and units. To attain this objective, it is essential that the conduct of all training point toward proficiency in (1) the ability to deliver immediate and effective fire with all weapons with which the unit and individual is equipped and (2) the tactical employment of the unit, including the ability of individuals and units to protect themselves and their equipment in combat.[21]

In May 1942 their objective was to raise more than 600 AAA battalions. Later that year, it was increased to over 800 battalions. In early 1942 there were forty-nine battalions in training, although there was the option to train seventy-six battalions at the same time.

In March 1942 the Army Ground Forces (AGF) were activated and an anti-aircraft artillery school was opened at Camp Davis. The AAA became separated from the Coast Artillery Corps. However, problems still existed within the AAA. For example, not enough 40mm Bofors guns were yet available. Units that were designated for deployment received a priority status and issued as much equipment as possible. Some units only received their fire directors once they were in the UK, while ammunition shortages were alleviated by mid-1943 and suitable aerial targets would be available by the end of 1943.

Chapter 2

Combat and Reflection

The first test: North Africa.

During the Imperial Japanese attack on Pearl Harbor, on 7 December 1941,

> there existed a shortage of AAA units. In order to expedite the activation of new units, the training programs at the Coast Artillery Replacement Training Centers were reduced to eight weeks. [...] At the same time, the shortage of anti-aircraft artillery armament throughout the United States Army made it necessary to remove most of the primary armament at the three Replacement Training Centers for the purpose of supplying units "being sent to the field during the emergency."[1]

The first time the AAA would truly be tested in combat, was in the battles of North Africa. The war in North Africa was not progressing in favor of the German Afrika Korps. In charge of the German troops was Erwin Rommel, who preferred *Blitzkrieg*-style tactics. These tactics relied on close cooperation between German armored units and the Luftwaffe. The Luftwaffe would perform reconnaissance and close air support for the units on the ground. In December 1942 the Luftwaffe strafed American command posts, troop movements, and attacked the field artillery positions. The German artillery weapons were outranged by the 105mm and 155mm weapons. In February 1943, the Americans had developed effective ways to counter the enemy tanks with their artillery, and Rommel upon realizing this, even gave orders to destroy as many American howitzers as could be located. Thus, the need for anti-aircraft protection was great.

The Allies also realized this. In February 1943, Major George Croker, CAC, reported to the AGF on the anti-aircraft artillery situation in North Africa. It was a week before the Battle of Kasserine Pass and it revealed a variety of things on which the AAA could improve.

The training of the ten separate AW and five AAA regiments in the U.S.A. had been unimpressive. They did not have enough training to become proficient with their weapons. Problems with aligning the directors meant that the guns were less accurate than anticipated. The officers were theoretically trained, but not able to pass on their knowledge to the soldiers they commanded. The platoons served alongside armored or infantry units but knew little about supporting these units. The first time the 105th CA Battalion supported a division was during the Kasserine Pass battle and the field artillery they were protecting moved twice without telling them.[2] Training in common aspects of soldiering, such as field fortifications, site security, and field sanitation were inadequate. The units needed more time in the field, and the soldiers hardened for combat as well as receiving training in combined arms tactics.

In his report, Croker also recommended that targets be tracked until identified and that the units opened fire to kill at a maximum range, not to drive off the hostile aircraft. He also argued for the use of the British "Stiff Key Stick", which could be adopted by the American units. This sight could be used on-carriage, it was a simple rugged aiming device that allowed the guns to start firing quickly and switch targets easily. Furthermore, no dead zone would be created because of the director which needed to be set up in the vicinity of the 40mm gun. The director had several additional issues, including the need for proper alignment before firing, which significantly reduced the mobility of the AAA units.

One of the problems Croker mentioned dealt with fratricide. Anti-aircraft units and combat units shot down a disproportionate number of friendly aircraft. One of the causes was a lack of an Air Defense Command, which was initially not present in North Africa. There was no doctrine of integrating close air support, interdiction and air superiority missions, and anti-aircraft artillery fire near the line of contact. Compounding the problem, aircraft identification was an issue for many units. Finally, the slow response of close air support meant that U.S. aircraft would sometimes arrive on site without warning hours after support was needed, thus catching everyone by surprise.

The automatic weapon battalions didn't have binoculars and also didn't have dedicated observers to warn of incoming aircraft. Thus AAA units opened fire as soon as possible, guided by the thought: "Shoot them down and sort them out on the ground."[3] During the Battle of Kasserine Pass, American planes would rock their wings while flying over friendly units and the combat units had yellow smoke to identify themselves to the aircraft.

Croker was also impressed with the 443rd Coast Artillery Battalion. This unit was equipped with two prototypes. Twenty-eight M15 prototypes were supplied with a 37mm gun/dual .50 cal machine gun turret mounted on a half-track, while fifty-two M13s were supplied with a dual .50 cal machine gun turret mounted on a half-track.

Meanwhile, the Anti-Aircraft Artillery Command had standardized the quadruple .50 cal machine gun M16. It would replace the M13, which lacked the necessary firepower. Their main benefit was mobility, allowing them to emplace and displace rapidly. In the months that followed, towed units proved to be satisfactory for stationary targets, such as assembly areas, but a division on the move needed self-propelled AAA protection.

Gun crews learned to be better at aircraft identification and observers reinforced the process. Combat in North Africa also indicated that AAA units needed to keep up with the units they were supporting to provide adequate protection. Whereas a mobile mass of AAA was suitable for certain situations, anti-aircraft artillery needed to be present in every division as well. An onboard fire control system for the Bofors gun was created, and a new carriage for the 90mm guns developed. The Army Air Force and the AAA units exchanged more information to prevent friendly fire. AAA had proven itself in battle. It had learned from its first engagements and it would continue to develop new weapons and tactics.

Training cycles for the units initially had been twelve weeks, but this was increased to twenty-two weeks. The units that took part in the invasion in Europe in June 1944 were better equipped and better trained than the units that deployed in North Africa. They had plenty of ammunition and had the opportunity to participate in the Tennessee or Louisiana maneuvers.

The units were also supplied with better equipment. The automatic weapon battalions now had dedicated observers, the weapon crews had binoculars, more radios, and a new weapon. The M-51 or M-55 trailer, a quadruple .50-caliber machine gun on a trailer. Thus, in total, the battalion had thirty-two 40mm guns and thirty-two M-51s or M-55s at its disposal. The 452nd AAA used the M-51 trailer.

However, this mobility was not enough for Colonel Charles G. Patterson, the First Army's AAA officer and stationed in England in anticipation of D-Day, and his automatic weapons staff officer, Major Fred Jacks. They acquired 700 excess halftracks from the First Army Ordnance Officer. The quad mounts were taken from the trailers and bolted on the half-tracks, becoming the M16B, because there were sixteen per AW battalion. It again added an element of mobility to the AW battalions, allowing them to operate on a fluid battlefield. Some battalions, such as the 457th Anti-Aircraft Artillery Battalion, which would operate alongside the 452nd AAA, did receive them and thus could keep up with armored units or provide protection almost immediately after an objective had been seized. However, it seems that the 452nd AAA didn't receive them. This meant that they were less mobile than the 457th AAA and thus the battalions received different missions on the battlefield.

The AAA also incorporated tactics of Allied armies. For example, they adopted the different movement method used by British units. Battery officers would go ahead as soon as they received the new mission, scouting ahead and selecting new gun positions, while the unit would depart under the command of the battalion executive officer. The route was identified in broad strokes and the officers would leave markers behind for the battalion that followed them. When arriving, the unit could immediately go into position. The benefits were that the unit didn't have to wait for the battery officers to return, and the quickest route was taken, since the battalion followed the recon element closely. The unit officers needed to understand the assets they were defending so that the battalion could deploy in swift order, and that the march column was standardized so that the officers knew which guns would arrive where.[4]

The automatic weapon battalions would be employed to defend field artillery units or they would defend command positions, ammunition dumps, or river crossings. The directors were abandoned in favor of more mobile options, while the men needed to be trained in relocating frequently. The units on the ground and in the air needed to be improved to reduce instances of friendly fire.

Fratricide and attempts to prevent it

Anti-aircraft guns are meant to engage hostile aircraft. However, due to the "fog of war" as Clausewitz called it, this is not always the case. It was three days after the declaration of war on Germany when the first British AAA kill was made. It "was unfortunately a friendly aircraft that had even given the correct recognition signal".[5] It was only a month later, on 19 October 1939, that it downed its first German aircraft.

More costly mistakes would be made throughout the war, for example during the invasion of Sicily, Italy, on the night of 11/12 July, elements of the 82nd Airborne Division overflew the invasion fleet. Arriving shortly after an Axis bombing raid, the division's planes were engaged after a single gun opened fire. Shortly afterwards all Allied anti-aircraft guns opened fire. Twenty-three of the 144 aircraft involved were destroyed, while another thirty-seven were badly damaged. A total of ninety-seven paratroopers were killed or missing, while 132 others were wounded. Sixty persons from the air personnel were killed or missing, while thirty more were wounded.[6]

This would not be the end, because two nights later British and American troop carriers tried to drop British paratroopers near a bridge and establish a bridgehead on the east coast of Sicily. Again, friendly naval and ground fire engaged the transports, causing eighty-seven aircraft to press on and allowing thirty-nine to drop their troops within a mile of the designated drop zone. Of the other aircraft involved, eleven were destroyed, fifty were damaged, and twenty-seven were forced to abort the mission. Despite all this, the paratroopers who landed managed to carry out their mission.

Because of this harsh lesson, during D-Day special invasion markings (white stripes) were painted on the aircraft, but again Allied anti-aircraft gunners engaged and downed Allied aircraft. American pilot George Preddy, with at least twenty-six kills to his name, was one of the U.S. best fighter pilots. On 25 December 1944, while chasing German aircraft, Preddy was killed by friendly anti-aircraft fire. The AAA battalion had attempted to fire on the Fw 190 that Preddy was chasing but hit him instead.[7]

Even generals were not safe, because "on 1 January 1945, U.S. AAA units fired on an aircraft carrying Army Air Force Generals

Carl A. Spaatz and James H. Doolittle. Spaatz informed General George S. Patton Jr. of his gunners' poor aircraft recognition and shooting skills."[8]

All warring nations suffered from this problem. Germany lost 229 fighters in 1943 to friendly flak. On the night of 31 December 1944 to 1 January 1945, during Operation *Bodenplatte*, more than 1,000 German aircraft were supposed to attack sixteen different Allied airfields. At least seventeen airplanes involved were confirmed as shot down by German flak, though estimates assume that it might possibly be thirty to thirty-five aircraft.[9]

Friendly fire was costly because valuable aircraft and pilots were neutralized by their own forces. Electronic identification devices, recognition signals, and restricted areas were introduced. Although fratricide was drastically reduced during the Second World War, it never entirely disappeared.

Automatic weapon battalions

During the Second World War, American AAA employed several types of battalions. Each battalion was a self-contained administrative and tactical unit. The most common types were the gun, searchlight, and automatic weapons battalions. The gun battalions used the 90mm gun, while the searchlight battalions operated large searchlights to illuminate hostile aircraft. Lastly, the automatic weapon battalions used 40mm Bofors guns, which were again divided into several categories, such as self-propelled units, like the 443rd AAA, and towed battalions, like the 452nd AAA. The task of an AAA AW battalion is simple. As formulated by the Field Manual of December 1944:

> PRIMARY MISSION. The primary mission of automatic weapons is to attack all enemy aircraft within range, particularly low-flying aircraft to destroy them, cause them

> to abandon their missions, or to decrease the efficiency of their operations.
>
> SECONDARY MISSION. The secondary mission of automatic weapons is to attack and destroy enemy mechanized or other ground targets within range, particularly light and medium tanks and armored cars; in coast defenses, to attack and destroy enemy motor torpedo boats or other light naval craft within range; or in support of infantry, to act as reinforcing infantry weapons or tank destroyers.
>
> PRIMARY VS. SECONDARY MISSIONS. Although AAA automatic weapons are not primarily designated for fire against ground or naval targets, automatic weapons units may be diverted from their primary mission and employed on their secondary mission. *It is not normal, however, for field commanders to divert automatic weapons from their primary AA mission as long as there is a threat of enemy air action.*[10]

The appropriate division commander decides when the AW will be employed in their primary or secondary role. However, these secondary missions were not without risk due to the size of the anti-aircraft guns. "When AAA automatic weapons are engaged solely on their secondary mission, the high silhouette and relative immobility of most automatic weapons make them extremely vulnerable targets. In addition, the normal methods of technique, fire control, and fire direction cannot be used against ground or naval targets in most cases."[11]

To measure the destruction of hostile aircraft, three categories were introduced, which was universal through all theaters of operations:

> Category I: Planes destroyed in air or seem to fall to ground or into the sea. This report has to be confirmed by written statements of disinterested parties.

Category II: Plane damaged in air so severely that it is very unlikely that the plane could have reached its base. The planes damaged condition must be observed by a disinterested party.

Category III: Plane damaged, but not so severely enough to prevent it from reaching its home base. The plane should be seen to trail smoke or pieces of the plane fall. This again has to be witnessed by an impartial observer.[12]

Although all AAA units used the same categories, there were certain differences in organization. Even within the automatic weapon battalions, there were for instance mobile, airborne, and semi-mobile units. As the Field Manual stated: "There are six types of automatic weapons battalions: mobile, semi-mobile, self-propelled, airborne, air-transportable, and machine gun (light)."[13] The 452nd AAA Battalion was a mobile unit. The personnel was divided between a range section, a gun section, and a machine gun section.[14] The battalion used a 40mm Bofors AA gun on an M2 carriage and it had a quad .50 caliber machine gun trailer, the M-51. Each of these weapons was described as follows in the Field Manual:

40mm gun. The 40mm gun is fully automatic, and can deliver short bursts at the rate of 120 rounds per minute. It is air-cooled, and if fired at full rate may begin to overheat after firing about 100 rounds. When overheated, fire must be suspended and the barrel changed (30-40 seconds). The gun can be fired full automatic or by firing single shots. The best results are obtained if the gun is single-fired at a rate of 80-100 rounds per minute. [...] The gun will elevate from -6 degree to 90 degrees and will traverse through 360 degrees.

Caliber .50 machine gun. The caliber .50 machine gun fires at a rate of 450-600 rounds per minute. Its effective range is

> dependent primarily on the gunner's depth perception. [...] In most automatic weapons units, the caliber .50 machine gun is used in electrically operated multiple (quadruple) machine gun mounts, thus greatly increasing the fire power. These multiple machine gun mounts can be traversed and elevated at maximum rates of about 600 per second by a single operator.[15]

Both of these weapons had their own carriages or trailers, making it easier to transport them. For the 40mm gun, there was the M2 carriage, which took between two and three minutes to emplace. Firing from the wheels with direct sights was possible, but more effective fire was given when the gun as emplaced.

The ammunition for these weapons consisted of several types, as defined by the Field Manual:

> The principal classes; of combat ammunition are ball, armor piercing, incendiary, armor piercing incendiary, and tracer for caliber .50 machine guns and high explosive shell and armor piercing shot for 37mm and 40mm guns. The tracer element of caliber .50 tracer ammunition burns out at a range of about 1,850 or 2,450 yards [1,690–2,240 meters], depending on the type. Both 37mm and 40mm high explosive shells and AP shot contain tracer elements and both 37mm and 40mm high explosive shells are self-destroying. (Self-destroying ammunition explodes after a certain definite time of flight, or upon impact.) [...] 40mm high explosive shells are self-destroying at ranges of approximately 3,500 yards [3,200 meters] or 5,500 yards [5,030 meters], depending upon the type of tracer element used.[16]

The types of ammunition were for different targets. The .50 cal ammunition and 40mm high explosive rounds were to be used against personnel and light materiel. The .50 cal and 40mm armor piercing (AP) ammunition were for use against armored vehicles, concrete shelters, and similar targets. Incendiary ammunition was used for inflammable or explosive targets. Lastly, tracer ammunition was primarily for the observation of the fire. The .50 cal ammunition was usually belted with two armor piercing, two incendiary, one tracer, although the combination could be altered to suit the mission.

The automatic weapon battalions used explosive shells against hostile aircraft. The biggest flaw of this ammunition was that the 40mm shells needed to hit to destroy their target instead of exploding in proximity like shells with a time fuse. Close fire, such as tracer streams, might have a deterrent effect on the enemy, but it would not destroy them.

There were four categories of ranges at which the enemy could be engaged, defined as follows:

> Extreme deterrent range is defined as the tracer burnout range of automatic weapons projectiles. Fire at this range is not accurately aimed fire, and cannot be expected to make any given round a hit. Deterrent fire delivered at extreme ranges, and with maximum density, can decrease the efficiency of operation of enemy aircraft by making them break formation, take avoiding action, or, in some cases even abandon their mission. [...]
>
> Maximum hitting range is defined as the longest range at which, under average conditions, the various weapons and methods of fire control can produce hits. Maximum hitting range depends on visibility of tracers when tracer observation is used for fire adjustment; on the approach angle of the target; on the speed of the target; and on the type of fire control employed. [In the case of .50 cal machine

> guns, this is 800 to 1,000 yards [730–910 meters]. For 40mm guns, it is 1,500 to 1,800 yards [1,370–1,650 meters].]
>
> Effective hitting range is defined as the range within which weapons can execute effective fire and hits can be expected. It forms the basis for doctrines concerning tactical employment of automatic weapons.
>
> Effective hitting range depends mainly on aiming tolerance, which can be defined as the mil angle subtended at the gun by the target. The actual physical size of the target causes the target to subtend a greater angle at the gun at close ranges than it does at distant ranges. Therefore, there is more aiming tolerance at close ranges. The target must be close enough so that tracer sensings are fresh and reliable. Positive tracer observation is more necessary while using tracer control or on-carriage sights. [In the case of .50 cal machine guns, this is 500 to 800 yards [460–730 meters]. For 40mm guns it is 1,000 to 1,200 yards [910–1,100 meters].]
>
> Minimum tracking range is the smallest range at which gun pointers can continue to track close-in, high speed targets. As the approach angle of such targets increases, the angular rate of travel may be so great as to make tracking inaccurate or impossible. The powered-operated caliber .50 machine gun turret mounts have virtually no minimum range limitation. [The 40mm guns were usually incapable of dealing with high-speed targets within 400 yards [365 meters].][17]

The benefit of the AW is that they can swiftly switch from one target to another and they deliver a high volume. Thus the weapons were frequently employed against other targets than hostile aircraft.

The battalion consisted of several key individuals. The battalion commander is responsible for the tactical employment of the battalion as well as the unit's training, administration and supply. He must deploy to the best of the current circumstances as well as "estimate the probable future situation based on the information available".[18] His job is complicated by the fact that the units under his command may be widely dispersed. Most important is that he keeps the battery officers informed on the friendly and enemy situations.

Luckily, the battalion commander is not alone, because he is assisted by the staff around him. This staff works out details regarding the CO's plan. These staff members also advise the battalion commander on a host of different issues.

The AAA AW battalions consisted of four batteries: A, B, C, and D. Each of these batteries consisted of two platoons. Every platoon was further broken down into four sections, centered around a gun and a trailer. All batteries were commanded by a battery commander, generally a captain. He needed to take care of the training, administration, supply of the battery, and the defense of the objectives assigned to the battery. He selected the positions to be occupied by the battery. Additionally, the battery commander was responsible for the local security, inspection of weapons, sanitary facilities, equipment, and personal cleanliness of the troops. The battery commander was assisted by the other junior officers under his command.

If not enough time was available, the battery commander could select sites on a map and then rely on his platoon leaders and section chiefs to work it out. The positions depend on the mission assigned. The battery commander also selected the position of the command post, the motor park, the maintenance section, and the bivouac area. The battery command post facilitates communication with the platoon. If the battery is detached from the battalion and attached to another unit, the command post is near the command post of the attached unit.

At a lower level, the platoon leader, usually a lieutenant, performed similar duties as the battery commander. However, the focus was on the platoon instead of the battery. He positioned each firing unit and the routes to the positions. He also selected the site for the platoon command post. The positions for the gun, the director, and the power plant were selected, as well as the positions for the machine guns, the AA lookouts, the truck park and bivouac, and the ammunition storage. The platoon command post was often located near the platoon, usually 50 yards [45 meters] from one of the fire units. It allowed observation of the fire of the guns in the platoon and was located near the command post of the unit to which it is attached. The battalion would often be split up and batteries or platoons be assigned different objects to protect. For the purpose of administration and supply, the platoon or battery, would be under the control of the unit to which they were attached. This also included censoring their mail. Barrett James Whiteley, an officer in the 191st Field Artillery Battalion, to which a platoon of the 452nd AAA was attached, recounted a humorous incident regarding this:

> The other soldier that I wanted to mention might have been in even worse trouble when he came back to the States after the war. He was one of the crew members from the anti-aircraft unit that was attached to us, and we had to handle their mail as well. When he wrote letters, he wrote five of them to five different girls, scattered around the United States, and the letters were identical.
>
> There was no change in them. He would write five identical letters, and send them to each of these five girls. To each one he assured her that as soon as the war was over he was coming back to her, and they were going to get married. These were amazing letters, and I was very tempted to offer some advice, but that was not my job, and I would have been amiss in commenting on anything that was in the letters, as long as it didn't break our silence on the secret matters,

> so I had to send the letters on. But, you know, I've often thought since the war that for that soldier, the war would only just be beginning when he got back to the United States with five women expecting him home to marry them.[19]

The 40mm guns were located where they had a good field of fire on the air and ground targets. If it was not possible, AAA lookouts were placed on the other side of the obstruction and communicated back. Each automatic weapon fire unit was assigned a specific sector but engaged planes regardless of the direction. The machine guns supplemented the 40mm guns, but could also be used as separate units in the defense. Camouflage was recommended against ground and air observation. In the case of obvious positions, such as at a road intersection, it was possible that hostile artillery could engage the AAA guns. At such times, alternate positions must be taken. Foxholes and trenches supplied additional defense measures.

Selecting the gun positions relied on good reconnaissance before the guns were deployed. Good positions afforded a wide sector of fire, good ground cover and maximum concealment. They should be situated to take advantage of ground protection afforded by other troops, be able to move out equipment quickly, and mutually support neighboring friendly fire units.

Using AAA weapons on elevated sites were only used with caution since the guns could not easily be displaced. Occupying a position on the crest of a hill was not recommended as the profile was visible and the gun in an exposed position; a little behind the crest was better, allowing soldiers the benefit of cover.

In addition to terrain which affected the deployment, also the type of object that needs to be defended, and the tactics of the enemy needed to be taken into account. A single objective could be a bridge or a field artillery battery, while a vital area might be several field artillery batteries, an airfield and the buildings around it, or a railway marshalling yard.

It was recommended that the 40mm guns be sited around 300–400 yards [275–365 meters] from each other, and no more than 1,000 yards [915 meters] from the other guns. The guns could be sited to cover the dead areas of each other. The .50 caliber guns would be sited to protect against minimum altitude attacks and to supplement the fire of the 40mm guns.

From there the AAA guns waited until a target presented itself. For effective engagement, an early warning system was important. The AAA communications were done by a variety of means, but mostly radio. The battalion headquarters had a SCR-177, which is employed in the group net. The SCR-543s were used to communicate between the battalion and batteries and platoon headquarters, as well as the observation posts. Additionally, wires could be used to maintain communication.

When a single target did present itself, it was engaged. If two or more targets were within the field of fire of the unit, the "most dangerous threat to the mission of the defense of which the fire unit is a part" was engaged.[20] The fire unit commander would select the target if two or more targets presented themselves.

Targets that were obscured by fog, darkness or smoke could still be engaged by barrage fire. However, this barrage fire mostly worked as a deterrent due to the tracer ammunition. The same applied to targets that were diving out of the sun.

There were three types of attacks against which the AAA commonly defended the units to which they were attached. These were dive bombing, where the hostile pilot dives on its target to release a bomb; minimum altitude attacks, such as strafing or skip bombing; and low-level horizontal flight attacks, such as firing rockets or jet-propelled bombs.

Besides active AAA defense, there were also passive air defense options, such as using available cover, close liaison between the units, and concealment or dispersing the vehicles or troops that needed to be defended. This didn't always apply, however; for example, an intersection or a bridge couldn't easily be hidden.

The main difference between static deployment and mobile deployment is that static is permanent or semi-permanent, whereas mobile is in a moving situation. All units could perform in a static role and this could be the defense of an area deemed of vital importance, such as a port, an airbase, or a depot. The protection of airdromes was one of the most important types of missions. In the case of mobile employment, the units were called upon to protect assets or elements that would relocate frequently, such as armored divisions.

Each of these objects that needed protection came with their peculiarities and dangers. The AAA commander could advise the armored unit about AAA defense. Units on the march had AAA guns placed throughout the column. In the case of field artillery a single battery or platoon would be attached to a single field artillery battalion. In the case of protecting a field artillery battery, counterfire would pose a risk and the automatic weapons should not be sited within 100 yards [90 meters] of the nearest field artillery gun.

In addition to the types above, there were supply dumps that needed to be protected. These were organized into different classes. Class I supply dumps consisted of rations. Class II supply dumps consisted of equipment that the soldiers might need, such as clothing and shoes. Class III would consist of oil and gasoline supply dumps. Empty containers would be swapped for full ones. Class IV supply dumps consisted of various materials, such as construction materials. Class V supply dumps consisted of ammunition dumps.

In the case of an attack by friendly forces, the AAA would operate in support. Their main tasks were to guard against air attacks that attempted to stall the offensive, or deny the enemy observation of friendly operations. In defensive operations, the AAA is important, because usually the friendly forces are outnumbered by the enemy. Also, in this case, the automatic weapons protected against hostile air attacks and observation. Dummy positions could even be established.

When there was no hostile air threat, the AAA guns could be deployed against ground or naval targets. However, these targets would not be engaged if there was still a bigger aerial threat. The self-propelled weapons were more suited for this since they didn't depend on their prime movers as the towed units did. The high silhouette, lack of protective armor, and the fact that the weapons had a flat trajectory made the AAA guns ill-suited for ground targets. Concealment was even more important for the towed units since they could not be displaced rapidly.

However, their high rate of fire and their firepower might make them the best gun available in a given situation. During an attack, the AAA might operate as close support for the infantry or against a machine gun or fortified position that holds up an advance. In the case of engaging mechanized targets, it was recommended to engage medium armored vehicles up to ranges of 600 yards [550 meters], while heavily armored vehicles were not common targets. Tanks would need to be engaged from the side, not the front. If the AAA gun was deployed as a tank destroyer, it was better suited at removing threats against the flanks and the rear. The organic anti-tank defenses can be deepened by employing AAA guns in a ground role. However, when used in a ground-attack role, the ammunition expenditure is much higher than when used in an anti-aircraft role.

Segregated units

The U.S. was a segregated country, limiting the opportunities for Black and Asian people within the nation. Segregation was intended to treat Black people as separate, but equal to white Americans. This was derived from a U.S. Supreme Court decision in the case of Plessy v. Ferguson in 1896.

White supremacy, the prejudice that white people were naturally superior to other races, was present throughout U.S. society and manifested itself in various ways. After the American Civil War in 1865, the Thirteenth, Fourteenth, and Fifteenth Amendments were added to the American constitution. Slavery was illegal. Every born or naturalized citizen of the United States received equal protection from the law. Lastly, everyone would be allowed to vote. The purpose of these rights was to give people equal rights, regardless of race.

These equal rights were challenged when the state of Louisiana passed the Louisiana Separate Car Act in 1890. This law claimed to provide "equal but separate" cars to white and Black Americans. Passengers were also prohibited from entering the coaches for other races.

Two years later, Homer Plessy, who was of mixed descent, boarded a whites-only car and refused to leave. He was arrested and the case escalated to the Supreme Court. In 1896 the Supreme Court decided that Plessy's rights hadn't been violated, thus ruling in favor of the Louisiana Separate Car Act, 1890.

Segregationist laws were then enacted in the Southern states. Many of these racial segregation laws became known as "Jim Crow" laws. The name was derived from a racist minstrel song that mocked Black people, and over time it was used to refer to Black people themselves. Any racist law that established a difference between white and Black Americans became known as a Jim Crow law.

In practical terms, it was often "separate and unequal" rather than "separate, but equal", since facilities for Black Americans would often be less than those of their white countrymen. However, segregation could be stricter or less strictly enforced in different areas due to local practicalities. Throughout their combat career, Black American units would be marked with an asterisk, which would denote "Negro enlisted personnel", or similar remarks to indicate that they were different to the white units.

Another way in which white supremacy could be manifested was through lynching. Although there were fewer lynchings in the 1930s than in previous decades, six Americans were lynched in 1938 and three in 1939. In 1941 there was a lynching at an American military base; near Fort Benning the corpse of Felix Hall, of the 24th Infantry Regiment, was discovered with his hands tied behind his back and a noose around his neck. The perpetrators were never caught.

During the Second World War, racial tensions also flared up when all Japanese Americans were suspected of being disloyal. They also had their own unit, the 442nd Infantry Regiment, consisting of Americans of Japanese descent. While this unit fought in Europe, it resulted in an unusual situation, because their families were in internment camps.

Segregation was another difficulty with which the American army had to contend during the Second World War. From March 1941, the Army General Classification Test (AGCT) was conducted. It had been designed to measure the speed at which people could learn, but instead was often interpreted as an intelligence test.[21] This test consisted of three tasks: First to sample a person's grasp of the meaning of words and their differences; second, solving arithmetic problems and mathematical calculations; third was some items which required the ability to visualize and think about connections between things in space. The test measured the rate of learning through four elements: native capacity, schooling and educational opportunities, socioeconomic status, and cultural background. The learning could come from a school, but also listening to a radio, reading a newspaper, or watching a movie.

Black Americans, being segregated from white Americans, often had fewer opportunities to learn than white Americans. Thus they scored lower than white Americans. Since the test was interpreted as an intelligence test, rather than measuring the speed of learning, it caused tensions in the training of Black American units.

As a prejudiced study mentioned:

> although economic, political, and social factors loomed large in the background of the task in which they determined the milieu in which was formed the raw material out of which General McNair and his successors were required to make soldiers, it was not clearly the province or the responsibility of the Army Ground Forces to change the pattern of society. A strictly military and therefore pragmatic view of the operation and consequences of these factors was the only one which General McNair could take, faced as he was with the task of making effective soldiers out of the material given him, in a time that was critically brief.[22]
>
> It should be borne in mind that in these and other recommendations for the utilization of Negro troops General McNair was thinking primarily, if not exclusively, in terms of fulfilling the AGF mission of producing a fighting force of the highest possible combat efficiency. He was in thorough accord with the policy repeated stated by the War Department that the promotion in the Army of social aims which had not been attained in the country as a whole would materially impede the effort to build and maintain a force capable of defeating an efficient and determined foe. In short General McNair's concern was military effectiveness and not social reform.[23]

The purpose of all armed forces training was clear:

> The policy of the Army Ground Forces with reference to colored troops was based on War Department requirements that Negroes be taken into the Army in numbers proportionate to their share of the population, that colored

> organizations be stablished in each major branch of the service, and that Negroes be given an opportunity to qualify as officers. These requirements were to be reconciled with the fundamental mission of the Army Ground Forces, which was to deliver to ports of embarkation units capable of meeting a highly efficient foe. Limitations of shipping increased the importance of sending only the most effective units.[24]

As the paper admits, there were a multitude of problems with regard to Black American soldiers. Not in the least, these were a result of their disenfranchised position in society, being less capable of following good education and developing professional skills. However, even if the purpose was to send only the most effective units overseas, the Army Ground Forces did make serious mistakes. Well-prepared units, such as the 795th Tank Destroyer Battalion, were deactivated and the men were sent to other outfits, while sometimes ill-prepared units, such as the 827th Tank Destroyer Battalion, were sent overseas.

Additionally, for a Black American unit to operate effectively, it needed in some cases an extended training period. Unit commanders were encouraged to develop special techniques for teaching the personnel that had received little education and to fill the command positions with officers qualified to serve with Black American soldiers. If these conditions were met, a unit could be effectively employed, but this was not always the case. Inadequate unit commanders, or unit commanders incapable of adjusting to commanding Black American soldiers, could demolish a unit in training, while similarly, teaching methods needed to be adapted to the students rather than the teachers.

> As the army expanded, so too, did the segregated units increase. The army had historically maintained four

> segregated units, being the 9th and 10th Cavalry Regiment, and the 24th and 25th Infantry Regiment. Within the National guard were three segregated units, the 184th Field Artillery Regiment, inducted in 1941, the 369th Coast Artillery, inducted in June 1941 and the 372d Infantry Regiment, induced in March 1941.

However, this was not all,

> as the field forces were expanded in 1941 old colored organizations increased in strength and new units in nearly all the Arms and Services were called into being. [...] Combat units activated during the General Headquarters (GHQ) period (26 July 1940 – 9 March 1942) included three infantry regiments (the 366th, the 367th, and 368th), five Coast Artillery regiments (the 54th (155mm Gun), TD), 76th (AA), 77th (AA), 99th (AA), and 100th (AA), one field artillery brigade (the 46th) and four field artillery regiments (the 349th, 350th, 351st, and 353rd), and one light tank battalion (the 758th).[25]

More units were scheduled, such as the 105th Infantry Division in 1943, but several things prevented this, including the planned reduction of the army strength, the opposition of Army Ground Forces to organizing Black American soldiers in large units, and the preferences of theater commanders for white units.

In 1944 the war was changing, going from a defensive war to an offensive one. As such, the combat conducted was changing and so different units were needed. Both white and Black units in training needed to adapt to the changed circumstances. As a result, more service units were needed, for which predominately Black units were chosen, as well as a diminished need for certain types of combat units, such as Anti-Aircraft and Coast Artillery.

Throughout the training of Black American soldiers, it was stressed that in general they had less education and had less mechanical aptitude than white Americans, both things that were a direct result of the social circumstances in which Black Americans lived. This reflected the jobs that were available to Black Americans in society. In the same report, it is noted: "The occurrence rate of other technical specialists among colored inductees was woefully small," and also, "As with all other skills, except cooks, there is a great disparity between what is needed and what is available."[26]

To remedy this, the army trained the soldiers under their command, but many of these soldiers were never given a fair chance due to the reigning prejudices:

> Unit commanders and higher headquarters made gargantuan efforts to train the required specialists. But results fell considerably short of the needs. A crux in the situation was the lack of a satisfactory foundation on which to build. The social and economic system prevailing in peacetime afforded only limited opportunity for participation by Negroes in technical pursuits. The race was ill-equipped, therefore, for full participation in a war conducted to a large extent with machines. It was a case of calling on an agricultural and laboring people, accustomed mainly to plows, shovels, and hoes, to enter an activity where essential tools were automatic weapons, motors, and radios. The commanding general of the Anti-Aircraft Command summarized thus the situation confronting him. "Each of the three types of anti-aircraft battalions is equipped with a large amount of electrical, radio, and mechanical equipment… The great majority of (colored) men are unable to grasp the barest fundamentals of the gunnery problems involved, and to care for and properly man the complicated equipment inherent in anti-aircraft units. There are in the 16 colored anti-aircraft battalions

> approximately 10,000 men whose opportunities for mental development have been so restricted as to necessitate their classification in AGCT grades IV and V. Of this number only about 3,000 could be employed to useful advantage within the 16 battalions were all to be continued active."[27]

The racism is even more obvious when this study tries to explain the failures of the Black American soldiers:

> The colored soldier's abuse of equipment was attributable in part, if not largely, to the character of his civilian background. A staff officer with wide experience in two Negro divisions remarked: "Negroes have never had much equipment of their own to look after. The equipment that they used in their farming and other activities usually belonged to the 'boss man' and they felt no responsibility for looking after it. The thing has carried over into the army. It will take a long time to make the Negro property conscious."[28]

> A considerable number of white officers testified to a lack of honesty and forthrightness among the colored troops. This seems to have been attributable in large measure to a defensive attitude, springing from longstanding subordination to the white man. It sometimes took the form of an individual covering up small errors until they developed into major mishap. The point may best be illustrated by a hypothetical but typical instance: A truck driver runs over a stump and tears a hole in a rear tire. For fear of being blamed and upbraided he fails to report the damage, but lets things drift along until the tire blows out and wrecks the truck. When questioned then as to whether or not he had observed the hole before the blowout he answers negatively and proposes some other reason for the wreck.[29]

Additional racist comments included:

> The defensive complex was also manifest in the reluctance of colored men to reveal delinquencies of their fellows, even when these delinquencies caused them injury or inconvenience. Cases of theft, sodomy, and destruction of property which would have come to light almost immediately in white units evaded detection for months in colored organizations because of the prevalent unwillingness to expose the guilty parties to the Army's counterpart of "the law".[30]

However, rather than just blaming the troops, officers needed to be aware of the effects of segregation and the impact this might have on the morale of their troops. Additionally, an officer needed to be aware of the social issues affecting Black American soldiers:

> Another shortcoming of colored trainees was a lack of interest on the part of many of them in their military activities and in the war itself. The commander of a colored cavalry brigade wrote in December 1943: "The most difficult thing in all our work here is trying to instill a desire or determination in these soldiers' minds that they must and will fight. Approximately 95% 'just don't want to.' In some instances the lethargy sprang from a conviction that the Negro had little to gain from the war; that the United States was a white man's country and that it would be no less so after the conflict than before. This conviction was nourished by instances of abuse and discrimination. Some white officers of Southern background offended their men by referring to them as 'boys', 'shines', 'darkies', and 'jigaboos'. Negro soldiers and their families sometimes were crowded off buses by whites, and those who dared protest were abused by drivers, policemen, and other civilians.

> Colored troops traveling in the South sometimes had to go hungry: those riding the train, unless traveling in convoy, were usually excluded from dining cars; those who rode in buses sometimes did not have time during allotted stopovers for meals to find their way to 'Negro-town' and back to the station. Time Magazine reported that 'Negro troops being shipped through El Paso, Texas, were barred from the Harvey House restaurant at the depot and given cold handouts. They could see German prisoners of war seated in the restaurant and fed hot food.' Negro soldiers visiting towns on passes were sometimes beaten without just cause by civilian police. Incidents of mistreatment were given wide publicity by the Negro press; usually the accounts were exaggerated and distorted. Sensitiveness to discrimination, whether real or imagined, was more common among educated soldiers than those of little learning, and among those from the North more than those from the South."[31]

Ironically, while at the same time Black American soldiers were considered inadequate, due to their lack of mechanical aptitude, "some artillery commanders found Negroes better than whites in the service of the piece."[32] Elsewhere Black American soldiers were similarly praised:

> The commander of an anti-aircraft unit wrote in February 1943: "They are without doubt the most responsive of any people … The thing to do is to appeal to that responsiveness … (by) passing out of compliments and the good word, giving them 'color', always showing an outward humanness." As might be expected there was a close correlation between responsiveness of the troops and the quality of their leadership.[33]
>
> Still other commanders thought the Negroes more responsive to individual notice, to flattery, and to competition

> than the whites, and the more successful ones capitalized on this characteristic in numerous ways. Drivers who had no wrecks for stipulated periods were given "safe driver" signs for their vehicles. One officer gave "Good Conduct" ribbons to every man "who had just stayed out of the guard house for three years." Other commanders stressed weekly competitions between units for "bests" in every conceivably category – "best mess", "best company area", and "lowest venereal rates". Winning units were given placards, published in bulletins, and cited at formations.
>
> Loyalty to officers whom they admired was another virtue attributed to colored soldiers. One officer, whose testimony was generally unfavorable to Negroes, remarked: "I'll say this to their credit – when you win the friendship and affection of one of them, he will be very loyal to you … Even the bad ones can be loyal." In summary, it should be noted that the quality of Negro trainees was not a constant thing, but varied with changing influences and circumstances. A "good unit" might deteriorate into a troublesome, inefficient, undisciplined mob when transferred from North to South, particularly if it contained a heavy admixture of racially sensitive men imbued with the attitudes of the Negro press, and was moved into a community where lines of segregation were tightly drawn and recreational facilities limited. A unit was almost certain to degenerate when capable officers, experienced in dealing with colored troops, were replaced by novices lacking in command ability. Conversely a poor unit might sometimes be brought to an efficient status by replacement of unsatisfactory or inexperienced officers with leaders of proved ability to command Negro troops.[34]

Meanwhile, the commander of the 99th Anti-Aircraft Regiment, which was already overseas, shared his thoughts with a sense of wonder:

> It is funny. I have been thinking over what is in this letter and it applies, all of it, to white troops as well as colored. I guess it is merely the details that count. Nevertheless, I am sincere in my admiration for these troops and I say that with full knowledge, that if I get a chance to take them into battle my own life and all that I have to live for will depend on them. I am supremely confident of their ability. There is not one iota of doubt in my mind that you people in Washington are building a mountain out of a molehill when you speak of "The Negro Problem in the Army." My God, these men are human and only waiting to be led. They are actually eager to do what is right. That sounds as though I am a negrophile whereas I am not. I am only a realist wanting to see the army make full use of this vast reservoir of man power. It must be used.[35]

The promotion of Black American officers was difficult. Although they might merit the promotion, based upon their skills and their achievements, the fact that they would be placed over white troops or white officers caused a problem. As the report summarized, "In no cases will white officers be commanded by Negro officers."[36] In other cases, Black lieutenants deserved promotion to the rank of captain, but since there were no vacancies available and the unit commander was reluctant to lose a capable officer, the Black lieutenant was left in his current position.[37] An example, "one case – involving two officers of the 646th Tank Destroyer Battalion – was it said that promotion was prevented by the War Department policy, the prohibitive provision being that which forbade colored senior officers serving in the same unit with white junior officers."[38]

When talking about the issues of race and Black officers:

> most of them were from the North. When stationed in the South, as the overwhelming majority of them were, they

> were brought face to face, both in camp and out of camp, with mores which assumed the white man's superiority – an assumption to which they were not accustomed. Their reaction was naturally one of protest and defense.[39]

However, this too was explained in the study:

> Still another factor which aggravated racial sensitiveness was the conviction that white officers were prejudiced and unfriendly. This feeling was not without foundation. Many white officers look with disfavor upon the assignment of Negroes and whites to the same unit. They were not accustomed to intimate association on an equal basis with Negroes in civilian life and they resented any pressure to that end in the army. Most of them met the minimum requirements of War Department orders prohibiting segregation in messes, barracks, and theaters, but the conformity of many was on a "duty" or "good soldier" basis. Efforts of commanders to intermingle their white and colored subordinates in officers' clubs were steadfastly resisted. White officers of one regiment when ordered by their colonel to admit recently assigned colored lieutenants to their club declared it disbanded; a little later they joined a private riding club beyond the camp limits which barred Negroes from membership.[40]
>
> If officers of colored units made poorer showing than their opposite in white organizations in 1942, it seems likely that the reason was lack of experience in dealing with Negroes rather than a deficiency in the qualities of leadership.[41]
>
> It seems incontrovertible that the command of colored units, particularly of combat organizations, was one of the Army's toughest assignments. To make good at it, an officer had to have sound judgment, common sense, tact, aggressiveness, initiative, self-confidence, and the other

> qualities usually associated with leadership. But he had to have more.[42]
>
> The officer had also to have an understanding of the peculiarities, the weaknesses, and the virtues of his men. He had to know how to blend firmness with kindness, to punish promptly but without show of bitterness or rancor, to avoid sarcasm, and to "kid" the men without seeming to get down on their level. To get the best results he had to call them by name, know something of their families, and establish himself as protector against all who might seek to abuse them. He had to be aware of their sensitiveness to such terms as "nigger", "boy", "shine", and "darky". He had to demand neither too much nor too little of them. And last but not least he must not be upset by unpredictable turns in their attitudes or actions. Rare indeed, and usually inexperienced, was the small unit commander who was bold enough to say: "I know the Negro."
>
> The officer who had a genuine fondness for Negroes, and whose interest in them was real, was apt to be more successful than one who posed his relationships on an abstract or pure duty basis. For Negroes were quick to detect a difference between artificiality and the real thing.
>
> The officer of colored troops needed also to differentiate between Northern and Southern Negroes, between college graduates and those of little education. The rustic Southern recruit, accustomed to strawbosses and white patriarchy, would brook, and perhaps even like, an assumed roughness of command that would provoke sullenness or revolt from educated Northerners, particularly those whose attitudes were shaped by the Pittsburgh Courier or the Chicago Defender.[43]

However, white and Black officers rarely associated outside of their duties:

> At Fort Huachuca and elsewhere, white and colored officers lived under the same roof and ate at the same messes. But they rarely got together for drinking, conversation, and yarn-swapping as was the custom in groups made up solely of white personnel. In mess halls they usually ate at different tables and in separate portions of the room. Segregation was hardly less real under rules which sought to prevent it than it would have been had the rules not existed. It was only natural that colored officers, especially those of Northern upbringing, should chafe greatly under this order of things. Some of them openly challenged it. At Camp Stewart, for instance, they would ride up to white officers' clubs to seek admission, leaving their drivers outside, in anticipation of certain refusal. In the 92d Division on one occasion, white officers of a regimental mess on coming to breakfast found a colored lieutenant sitting at each of the tables usually occupied by the whites. The white officers took their accustomed seats and ignored the "token visitors". After a few days the Negroes went back to the places they had previously occupied. Never again did they cross the aisle separating the colored and white officers in this "non-segregated" mess.[44]

When asked about his personal opinion, a Black lieutenant responded to questions about postponing agitations of racial rights until victory over the Germans and Japanese:

> To retard the war effort is a serious thing. However, I feel it is asking a little too much of me as a colored man … to enter wholeheartedly into that struggle … when I am not accorded the treatment to which my conduct entitles me … I do believe that if the army requires me to be a member of it, it ought to accord me the same protection which my status entitles me. If it doesn't do that I cannot have the

> right attitude towards it … I believe that a man should be treated as a man, whatever his complexion or color may be. That is not asking too much of the army … I think that an officer in the U.S. Army … ought to be able to go anywhere and do anything that any other officer is able to do.[45]

Meanwhile, assignment to a Black unit was not always regarded as a positive step in the careers of white officers. Some were sent to these outfits as a punishment or because they fell out of favor with their superiors:

> A new officer reporting to a colored unit sometimes was greeted with the query: "Well, what did you do to get sent here?" The apprehension was rather widespread among officers serving with Negroes that they were regarded by officers at large as inferiors – as men who had failed to make the grade with white troops.[46]

In hindsight, Black Americans were treated unfairly. During a racial flare-up, the official reports about it, one being a study on the Anti-Aircraft Artillery Command and the other a study about the training of Black American troops, are full of invective and view the incident from a certain perspective, thus failing to grasp the actual problem. The Anti-Aircraft Artillery Command study opens with:

> The tendency of the Negro to react to mob psychology and unfounded rumor was a direct cause for serious trouble in more than one case within the AAC. For example, during June 1943 there was a serious disturbance approaching race riot conditions among colored troops at the AAATC at Camp Stewart, Georgia. Subsequent investigation disclosed that the trouble was caused by a false rumor concerning treatment of colored personnel.[47]

The same incident is mentioned in the study regarding Black American soldiers:

> The affair at Camp Stewart, Ga., in June 1943, provides the profile of a typical outbreak. At the time of the disturbance there were about 15,000 Negroes stationed at Stewart. Recreational facilities in the colored portion of the camp were grossly inadequate. The nearest towns having any considerable population were Savannah, 42 miles [68 kilometers] from camp; Waycross, 60 miles [97 kilometers]; Brunswick, 66 miles [106 kilometers]; and Statesboro, 40 miles [64 kilometers]. Limited transportation facilities made these towns inaccessible to the great majority of Negro soldiers.
>
> No serious trouble had arisen before the spring of 1943. At that time two groups of Negro soldiers arrived at camp whose presence greatly influenced the attitude of other colored troops. One of these groups was the 100th Anti-Aircraft Artillery Regiment. Over half the members of this unit were Southerners, but their original ideas of race had been changed by association with comrades from the North and by a year of service in Sault Ste. Marie on the Canadian border, at which place they had intermingled with the whites freely, and some of them had married white women. Transfer of the unit to Georgia placed the soldiers in contact with a social system which most of them regarded as intolerable. Some of them boasted that they were going to break down the local barriers of racial prejudice. Their stories of equality in Canada and their success in building up a reputation for toughness at Stewart tended to make them popular champions among other Negro troops. Their influence was diffused by the breaking up of the 100th Regiment and the dispersion of its members among other units at Stewart.

The other provocative element was a group of soldiers of the 369th Anti-Aircraft Artillery Regiment, originally from New York, who had served in Hawaii where they had been well treated by the natives and the non-belligerent Japanese. When subjected to Georgia conventions and the unpleasant conditions at Camp Stewart these soldiers became disgruntled. Some of them raised the question whether the Japanese would not treat them better than the Georgians. Resentment was sharpened by designation of certain camp latrines and other facilities as "white only", in violation of War Department policies.

The discontented Negroes wrote letters of protest to their friends in the North. Some of the complaints fell into the hands of colored newspapermen who used them as grist for exaggerated and inflammatory articles about "the hell-hole of Georgia". Copies of the *Chicago Defender, The Afro-American, the Pittsburgh Courier*, and other papers featuring these articles circulated at Stewart and added fuel to the smoldering fire of resentment. Negro officers contributed to the unrest by manifestations of sympathy for aggrieved soldiers. They also challenged the existing order of things by attending camp theaters and exchanges in white areas contrary to the customs of the Post. Discontent of the officers was aggravated by the fact that many of them had served for long periods without promotion, under white executives who had been advanced with comparative expedition.

[...]

Some of the white officers contributed to the discontent by expressing their distaste for Camp Stewart and an earnest desire to leave the state of Georgia.

The presence of white military policemen among them was also an irritant to the Negroes. Whether justifiably or not, colored soldiers at Stewart, and in general, regarded white military policemen as more cruel and oppressive than those of their own race. Resentment at Stewart was heightened considerably by reports that white military police used a machine gun to disperse a crowd that had assembled outside a Negro service club.

For several weeks in the late spring the Negroes surreptitiously collected weapons and ammunition. It seems likely that supply sergeants in some instances permitted the soldiers to obtain arms and later made up the tale that the weapons were taken by force.

Emotions were heightened from time to time by minor interracial incidents in and out of camp and by rumors of mistreatment and abuse.

On 9 June 1943 the Negro portion of camp was electrified by a rumor that white soldiers had raped and murdered a colored woman and killed her soldier husband. One version of the report was that the assailants were white military police. It mattered little that the rumor in all its versions was false. About 9:30 that evening a mob of approximately one hundred colored soldiers, some with guns, assembled in the east wing of the camp. As officers attempted to disperse the group a wild shot was fired from the mob and military police were called. Excitement mounted and the crowd increased. During the next half-hour some of the Negroes raided supply rooms for ammunition, rifles, and machine guns, while others took to the woods in fright. Confusion was heightened by the unauthorized sounding of a gas alarm.

About ten o'clock an MP vehicle approached the scene of disturbance and received a heavy fusillade from elements of the 458th Anti-aircraft Artillery Battalion. Four military police were wounded. This initiated a general firing in the 458th and other areas which lasted for two hours. Much of

> the shooting was in the air, but several vehicles were fired on and a civilian bus driver was wounded.
>
> Just before midnight the MP detail was fired on while marching across a firebreak and one of the members was killed. The military police fired one shot in return; this and two others, one of which was accidental, were the only shots fired by the military police during the entire melee. It was estimated that the rioters fired from 600 to 800 rounds.
>
> Shortly after midnight two white battalions came to the area in half-tracks and the firing ceased.
>
> A board of officers investigated the riot, and courts-martial meted out punishment to some of the ring leaders. The board's recommendation to disband the 458th Battalion, principal offender in the affair, was overruled because the unit had already been alerted for overseas movement, but steps were taken to quietly to reduce the number of Negro troops at Camp Stewart to about five thousand.[48]

Disbanding the 458th AAA, which had been alerted for overseas movement, would have been a waste of time and money. The training that the unit had received would be for naught. Unfortunately for the Black Americans, the real problem, social inequality, was not addressed.

Although the study did admit that there were serious errors and patterns to detect:

> The factors which produced the outbreaks were numerous and complex. Inadequacy of transportation facilities and of opportunities for recreation, particularly on weekends, was undoubtedly a source of much unrest among colored troops. In the South, Negro troops were often unable to secure seats on commercial buses because of the higher priority of white passengers. The government provided

vehicles in some cases, but rarely in numbers adequate to demands. Even when colored soldiers were able to secure transportation, there was frequently no suitable place for them to go. Towns near the camps were usually too small to accommodate large crowds of soldiers, and entertainment facilities consisted mainly of dilapidated beer dispensaries, gambling dens, theaters, "juke joints", and bawdy houses, all of which were greatly overcrowded. Most soldiers who went to town seeking recreation were reduced to the necessity of roaming the streets. The lack of diversion made them moody and irritable. Competition for such entertainment as existed often produced fights. This in turn led to intervention by "the law" and the situation was ripe for a riot.[49]

The character of "the law" increased the tension, for in most Southern towns the police force consisted in part at least of ignorant, tactless, underpaid men drawn from the stratum of society which had the strongest race prejudice. These qualities combined with fear in some instances to make the law enforcers unduly quick with club and bun/gun.[50]

[...]

Many Southerners strongly opposed the stationing of colored units in their midst. A Texas mayor, for instance, on hearing that several thousand Negroes were to be brought to a nearby camp, asked his congressman to inform the President that he would personally shoot the first colored soldier who came to town.[51]

Over against the Southern conviction that colored soldiers, especially those from the North, were "uppity", boisterous, rapacious, trouble-bent, and in general a menace to the traditional order of life, was a feeling equally strong among Negro troops hailing from the country north of the Mason-Dixon line that Southern ideas and customs of race were cruel, oppressive, and more akin to Nazidom than to democracy.[52]

[...]

Cleavage was also sharpened by conviction of the Negroes that it was illogical for them to submit to a discriminatory social system at home while preparing to fight for the four freedoms overseas.[53]

[...]

Some commanders in the field regarded the formula – if you have the right kind of leadership you will not have racial outbreaks – as having too much of an armchair slant. Their attitude was that, given certain conditions – such as placing a unit composed of racially sensitive Northern Negroes in the deep rural South, with limitations of transportation and recreation – the most effective command may not be able to forestall a racial flare-up.[54]

The total experience of the Army Ground Forces indicated that the following measures were of greatest efficacy in preventing racial disturbances: (1) filling command positions in colored units with strong leaders – officers who combined outstanding qualities of command with an intimate knowledge of Negro troops; (2) a generous program of camp recreation including movies, sports, and music; (3) stationing of Negro troops near towns having a sufficiently large colored population to "absorb" them on weekends and provision of ample facilities for transporting troops from camp to towns; (4) programs of training sufficiently strenuous to prevent accumulation of excessive energy; (5) use of colored rather than white military police, and the sending of large numbers of military police to towns frequented by colored troops, particularly on weekends following payday; and (6) a rigid system for safeguarding weapons and ammunition. The Commanding General of

> the 92nd Division, who reported considerable success with the policy regarding military police, had a double quota of military police, all of whom were husky Negroes ranging in height from 6 feet to 6 feet, 6 inches. Said this commander of the value of colored military police in forestalling difficulty: "If trouble starts brewing and a flock of white MP's appear, the Negro's resentment will be aroused. If the colored MP's show up, the Negro troublemakers will more than likely decide to move on."[55]

Whereas the study did acknowledge some of the errors, it wasn't above blaming the Black American press for the errors, "which agitated steadily for the overthrow of segregation within the army and out of the army."[56] Black American units were different to white American units, in that these units needed more than being treated as strictly military. There was also a racial asset to them and commanders needed to be aware of them as well as be able to handle these situation. Not every commander could rise to the challenge:

> As a commentary, it may be said that the experience of the AAC has indicated that officers assigned to duty with Negro troops must he carefully selected for such assignment. These officers must be firm but patient, and they must possess leadership abilities to a marked degree. The common belief that only those officers who have lived in the South are qualified for duty with Negro troops has been found to be without basis. A complete understanding of the average Negro, however, is essential to the successful handling of colored troops.[57]

Even other Anti-Aircraft Command units had the necessary problems:

> Subsequent investigation disclosed that the trouble was caused by a false rumor concerning treatment of colored personnel.

> During May and June 1943, there were three incidents involving colored troops at the AAATC, Fort Bliss, Texas. On 11 October 1943, a very serious incident occurred at the Barrage Balloon Training Center, Camp Tyson, Tennessee, the aftermath of which involved the trail by General Court Martial of sixty-four colored soldiers, a large proportion of which were non-commissioned officers. The charges involved the unlawful taking of rifles, ammunition and trucks for the purpose of engaging in activities which could have had very serious consequences. All sixty-four of these defendants were found guilty by the General Court Martial, the accused receiving dishonorable discharges and sentences ranging from one to five years confinement at hard labor.[58]

Black soldiers and the threat of hostile aircraft

Despite being largely relegated to service units, Black Americans served from the first until the last day of the Second World War. Segregated units consisted in all services. The 332nd Fighter Group flew in support of the Allied bombing campaign. The 92nd Infantry Division (ID) fought in Italy, while the 93rd Infantry Division was deployed in the Pacific. The 555th Parachute Infantry Battalion didn't fight in combat but fought forest fires. The 761st and the 784th Tank Battalion rolled into battle with their M4 Sherman tank in the European Theater of Operations, while the 758th Tank Battalion fought with the M5 Stuart Light Tank in Italy. The 614th and the 827th Tank Destroyer (TD) Battalions fought in Europe, while the 679th TD was deployed with the 92nd ID in Italy. Segregated artillery battalions, like the 333rd, 349th, 350th, 351st, 578th, 686th, 777th, 969th, and 999th Field Artillery Battalion, fought in Europe or in support of the Black infantry divisions.

The 320th Barrage Balloon Battalion, the 3275th Quartermaster Service Company, the 582nd Engineer Dump Truck Company, the 385th Quartermaster Truck Company, and the 490th Port Battalion, landed on the shores of Normandy on D-Day. Third Platoon, C Company, 614th Tank Destroyer Battalion earned the Distinguished Unit Citation during the battle of Climbach. The 969th Field Artillery Battalion earned one for their valiant stand at Bastogne together with the 101st Airborne Division. Even Black women served, such as the 6888th Central Postal Directory Battalion, or worked in one of the many war factories.

However, these units were the exception. Many more Black combat units were established, but they never reached the frontline. The first two segregated tank destroyer battalions to be activated, the 795th and the 846th, were broken up and converted to service units. This was the fate of the majority of the Black combat units in training and most of the Black soldiers served in support or labor battalions, repairing roads or railways. They served in the quartermaster corps, drove trucks, loaded or unloaded ships, and hauled ammunition to enable the white soldiers to fight. Others worked as linesmen, fixing communications.

Although they were employed behind the frontline, where combat was unlikely, it didn't mean they never experienced combat. Planes continued to be a nuisance, hindering the American war effort often far behind the front lines, where service troops were working. One of the early decorations for valor in combat happened on 25 October 1942, when Mack B. Anderson, of the 823rd Engineer Aviation Battalion, engaged a Japanese aircraft. The airfield near Assam, India, where he was stationed, was engaged by eighteen Zeros, Japanese fighters. Single-handedly Anderson manned a .30 machine gun and engaged the hostile fighters. The airplanes made several passes to silence the machine gun but failed to do so. Eventually, Anderson's weapon jammed and he ran over to a trench, where he took cover. From there, he engaged the fighters with his .45 pistol. For his actions, Anderson was rewarded with the Silver Star with the following citation:

> On October 25, 1942, at an airdrome in Assam, India, during a violent strafing attack by eighteen Japanese fighters, Private First Class Anderson proceeded to single-handedly man a .30-caliber machine gun, when taking cover in a nearby slit trench would not have brought censure. His gun was in open terrain since the firing pit had not been completed. With utter disregard for his personal safety, being subjected to almost continuous fire from the attacking airplanes, he returned their fire until failure of a part put his gun out of action. He then continued firing with his automatic pistol. Several Japanese fighters definitely centered their attack on his position. His extreme coolness under fire was an example, in this initial attack, in keeping with the highest traditions of the Service and sets the highest standard in a branch of the Service not basically combatant.

Turning a machine gun skywards is one way to combat hostile aircraft, but the Anti-Aircraft Command also raised segregated units with dedicated training:

> during 1942 and 1943 the AAC activated and trained one regiment, four gun battalions, and fourteen automatic weapons battalions, all manned by Negro personnel. Four activated barrage balloon battalions were also designated as colored units. In addition, a certain proportion of the training batteries at two replacement training centers devoted full time to training of colored AAA enlisted replacements.[59]

One of the first Black Anti-Aircraft Artillery battalions to go overseas was the 450th AAA AW Battalion, which distinguished itself in combat before it had even landed on Italian soil. Their ships were still in the harbor in Naples when German bombers came flying over at night. Searchlights came on and located the bombers. Soldiers of the 450th manned its 40mm guns and fired upon the bombers, shooting down one of them.

Onboard another ship, Master Sergeant Johnson Clark of Detroit, Michigan, jumped into a loaded truck parked on deck and opened fire with a .50 caliber machine gun mounted on the cab. Others from that ship fired upon the hostile aircraft as well and a second bomber crashed into the water. Lieutenant General Mark Clark, commanding the Fifth Army, commented on the soldiers of the 450th Battalion for this accomplishment: "I am proud of the outstanding performance of duty of these soldiers in this baptism of fire. Their conduct was excellent and reflects the training and discipline of their unit. The Fifth Army welcomes such soldiers."[60]

Chapter 3

We Guard the Skyways

The 452nd Coast Artillery Battalion (Separate) (Automatic Weapons)(Anti-Aircraft)(Semi-Mobile)

On 9 May 1942 the 452nd Coast Artillery Battalion (Separate) (Automatic Weapons)(Anti-Aircraft)(Semi-Mobile) was constituted on the list of inactive army units. It had a long and unwieldy name. A letter from the War Department, dated 13 June, gave instructions that the unit would be activated soon and the activation was accomplished at Camp Stewart, Georgia, on 1 August 1942.

Originally the battalion numbered just five officers and ninety-two enlisted men. These soldiers came from the 54th Coast Artillery Regiment, operating 155mm guns, and at that time placed at Fort Ord, California. First Lieutenant Bruce Bass was in charge of the unit and he would be relieved on 15 August, when twelve additional officers arrived, among them Major Irwin I. Sanborn, who became the new commanding officer. On 26 August 1942, Lieutenant Colonel Allen M. Murphy assumed command of the unit. In the next couple of weeks more men arrived from Fort Eustis, Virginia; Camp Wallace, Texas; and Jefferson Barracks, Missouri. On 10 October 1942 the 452nd Coast Artillery Battalion was converted from a semi-mobile unit to a mobile unit.

On 5 December 1942, Major Raymond C. Cheal assumed command of the unit. The battalion continued to grow, although eventually some men were transferred out again. In December 1942 ninety-four enlisted men were selected to serve as the cadre for the 484th Coast Artillery Battalion (AA), at Camp Stewart, Georgia.

Thus, by the closing of the year 1942, the battalion consisted of fifty officers and 843 enlisted men.

On 10 January 1943, the battalion moved to Camp Atterbury, Indiana, where it was attached to the Second Army, XI Corps, 83rd Infantry Division. The purpose of this reassignment was to get combined arms training; recent experiences in North Africa had shown the importance of this as it allowed anti-aircraft soldiers to offer better protection to the units they were attached to. The battalion travelled there by train, the equipment and freight in one section and the soldiers in two passenger sections.

In March, during their training, the battalion received approval of their Coat of Arms. It consisted of four 40mm gun barrels, five indentures and two divisions, denoting the numerical designation of the outfit, 452, with the motto: "We guard the skyways". The lower division was scarlet, representing the Coast Artillery, while the other one was azure. The guns represented the crown of victory, to which this battalion would contribute.

On 1 April 1943, the battalion received orders that it would be moved to Fort Sheridan soon, departing Camp Atterbury, Indiana, on 3 April 1943 and arriving the next day at their destination. It was again under the control of Anti-Aircraft Command. The unit afterwards received notification that this was a permanent change of station.

On 13 May Lieutenant Colonel Lamar C. Ratcliffe would assume command of the unit, being the commander that would remain with the unit for the rest of the Second World War. Lamar Ratcliffe seems to have been one of those commanders who was fit for the job. Born on 6 February 1910, he was appointed to West Point as the class of 1933. Previous service included duty with the Coast Artillery in Texas, Virginia, California and on Corregidor, Phillipine Islands. He was married in December 1940 to Ruth Webster at the Panama Canal Zone. He was an early advocate of complete integration in the Armed Forces.

On 15 May 1943 orders came in that the name of the battalion was to be changed. It would be known as the 452nd Anti-Aircraft

Artillery Automatic Weapons Battalion (Mobile). A few days later, on 20 May, the battalion was reorganized with the new Tables of Organization. It was to have an authorized strength of thirty-five officers, three warrant officers, and 736 enlisted men. The battalion was reorganized again on 13 December 1943, keeping the officers and warrant officers at the same number but increasing the enlisted men to 779.

In August anti-tank firing, mobile training and seacoast target practice were completed. In September AA target practice with a towed sleeve was completed. In the temporary absence of Lamar C. Ratcliffe, on 24 August Major Ralph M. Roberts assumed command. In September orders were received that the unit would be moved overseas soon. Two officers and two enlisted men needed to go ahead as an advance detachment to prepare for the arrival of the unit. The advance detachment consisted of First Lieutenant George T. Waterhouse, Second Lieutenant Gerard A. Gobeille, Technician Fourth Grade John I. Cothrane and Technician Fifth Grade Alfred J. McGill. On 5 October the battalion moved to Camp Shanks, New York, where it would be made ready for movement overseas. In two trains the battalion went to the port of embarkation. From there it would board the ship that would carry them across the sea.

In preparation for going overseas, units were given other designations. This was done to prevent potential spies from learning about the movements of units. The battalion was temporarily assigned the code 5022-R. In preparation for the movement, it was explicitly stated that this code designation, both number and letter, was to be used for shipping purposes instead of the unit's actual designation. As such, "5022-R" would be the name of the battalion.

Battlefield England

On 3 November the battalion disembarked in the United Kingdom. It then proceeded to the staging area at Checkendon, Berkshire.

Around 14 November each battery went its separate way, deploying at different operation sites, including Cheltenham, Gloucester; Tidworth, Wiltshire; Ashchurch, Gloucestershire, and Thatcham, Berkshire.

The battalion set up to cover Services of Supply depots and one battery was deployed at each location. These depots consisted of different supplies and materiel which all needed to be guarded against possible air attacks.

The headquarters of the Services of Supply (SOS) was located at Cheltenham, where two office buildings were allocated to the SOS. These had been built by the War Office in case London needed to be evacuated. Brigadier General John C.H. Lee, in command of the Services of Supply in the European Theater of Operations, worked from one of these buildings.

Another location was Ashchurch (G-25), where an Ordnance depot needed to be protected. Ashchurch was 8 miles [13 kilometers] from Cheltenham and it was the most modern and largest of the five U.S. general depots activated on 11 July 1942. It had been built by the British Royal Army Service Corps as a depot for maintenance and automotive supply. There were ten large hangar-type warehouses and five smaller ones. They provided a total closed storage space of 1,747,998 sq.ft [162,394 sq. meters], of which Ordnance was assigned 378,200 ft [115,275 meters]. Another 1,014,200 sq.ft [94,222 sq. meters] were assigned to Quartermaster's Motor Transport Service. The large warehouses were of brick, with gabled roofs and overhead roller suspension doors. The roads were lined with fences, which had been painted in yellow and black to aid visibility during blackouts.

An Ordnance depot at Tidworth (O-640) also needed to be guarded. The depot was activated on 22 July 1942, featuring 133,000 sq.ft [12,356 sq. meters] of shop space and 50,000 ft [15,240 meters] of storage space in two buildings. The depot had good connections to the highways and the railways.

Thatcham (G-45) was a quartermaster depot. It had originally been a military depot that had been operated by the British Army, before being transferred to the United States Army. As was common, the storage areas were dispersed over a wide area. It was unique in that it was the only depot in the United Kingdom that handled women's items.

At each of these locations, it had already been decided where the anti-aircraft guns needed to be placed. In most of the cases the .50 cal machine guns could be placed nearby, although in a few cases it was better to site these guns a couple of hundred yards away.

While in position, the battalion was under the command of Air Defense of Great Britain (ADGB) and they would provide the battalion with an early warning in case of approaching hostile aircraft. The battalion came under the command of the 3rd AA Group, which was a British unit, and not the 3rd AAA Group, which was a U.S. unit.

At most locations, accommodation needed to be constructed for the gun crews and additional personnel. The orders stressed: "The battalion is now in an active theater of operations, and is subject to a move at any time to operate in a mobile role with front line ground forces."[1]

It recommended using the time available to bring the unit to a state of maximum combat efficiency. Aircraft recognition training needed to be undertaken, as well as physical conditioning exercises, which could be done while in the staging area. These exercises would also be carried out later, when in the operational sites, along with gun drill and other topics such as first aid or mine and booby trap detection. British 40mm gun crews could be visited to see how they conducted drill and what training methods they employed. Mobile training was possible if it didn't interfere with the primary mission of AA defense.

In December 1943 an inspection was made of the 452nd AAA. Battery C and B were inspected on 20 December, while A and

D were inspected on 23 December. The report was satisfactory, although there were some areas of improvement. The battalion was greatly hindered by operating over such a dispersed area. The Air Sentries were the biggest fault of the battalion. They acted more like telephone operators and didn't appear to be instructed in their duties. There were no dark glasses or binoculars, while also no log was kept of planes being seen. However, these Air Sentries also had no maps onto which they could plot the airplanes, or to warn the battalion from which direction aircraft would approach.

Additionally, there was no local security plan, an evacuation plan, an automatic weapons barrage plan or camouflage discipline. The guns were not dug in and there was no protection of sandbags. Ammunition was stored in one pile at the gun positions. No alternate or dummy positions had been planned. There was a shortage of ammunition and there we no machine guns for protection against fast low-flying hostile aircraft. The wires of the field telephone were not hung on poles or in trees, neither was it dug in. It was just left on the ground.

The soldiers had not yet adjusted to the life of a combat outfit at the front. Their old habits might not have been a huge risk back in the U.S., but now the situation was different. The inadequacies weren't helped by the lack of a visible threat, though there were few moments where the German Luftwaffe presented a credible threat.

It also noted that "Anglo-American relations are excellent. In general the only difficulty has been with American white and other colored soldiers in the areas concerned. Bearing, soldierly qualities, and appearance are satisfactory."[2] The men were described as being cheerful, contented and healthy, despite the rainy weather and the mud they had to struggle with.

While operating in the area, six-hour passes could be granted once per week and four twenty-four hour passes, or a forty-eight hour pass, every month. It could be increased to a seven- or eight-day furlough if soldiers wanted to save up their furloughs. Then they could visit London or another historical place. The men were regularly given permission to visit nearby cities and furnished with transportation. An officer of each battery was with the convoy and would remain in the city during the visit.

Anti-Aircraft Defense in 1944

On 1 January 1944 the 452nd AAA was still in England. The various batteries were deployed at different locations to protect against aerial attacks. The battalion was attached to the 54th AAA Brigade and consisted of thirty-seven officers and 736 enlisted men. The HQ and HQ battery were at Wootton, Oxfordshire, while the batteries served at different locations. Battery A was at Cheltenham, Gloucestershire, defending the Headquarters Service of Supply, European Theater of Operations. Battery B defended Depot O-640, located at Tidworth, Battery C was at Thatcham defending Depot G-45, and Battery D was at Ashchurch, defending Depot G-25.

On 19 January the 452nd was attached to the 111th Anti-Aircraft Artillery Group. On 30 January the Headquarters and HQ battery moved from Wootton to Thatcham. The unit waited for action and an article about this lack of action appeared in Black newspapers in the U.S.:

> The gun crews of a Negro anti-aircraft battalion whose guns are emplaced on high windswept hilltops and the flat grain fields of farms "somewhere in England" maintain a vigil by their 40mm Bofors guns that never ceases, praying that Nazi planes will come their way. Spread out over a dozen counties, this AA unit provides sole defense against aerial attack for some of the most important United States supply centers and headquarters sites in the European Theatre of Operations. Each battery is deeply aware that upon it rests

no small quota of responsibility for the protection of vast stores of vital Allied invasion equipment.

Indicated Determination

Each gun crew earnestly feels that should the Luftwaffe succeed in destroying any one of the VPs (Vulnerable Points) around which battery guns are situated the war might well be lengthened. These crack ack-ack men don't mean for that to happen, and their demonstrated accuracy of fire and enthusiasm at gun drill are indications of their determination. In these days when new ways of war are constantly being devised AA outfits are likely to be ordered to apply their fire power to a wide variety of targets, on land as well as in the air, and so their training stresses versatility of firing techniques. Before this battalion shipped from the States its name had become synonymous with the highest standards in AA circles. Phenomenal record firing at towed aerial and anti-tank targets at training centers in Georgia and Illinois made for its present excellent reputation, and before training had been completed it had received personal congratulations from Lieutenant General Lesley J. McNair, Commanding General, Army Ground Forces.

Confidence, therefore, was part of the equipment these youngsters brought with them when they came to the [European Theater of Operations] and proceeded to assigned operational sites. Chafing now for lack of action against "live" targets, hundreds of gun crew men wait for Hitler's raiders with a grim intensity, clean and oil their guns with religious solemnity, and race through gun drills several times daily with a seriousness of purpose that conveys the impression that they are actually "tracking" German planes.[3]

On 29 January two batteries were alerted. At 20:50 the alarm sounded at Battery C, at location G-45. Battery B, at O-640, manned their guns and were ready at 20:55. At 21:40 hours Battery C stood down again. At 21:45 hours O-640 also stood down. Battery C was alerted once more at 21:54 hours and stood down again at 22:08. No aircraft were seen, but they were expected to be within 15 miles [24 kilometers] of the VPs, approaching from the east and southwest. No shots were fired and the sky was overcast.

On 23 February at 00:37 one aircraft was fired upon. A plane was seen in the sky, coming from the southeast and going north, before departing in a southerly direction. It was around 1,500 yards [1,372 meters] above the gun positions and previously heavy AA guns fired at the airplane. Battery A opened fire and four guns shot at it. The action lasted one to two minutes and no hits were registered.

Things would soon change. On 29 February the battalion was detached from the previous units to which it had been attached and was attached instead to the 113th AAA group. That day the battalion moved by motor to Stafford, Staffordshire. New orders came in for training and on 11 March training started at the 11th LAA Training and Practice Camp (British) at Stiffkey, Norfolk. The camp had the same name as the Stiffkey Stick Sight. This AA Practice Camp was allotted to them from 11 to 24 March. An advance detachment of four officers and twenty-four enlisted men could be sent ahead, while the rest of the battalion, twenty-nine officers and 696 enlisted men came two days later. An additional week of training was requested and approved after deficiencies were revealed during the training exercises. This greatly helped the battalion to improve.

Target tracking was done with a Hurricane, a British fighter, while the British Hawker Henley was used for towed-sleeve target practice. The men were trained on the 40mm gun, as well as the .50 cal machine gun. A report after this second week of training revealed that the battalion had greatly improved. It additionally noted that: "the morale of the men appeared to be very good. They seemed to have a pride in their organization and in the fact that they were members of a combat unit. All were very willing to work hard and willing to learn."[34]

Similarly, the battalion was praised because there had been no trouble with the unit in the neighboring towns. The battalion made the most use of their time at Stiffkey, although the report did note that the battalion would perform better in a semi-static role. It explained that while the battalion performed well under favorable circumstances, it had difficulty adjusting to unfavorable or awkward situations. The report recommended doing away with the director and focusing on Stiffkey Stick and Eyeshooting methods. This change would remove the burden of maintaining and adjusting the director. Additionally, the men were found to be more proficient at using Stiffkey Stick and Eyeshooting techniques.

On 31 March the unit moved to Blandford Camp. On 1 April the battalion was attached to the 47th AAA Brigade and then further attached to the 92d AAA Group on 4 April. At Blandford Camp, under the command of the 92d AAA Group and the British Tactical Training Center Personnel, the battalion conducted four weeks of intensive mobile training under actual field conditions. Almost all the requirements for compliance with Preparation for Overseas Movement were completed.

New orders came in on 10 April and the battalion was alerted for overseas movement. The battalion was detached from existing units and attached to the First United States Army; it was then attached to the 49th AAA Brigade from 30 April.

The battalion was prepared for the coming invasion in Normandy on 6 June. On 10 May it was attached to the Third United States Army and Blandford served as the camp where the unit would be gathered and declared that the unit would need to be prepared to move with six hours' notice on or after 3 June 1944.

From Blandford, the battalion went to Shaftesbury, Warminster, Melksham, Chippenham, Malmsbury, and Sherston Pinkney Park.

MPs were provided to help with traffic along the way. The convoy consisted of 100 vehicles with seventy-six trailers. On 23 May the unit proceeded to Pinkney Park Bivouac Area, Sherston Wilts, and completed there the remaining requirements for the Preparation for Overseas Movement, Short Sea Voyage.

The battalion was also divided in two: the Assault Group and the Residue. On 12 June orders arrived that the battalion would be attached to the 18th AAA Group. The Assault Group, consisting of twenty-seven officers and 506 enlisted men, departed on 18 June 1944 and arrived that same day at Marshalling Area, Camp D-8, Portland Area, Southern England.

D-8 was also known as Downwood, and located to the north of the village of Bincombe. Previously troops that participated in D-Day had been based at the camp, but now they had landed in Normandy new troops had taken their place. According to a strict time schedule, new troops arrived until they too could be put across the Channel. Thus a steady stream of men and supplies was created that would be put across the Channel and onto French soil.

The next day, at 07:00 hours, Battery D left the Marshalling Area and embarked in Portland on two LCTs, LCT 485 and LCT 765 at 10:00 hours. Between ten to fourteen hours later, HQ battery and Batteries A, B, C, embarked on two LSTs.[5] Early in the morning of 20 June the ships left Portland Harbor and sailed for France. However, due to heavy storms in the English Channel, the convoy took shelter in the Solent Channel near the Isle of Wight. This storm had been one of the worst in many decades and succeeded in something the Germans had failed to do: destroy the Mulberry harbor at Omaha Beach. Once the storm had abated, the ships set sail again.

Festung Europa breached

The first unit of the 452nd AAA ashore was Battery D, which landed at Utah Beach in Normandy at 15:50 hours on 23 June. Two days later Headquarters and HQ battery, Battery A, B, C, landed at Utah Beach at 16:00 hours on 25 June. That day the entire battalion was deployed and provided anti-aircraft protection for the Omaha Beach Maintenance Area. The Battalion Command Post was located at Asnières.

On 26 June 1944 Battery D and First Platoon of Battery B moved to a Class V (Ammunition) Dump near Formigny. On 30 June the battalion was attached to the 207th Anti-Aircraft Artillery Group. At 02:15 hours on that day, a flare was reported half a mile south of Gun Section No. 7 of Battery C, burning for an estimated two minutes. Around 02:35 Battery A fired upon an aircraft, shooting four rounds with the 40mm. Starting at 05:15 and within five minutes of each other, the three other batteries engaged an aircraft. That same day a person was picked up who, based upon a description sent out by the Military Police, was suspected of being a German spy.

On 1 July, around 00:18 hours, a twin-engine plane dropped a flare and Battery C fired upon it, while Gun Section No. 8 fired upon it with permission of Lieutenant Loesch. Battery D also fired upon the plane, which was illuminated by the flare.

That same day the Residue, under command of Lewis J. Hutchinson moved from the Pinkney Park Bivouac Area and went to Marshalling Area D, Camp C-3, Southern England. At Falmouth they embarked on 6 July and disembarked on 9 July at Utah Beach. They joined the battalion the next day.

Meanwhile, in France, Battery A reported on 5 July that it had shot down a plane, though it might have been a flare; an officer was to be sent over to investigate. The sections were then all instructed to fire only when the aircraft could be seen to prevent squandering ammunition and potential fratricide. Later, Gun No. 3, Battery C, requested to go out of action to clear a stoppage.

On 8 July early in the morning, 2,000 yards [1,829 meters] east of Gun No. 3, Battery C, yellow pyrotechnics were seen. Later, four more yellow pyrotechnics were seen to the northeast of Battery

C. Early in the morning the platoon leader investigated the small arms firing at Gun Section No. 1 of Battery C, which was almost certainly a sniper. This is substantiated by Major Chesney, Battalion Executive of the 320th Barrage Balloon Battalion, who was present.

On 9 July, early in the morning, a suspicious man approached Gun No. 4 of Battery D from the south of their position. When he came within 25 to 30 yards, he was challenged and ran away. The guard fired his submachinegun at him. Battery C reported five yellow flares 1 mile [1.6 kilometers] south of their position. Around 02:30 Battery D fired at a single-engine plane at 1,100 ft [335 meters].

Early in the morning of 16 July a burning aircraft crashed down to the northeast of the Battery C command post. Battery B, C, D, engaged aircraft that came flying over. On 18 July all guns of the battalion were pointed skywards in the protection of the Class V dumps at Longueville, Trévières, Formigny, and Asnières.

On 20 July the unit was relieved of the 49th AAA Brigade. It came back under the control of the 2nd AAA Group, which reported to the 51st AAA Brigade, which in turn answered to the Third U.S. Army.

On 3 August the battalion was relieved from protection of the Class V dumps in the Formigny area and went on to protect the Petrol/Oil/Lubrication (POL) Dumps of the Third United States Army in the Saint-Jacques-de-Néhou Area, Cherbourg Peninsula. The battalion had an authorized strength of 791 men, but was below it with 747. Forty-two officers, three warrant officers and 702 enlisted men were present, meaning they were two officers and forty-two enlisted men short. On 4 August the unit came under the command of the 38th AAA Brigade and the 27th AAA Group.

On 6 August Private Harold K. Chambers died in a drowning. He was buried the next day. On 8 August 1944, orders of the 38th AAA Brigade attached the unit to the 24th AAA Group and the battalion were used to protect the Main Supply Route of the Third Army in the Gavray Hyenville, Montchaton, Coutances, Bréhal,

La Jourdannière Area. The Third Army had arrived later than the U.S. First Army, which had landed on D-Day and was advancing to the east. The Third Army, south of the First Army, was also breaking out. XII Corps was preparing for battle and would soon be committed to action.

Guns were also set up at important bridges, crossroads and road junctions in this area. The Luftwaffe made frenzied attacks upon armor and infantry columns as well as bridges, road defiles and dams up and down the Avranches supply route. First Platoon, Battery A, was defending a crossroads and road junction at Gavray. First Platoon, Battery B, was defending another road junction. Second Platoon, Battery B, was defending a road junction and bridge near Montchaton. Battery C was defending a road junction and crossroads near Coutances. First Platoon, Battery D, was defending a road junction and crossroads at Bréhal. Second Platoon, Battery D, was defending a road junction at La Jourdannière. On 9 August, Second Platoon, Battery D, relocated to Cérences, where they provided AA protection for a road junction and the battalion command post relocated to a new position.

The war was happening all around them and a frightening reminder came on 10 August when a P-47 crashed near the Battalion HQ. It once more showed the soldiers the deadly consequences of war. The plane was temporarily guarded by soldiers of the 452nd AAA.

The threat of the Luftwaffe

The Luftwaffe had been a formidable threat at the beginning of the Second World War. Since the Luftwaffe had been employed in a ground support role, they focused on fighter aircraft over bombers, meaning that the German bombers were a lesser threat than anticipated. However, the constant combat, both at the front as well as in defense against the Allied bombing campaign, had ground down the Luftwaffe. New pilots, with less and less training time, were rushed into combat. They tried to offset their disadvantages by technological innovations, such as the Messerschmitt Me 262 and other jet powered aircraft, but it was not enough to turn the tide. Later in the war, the Luftwaffe was plagued by a shortage of fuel and material.

In support of XII Corps

On 13 August the 452nd AAA Battalion was relieved from previous attachments and added to XII Corps. That same day Second Platoon, Battery D, started defending the road junction at La Jourdannière again, being relieved on 14 August. On 15 August all the batteries and the battalion headquarters moved to XII Corps area, where new missions would be assigned upon arrival. Each battery was split up by platoon to provide protection for different field artillery battalions. Starting on the 16th, the following assignments were given:

First Platoon, Battery A, provided protection for the 179th Field Artillery Battalion (155mm howitzer).

Second Platoon, Battery A, provided protection for the 558th Field Artillery Battalion (155mm gun self-propelled).

First Platoon, Battery B, provided protection for the 945th Field Artillery Battalion (155mm howitzer).

Second Platoon, Battery B, provided protection for the 731st Field Artillery Battalion (155mm gun).

First Platoon, Battery C, provided protection for the 191st Field Artillery Battalion (155mm howitzer).

Second Platoon, Battery C, provided protection for the 802nd Field Artillery Battalion (155mm howitzer).

Battery D provided protection for XII Corps HQ.

Later an order came through stating that the Battalion would remain under XII Corps control. For the rest of the war, the 452nd AAA remained attached to XII Corps, which was part of General Patton's Third Army. It was under the command of Major General Gilbert R. Cook, but he would be replaced by Major General Manton S. Eddy on 19 August. XII Corps was often the spearhead of Patton's Third Army. The armored divisions of this corps would be used to force a gap in the German lines, where the infantry divisions would be pushed through. To bolster the divisional artillery, the corps artillery could be employed to neutralize German resistance.

The Germans also realized this and the field artillery was one of the priority targets to be defended. Field artillery battalions could not always be well concealed and thus formed an attractive target for hostile aircraft. The units which the 452nd AAA protected were used in support of armored or infantry divisions, thus providing an essential service during the Second World War.

On 17 August, Battery C and Second Platoon, Battery D, was detached to provide AA protection for bridges at Fréteval and at Cloyes respectively. First Platoon, Battery D, provided protection for XII Corps Forward Headquarters. The battalion command post relocated, which it did once more on 18 August.

On 19 August First Platoon, Battery C, provided AA and ground protection for a flying bombs location (W500466). A launch site for V-1, German flying bombs, had been overrun and a platoon was detached to secure the site and preserve it for future research by Allied scientists.

During the mad dash across France, the battalion and the units to which it was attached frequently relocated. At some moments, even the battalion headquarters didn't know where all their platoons were. A remark is added in the unit report regarding 21 August: "Last reports were that the 179th Field Artillery Battalion and 191st Field Artillery Battalion were still moving eastwards."[6] Thus, the battalion commanders didn't know where First Platoon, Battery A, and First Platoon, Battery C, were exactly at the moment. Similarly the next day, 22 August, "Battery A, less 2nd platoon, last reported in vicinity of Sens with CCB," while "1st Platoon Battery C, last reported east of Sens with CCA."[7] Combat Command A (CCA), and Combat Command B (CCB) were combined arms teams employed by the armored units and typically the size of a regiment. That same day orders came in that the battalion would be attached to the 27th AAA Group and Second Platoon, Battery D, was used as AA protection for the 34th Ordnance Battalion.[8]

The next day Battery D provided protection for a POL dump. Second Platoon, Battery A, was used to provide protection for two river crossings at Souppes. That day, at around 14:30 and 14:45, thirteen Me 109s and two Fw 190s attacked the 191st Field Artillery Battalion. The aircraft approached from different directions at approximately 500 to 1,000 ft [152–305 meters] height. They took evasive action and flew at around 390 mph [628 kph]. All guns of First Platoon, Battery C, opened fire, using the 40mm guns with Stiffkey Stick and .50 cal guns with Mk 9 sight. No damage was done to the 191st Field Artillery Battalion, which was obviously the target. A total of fifty-five rounds of 40mm were used and 2,110 rounds of .50 cal. The platoon submitted several claims, two Cat Is, two Cat IIs, two Cat IIIs. This meant that the they claimed two aircraft destroyed, two airplanes as probably destroyed and two more damaged.

On 24 August Battery D provided protection for the river crossings at Sens. The battalion command post relocated. On the 26th, Second Platoon, Battery A, was again available to provide protection for the Corps Artillery. Early in the morning, 06:55, a Ju 52 flew from south to north at about 300 ft [91 meters]. It probably attempted to land at an airfield nearby, under the assumption that it was still held by the Germans. It was engaged by the M-51 of Gun Section No. 2, First Platoon, Battery A. The gunner on the plane returned fire immediately after the M-51 went into action, but inflicted no damage. The plane was riddled with .50 bullets and disappeared over a hill, burning. The plane crashed in the area and prisoners captured by the aircraft included seventeen German nurses and nine airmen, while the gunner was killed by the M-51. Major Irzyk of the 8th Tank Battalion took away the prisoners and papers to Combat Command B Headquarters; 360 rounds of .50 cal munition were used and a new claim, for a Cat I, was submitted.

On 27 August, Second Platoon, Battery A, provided protection for a Corps Supply Point. The following day, Second Platoon, Battery A, provided protection for of a bridge at Arcis-sur-Aube. First Platoon, Battery D, protected the 176th Field Artillery Battalion. Second Platoon, Battery D, provided protection for the 974th Field Artillery Battalion. That same day, 27 August, Private Samuel Peterson died.

On 29 August, at 16:30, five Me 109s, approached the artillery concentration near Chalon from the west and circled it. Among the units on the ground was the 191st Field Artillery Battalion, with First Platoon, Battery C, attached. After circling over the area, the flight split up, four planes going to the left and one to the right, each making a strafing attack. First Platoon, Battery C, fired upon them and the airplanes departed to the east. No claims were made and twenty-six rounds of 40mm and 200 rounds of .50 cal were expended.

On 30 August Second Platoon, Battery D, had not received much help from the 974th Field Artillery Battalion, whose commanding officer did not want anti-aircraft protection, but was only interested in ground protection. However, the commanding officer of the 775th Field Artillery, Lieutenant Colonel Waldrop did want the platoon. Thus, Second Platoon, Battery D, was moved to the 775th Field Artillery Battalion. Once more the 191st Field Artillery Battalion was attacked. At 16:10 two Me 109s approached low from the west and went to the east, after being engaged by First Platoon, Battery C. One plane was hit by .50 cal fire. A claim for a Cat III was submitted and nineteen rounds of 40mm and 280 rounds of .50 cal were expended.

These strafing attacks had a lasting impact on the cooperation between the 191st Field Artillery Battalion and the platoon that provided anti-aircraft protection. As recounted by Barrett James Whiteley, who served in Battery C of the 191st FA:

> After crossing Orleans, the next big objective of the 4th Armored Division was to capture the city of Sens on the Yonne River. This was done early in our period of activity. In fact, the city was captured on August 21st.
>
> While we were in position, supporting the 4th Armored Division in its efforts to take the city, our battery was attacked and strafed by six ME 109s, a type of German fighter plane. We noted with fear that they were equipped with rockets on their wings; small rockets that they could fire, as well as the machine guns.
>
> We wanted to take cover, but we had no cover. We hadn't really gotten to dig any foxholes, but we fell to the ground as best we could, and just lasted through it.
>
> There were no casualties, although I can still remember seeing the dirt pop up every few feet from a machine gun that was firing somewhat in my direction, but passed by me on one side. I sensed a great relief over that.
>
> Probably one of the most important things that happened to our unit, as a result of that escapade, had nothing to do

with the attack at all. The day before we had been joined by a support unit of the First Platoon of Battery C of the 452 AAA. As all units were segregated in those days, it was so designated with the word "colored" after it, because they were black soldiers. The Army referred to them as "colored" troops. They were not integrated except to have some white officers, but all of the men at our positions were black soldiers.

When they were assigned, I had some real questions about what this would do to our unit, because ours was a National Guard unit from the state of Tennessee. If you know your history of the Civil War, you remember that Tennessee was on the fence. Some had Southern loyalties and some had Northern loyalties. But there were, among these men, many of them who had very strong feelings against the "coloreds," as they called them. When we were in the States, and it was suggested that a unit of black soldiers was going to be stationed next to us, we heard all kinds of threats from within our unit about what they would do to them if they got there. They didn't want to live next to them so they made many threats. It never developed because they were not stationed next to us.

But now into combat we came, and immediately, on the very first day of action, we had a "colored" anti-aircraft unit attached to us. They were in our battery area, around our guns. They were stationed there to defend us against aircraft, and, consequently, they had to be right up by us.

They were attached to us for administrative purposes. We fed them, and they were there on this very first day of action when the German planes strafed us. Our boys from

> Tennessee, a few of whom had some strong feelings, were able to see these black soldiers jump into action, man their guns without leaving them, and fire at the German planes, acting with real bravery. From that time on, a camaraderie developed between those black soldiers and the Tennessee National Guardsmen, and all the other members of our unit, about half of which were from other places.
>
> I have thought many times since that God works in a mysterious way, his wonders to perform, and he had worked his wonders there, because it took just that strafing attack for everybody to realize that we were in this war together, and there was neither black nor white.
>
> Later, after that unit had left us and gone to another unit, word got back to us that they had been very heavily shelled. When word that one of the men, named Christenson, had been killed, I actually saw some of these who had been the most anti-black of the Tennesseans cry real tears over the loss of that man.[9] As I saw them from time to time sitting around talking to the AAA men, sitting at their little fires (when fires were permitted), I knew that things were happening that were going to change them in the years to come.[10]

Although the white soldiers might have been hesitant about service alongside the Black soldiers, combat experiences swiftly taught them the value of the protection that the 452nd AAA provided. The added platoon was a great asset and the relations between the individuals involved improved greatly.

In September the weather was poor and hostile air activity was light. Summer, with its warm weather, gave way to fall. On 1 September between 13:05 and 13:15 hours, three squadrons of

Me 109s and Fw 190s, each with an estimated eighteen planes per squadron, attacked the field artillery near First Platoon, Battery C. As Barrett James Whiteley recorded of this attack:

> We ran out of gasoline near Commercy in open fields with no cover, so our artillery pieces were simply put in position with a clear view from above. We covered them with netting, of course, or various other types of camouflage, disguising our position. All the vehicles were covered, if we had enough of the camouflage nets to do it. So there we were, out in the open.
>
> We had been there only a day or two when we noticed, one day, that a shepherd came by our area with his flock of sheep. We were interested in the ease with which he could maneuver them. He and his dog seemed to lead these sheep. He simply whistled a little, and the dog directed the sheep. We were quite intrigued while watching this shepherd. You must understand that we were in the region called Alsace, an area that had been under dispute between the Germans and the French for centuries, and at this time was held by the French. But we knew that there were many German sympathizers in Alsace. Most of the names near there were of German origin. So, we watched this shepherd, and then the next morning, as I awoke, I heard what I thought was one of our liaison planes, our little Cubs, flying.
>
> I got out of my pup tent and looked up and watched him for a little while as he flew around the area. Then it occurred to me that it didn't sound exactly like a Piper Cub. And then it dawned on me that the wing was wider, larger than on the Piper Cub. By that time our anti-aircraft men had spotted it, and we all, at the same time, came to the conclusion that we were watching a German liaison plane, called a Storch, flying freely around, looking at our positions. As the anti-aircraft artillery went to work, and after discovery, he quickly

> got out of the area and was gone. This is not the end of the story, however, because later that day, toward midday, we saw the results of what the Storch had seen, and what we always believed were the results of the spying done by the shepherd, because 51 German fighter planes attacked our positions in the open field. They flew in strafing missions over us ("strafing" meaning to fire their machine guns at the ground troops from a low level) for maybe five to ten minutes. And then our P-47s arrived in the sky and we stood and watched the dogfight in the air. Several of the Me 109s went to the ground in flames. I did not see any P-47s go down.[11]

The planes approached from the east at an altitude of 300 to 500 ft [91–152 meters]. Between seven and ten enemy aircraft came within range. After they were engaged, they dispersed and flew in different directions. The 191st Field Artillery Battalion to which First Platoon, Battery C, was attached, didn't suffer damage from the strafing or rocket firing attack, but another field artillery battalion suffered twenty-three casualties. Claims for three Cat Is were submitted, being all Me 109s. Once Second Platoon, Battery A, was relieved of its current mission, it would provide protection for the 738th Field Artillery Battalion.

On 2 September an informal note arrived for Lieutenant Colonel Ratcliffe from Colonel E.F. Adams, of the 27th AAA Group:

> The following is quoted from a personal note I received today from Colonel Chamberlain:
>
> "The Chief of Staff called me today and said in his travels he noticed that personnel of anti-aircraft units were conspicuous for their disregard of uniform regulations and untidiness of dress and person. He particularly mentioned beards, the wearing of knitted caps, the unnecessary wearing

> of fatigue clothes, the mixing of fatigue clothes and wool ODs, and having uniforms usually unbuttoned."
>
> I am sending you this note informally at his request. He stated that disciplinary action will undoubtedly be taken against battery and other commanders unless these conditions were corrected.

It seems that the soldiers of the 452nd AAA didn't dress appropriately according to the group commander.

That same day, at 21:45 hours, an Fw 190 was circling above the field artillery near Apremont, which included Second Platoon, Battery D, and the 775th Field Artillery Battalion. The field artillery opened fire on a ground target as the Fw 190 circled above. Second Platoon, Battery D, engaged the Fw 190, which disappeared to the southeast. The platoon used thirteen rounds and fifty .50 cal bullets. When moving to new positions the soldiers of Second Platoon, Battery A, who went ahead, managed to capture eight Germans 4 miles [6.4 kilometers] east of Coole.

On 3 September, Second Platoon, Battery C, moved to the 253rd Field Artillery Battalion, and the battalion command post relocated once more.

The next three days brought no big changes. On 7 September, around 13:00 hours a ¼ ton 4x4 truck of the battalion was hit by enemy small arms fire at Saizerais on the east side of the town near the edge of some woods. The truck caught fire and was left there and there were no casualties from this incident.

That same day orders arrived that there was an acute shortage of gasoline cans in the rear areas. This would prove a hindrance to the forces in the field since they did not have the tools to advance anymore. Various solutions were offered: All surplus cans were returned to the nearest Class III Supply Point. Unit commanders would make personal inspections after gassing operations and before leaving bivouac areas to ensure that no cans had been discarded. Vehicle drivers had to pick up abandoned gasolinc cans along the highway. The same number of empty cans needed to be sent as the number requested to be filled. The use of gas cans for other purposes was immediately discontinued.

XII Corps had been relentless in their pursuit of German forces, but they had outrun their supply lines. Most desperately they needed fuel and although they helped themselves to captured enemy stocks, it was not enough. The problem had been expected for several days, but to prevent the Germans from recovering, the vehicles were simply driven as far forward as possible. However, eventually, the corps did need to stop so that the supply lines could catch up with them. The same supply issues also plagued the other American units at the front. After a few days, the Americans could advance again.

The Germans had hoped to stop the Allied advance at the Moselle and Meurthe rivers, but to the north and south of the city of Nancy, the fifth largest city in France, a gap had been forced in their defensive lines. This allowed XII Corps to envelop Nancy and trap the enemy forces within, as well as rupture the planned German winter line.

On 8 September, at 19:50 hours an Me 109 circled above Second Platoon, Battery D, and the 775th Field Artillery Battalion. The plane made two circles above the clouds and then came below them, flying from the northeast to the south. Both of the platoons of Battery D engaged the plane and when fired upon the plane immediately climbed back into the clouds. A claim for a Cat II was submitted, because a 40mm hit was observed and an artillery observation post reported that the plane crashed, however, the wreckage had not yet been found.

The battalion command post relocated on 9 September.

The next day, around 20:00 hours, Sergeant Mark Sherrod, of First Platoon, Battery B, was wounded by 88mm shell fragments. The next two days were calm. On 13 September, Battery Headquarters and First Platoon, Battery C, were under 88mm and mortar fire while crossing the Moselle River, but suffered no casualties. The next day was even more eventful, because at 16:00 hours, Battery Headquarters and First Platoon, Battery C, were on the way from Château-Salins to Arracourt when they were attacked by a truckload of Germans (around thirty). Lieutenant Brienza in the lead vehicle opened fire with a .50 cal machine gun, killing three Germans and wounding several others. No casualties were reported by Battery C. An hour later, an armored car was seen at a distance of 500 yards [457 meters] and going around 25 mph [40 kph]. It was swiftly engaged by First Platoon, Battery C, but no claims were made and the armored car sped away.

On 15 September, the city of Nancy was liberated by XII Corps. A month earlier, on 16 August, XII Corps had liberated Orléans, a city south of Paris, and then advanced eastwards to Nancy, a distance of some 220 miles [350 kilometers]. Along the way, XII Corps had also liberated Troyes. This rapid advance was partially made possible by the field artillery battalions, which softened up enemy points of resistance. That same day, the 253rd Field Artillery Battalion was subjected to mortar and small arms fire, causing one battery to withdraw. During this engagement, Private E.V. Lee killed two Germans with small arms fire.

On 16 September, a warning went out that the Mosquito bombers had new external fuel tanks; these were larger than the ones previously used. The units had to be aware of these changes to prevent a friendly-fire incident. On 17 September, all units except for Battery D and Second Platoon, Battery B, were on the move.

On 18 September, around 04:30 in the morning, No. 2 M-51 of First Platoon, Battery C, was fired upon by a bazooka. The gun crew, Corporal Cary, shot the bazooka gunner and wounded two more Germans. Nine others were taken prisoner. One of the injured later said that they had intended to knock out the M-51 and the field artillery battery. The battalion command post relocated once more.

On 20 September, between 15:00 and 16:15 hours, the 179th Field Artillery Battalion was shelled twice by German 88mm guns. At around 15:00 twelve shells fell and Private First Class Essex F. Hewitt, of Battery A, was wounded. Around 16:15 six more shells came down upon them. An officer, Daniel G. Pevarnick, of Battery A, was injured by shell fragments.

At 17:30 hours, four P-47s circled Haraucourt twice, at an altitude of 1,000 ft [305 meters]. The planes must have made a navigational error and assumed they were already over their target. On the third circle, two of the P-47s dropped two bombs about 750 yards [685 meters] northwest of the town, just missing the 735th Ordnance Company. After dropping the bombs, the lead plane made another circle and came in from the northwest at 500 ft [152 meters] to strafe. Just as the plane started strafing, Second Platoon, Battery A, opened fire with a 40mm gun and when the plane stopped shooting, one M-51 opened fire.

Fluorescent signal panels were displayed before the attack started, and during the attack, more panels were shown, red smoke grenades were ignited, and a yellow pyrotechnic was fired. The planes all had U.S. markings and several witnesses claimed that one or two of the planes had red and white striped rudder surfaces. One of the bombs came within 75 yards [69 meters] of the 735th Ordnance Company and continued to strafe toward the M-51, which eventually engaged the plane. Even though certain measures were taken, friendly fire was still a threat.

On 24 September, First Platoon, Battery A, and Second Platoon, Battery C, were subjected to artillery and mortar fire from 06:00 hours to 16:00 hours, when the 179th Field Artillery Battalion, protected by First Platoon, Battery A, and 253rd Field Artillery Battalion, protected by Second Platoon, Battery C, moved to the south. The two platoons were in the vicinity of Fresnes-en-Saulnois during the shelling. First Platoon, Battery A, got off without any casualties. They just had a damaged M-51. From Second Platoon, Battery C, Private Joseph Cobb was killed and Private Miller Brown was wounded. A Dodge WC, ¾ ton truck, of the battalion was destroyed. Two more casualties were reported that day, both of Battery C: Corporal Floyd Pace and Technician Fifth Grade, Osie Layton.

It was most likely on this day that the attack described by Barrett James Whiteley occurred, in which he assisted a wounded Black American gunner:

> During this shelling, I saw a man go down not far from where I was, so I crawled out and went over to him as the shelling was continuing. He had been hit in the chest, and I got the emergency bandage out that we all carried and began to treat him. He was one of our anti-aircraft gunners, and he was, I think, not fatally hurt; although, he was taken from us, I think he would have lived from the wound.
>
> While I was there I noted one of our men, his name was LaHood, he was a Tec 5. I noted that he was running around checking on men, although he was not given that responsibility. He was not a sergeant in charge of a section, but nevertheless, in the midst of the shelling, was looking for people who might be hit, and trying to help them. When I saw him, he saw me about the same time. He came over and proceeded to do as I was doing, giving aid and help to a wounded anti-aircraft man. I thought it was a particularly brave act for him to be out trying to do this. He managed to do it without being hit himself. Later on, when the opportunity arose, I was able to recommend him for a Bronze Star, which he received for his bravery at that time.[12]

It's an example of the close cooperation that existed between the soldiers at the front, where no distinctions were made in the color of someone's skin. Similar incidents will occur throughout the history of the 452nd AAA.

On 25 September Second Platoon, Battery C, protected a bridge at Dombasle on the east to west main supply route. This was an important assignment since all of the supplies went along this road. Battery D provided protection for five bridges. Three bridges were at St Nicholas, and two more were close by.

On 27 September, at 09:00 hours Second Platoon, Battery C, was relieved of its mission and provided protection for the 752nd Field Artillery Battalion. An hour later Battery D was ordered to provide protection for the 176th Field Artillery Battalion, to which First Platoon would be attached, and 278th Field Artillery Battalion, to which Second Platoon would be attached.

At 13:11 two Fw 190s approached from the south and flew north in the vicinity of First Platoon, Battery B, which engaged them. The planes changed course and flew off to the east. At 13:25 two Me 109s approached from the north and strafed the area of the 738th Field Artillery Battalion, which was protected by Second Platoon, Battery A. Gun Section No. 8, led by Corporal Warren Barker, fired four rounds of 40mm at one of the planes and obtained a direct hit on the cockpit of the plane. The plane burst into flames and was out of control. It crashed into the ground beyond a hill in hostile territory. During this encounter, two other Me 109s approached from the west, and a soldier of the 738th FA was wounded in his leg.

A Cat I was claimed by the Gun Section and this was even written about in the *Anti-Aircraft Artillery Notes*, a paper distributed among the AAA to stay updated about changes in equipment and tactics, or to receive advice on how to combat the aerial threat in Europe. It also included cases of efficient shoots, where little ammunition was used to take down hostile aircraft. It included: "The 452nd AAA AW

Bn (M), commanded by Lt Col L.C, Ratcliffe, produced another economical shoot. While defending XII Corps artillery, section 8, Battery 'A', of this battalion caused the destruction of an ME 109 with four (4) rounds of 40mm ammunition."[13]

On that same day, Staff Sergeant William Campbell, of Battery C, and Zeno H. Ellis of the Medical Detachment, distinguished themselves. At 14:00 hours a field artillery battalion was fired upon by hostile artillery. Several men of the battalion were severely wounded. Upon realizing that the present aid men were unable to immediately give adequate attention to all these casualties, both men rushed over to help, despite the shelling around them. The enemy shelling became so intense that the AAA platoon and the artillery battalion retreated. Instead of withdrawing to comparative safety, both men stayed behind to help with the evacuation of the wounded. The two men were initially awarded the Bronze Star Medal.

Curiously enough, the unit is identified as the 171st Field Artillery Battalion, however, this battalion is not listed as a unit that Battery C protected during its service. The General Orders, which includes the citations for the men, doesn't mention the unit in which both men served, and neither does it include the artillery battalion that they protected. It could be the 191st Field Artillery Battalion. However, two books mention the 171st Field Artillery Battalion. It could be that an error slipped into the award process, which obscures the true historical facts, the two men assisted a battalion in the vicinity, or that other historians had access to material that's no longer available.[14]

At 15:30 an airplane dove out of the clouds at an observation plane. It was engaged by Private Brown Ferguson with the M-51 of Gun Section No. 2 of First Platoon, Battery B. It was only after the plane pulled out of its dive that it was recognized as a P-47 and the M-51 ceased firing. The P-47 was smoking and is believed to have crashed.

Later that day an order came through that Red Cross markings on helmets had to be removed immediately.

On 28, 29 and 30 September, as well as 1 October, the battalion performed its normal operations. Private John A. Lewis, Battery C, was reported as wounded.

Starting in on 2 October, one 40mm section per battery was pulled into battalion headquarters for some rest and a check of equipment, but the next two days there was nothing of significance to report either.

On 5 October, around 14:15 hours, 191st Field Artillery, with First Platoon, Battery C, attached, was fired upon by hostile artillery. First Platoon, Battery C, suffered one casualty and one 2½ ton truck was slightly damaged. Additionally, one more soldier, Fountain Christian, was reported that day as being wounded.

On 8 October First Platoon, Battery B, moved temporarily to a new location for an attack that the 945th Field Artillery Battalion was supporting in the vicinity of Bioncourt. They returned afterwards.

At around 17:50 on 11 October four P-47s started circling above a bridge near Second Platoon, Battery A and Battery C, and First Platoon, Battery D. After being in the air for some twenty-five to thirty minutes the four planes came gliding in and headed for the bridge, where the four of them dropped one bomb each, although only two were heard to explode.

Recognition signals were put up all the time and yellow pyrotechnics were fired immediately after the bombing, but one plane continued to strafe elements in the vicinity. The planes were engaged by anti-aircraft in the area and Second Platoon, Battery A, fired ninety .50 cal bullets when it came in range, while Second Platoon, Battery C, fired five 40mm rounds and 403 rounds of .50 cal. First Platoon, Battery D, fired 250 .50 cal bullets at the P-47s. One of them was hit but continued in formation.

On 12 October, around 09:35, two Me 109s flew from south to north at a constant altitude of 1,500 yards [1,370 meters]. The Gun Sections No. 1, 3, and 4, of First Platoon, Battery D, fired upon them with 40mm and the M-51s. However, due to the clouds, visibility was poor.

At 10:15 a lone Me 109 flying northwards at an altitude of 1,500 yards [1,370 meters] attacked a Piper Cub, an artillery observation plane, in the vicinity of Gun Section No. 7 of Battery B. Two rounds of 40mm were fired and the Me 109 was chased away.

At 14:40 two Me 109s flew east to west at an altitude of 2,500 ft [762 meters] over an area covered by both First Platoon, Battery B, and Second Platoon, Battery D. Although the planes made no hostile actions, First Platoon, Battery B, fired two rounds of 40mm and when the two planes were in range of Second Platoon, Battery D, they fired eleven rounds of 40mm. No claims were made.

At 15:10 two Me 109s were engaged by Second Platoon, Battery A, while flying eastwards. The planes were engaged with 40mm and M-51s, but no damage was observed.

All the planes appeared to be merely passing through the skies guarded by the 452nd AAA and proceeded towards the rear, except for the Me 109 that attacked the Piper Cub.

On 13 October, 15:10 two Fw 190s flew over the area guarded by First Platoon, Battery C, and were fired upon by Gun Sections No. 1, and 3, both using the 40mm Bofors.

That same day First Platoon, Battery D, Second Platoon, Battery D, and Second Platoon, Battery C, engaged two planes flying from north to south between 10:45 and 11:00. Curiously enough, the planes were identified as either Me 109s or P-51s with German markings. Twenty-three 40mm rounds were used, as well as 768 rounds of .50 cal, although no damage to the planes was observed.

The next day was calm again and nothing of significance was reported.

On 15 October a reminder went out that watches had to be synchronized twice per day. During a shelling in the morning of First Platoon, Battery A, an ammunition chest and seven rounds of 40mm were damaged, as well as a vehicle tire punctured. First Platoon,

Battery A, engaged two Fw 190s at 13:35, which were strafing at an altitude of 200 ft [61 meters] and going after the field artillery and troop concentrations. They circled the area at Arracourt. The two planes were flying from northwest to southeast. They dived and strafed, when at first Gun Section No. 3 opened fire, followed by the M-51s, and later by AA guns in the area. One plane crashed and the pilot burned to death, while the other plane was seen to crash by an artillery observer east of Ley. Two Cat Is were claimed.

Things settled down again and during that week there was little to report. On 23 October the battalion command post moved once more. Additionally, on 24, 25, and 26 October there was nothing to report.

On 27 October Second Platoon, Battery B, and First Platoon, Battery D, moved with the artillery battalions they were protecting to a new location. Only Gun Section No. 6, of Battery B, remained at the old area, together with the battery to which it was attached.

On 29 October First Platoon, Battery D, moved to the 267th Field Artillery Battalion. At 06:10 on 31 October, a V-2 was seen flying from west to east at 1,500 ft [457 meters]. By the end of October, the 452nd had been credited with 9⅓ enemy planes destroyed.

During November the weather limited air operations. The German forces continued to stall for time, hoping to fight the Allied soldiers to a standstill so they could recover and resupply their battered units. When the Luftwaffe appeared, it was mostly reconnaissance flights and strafing attacks. The weather hampered XII Corps as well since their air support was limited. On the ground, the 452nd AAA had difficulty with the rain and mud. The first couple of days there was little to report. On the 7th a warning went out to all soldiers that small arms had to be carried at all times.

However, on 8 November, Third Army upset the German plans for rest and refitting their units when it launched a new offensive. At first XII Corps would attack, while the next day XX Corps, to the north of XII Corps, would strike the German lines. XII Corps issued an order for the "operation with XX Corps to destroy enemy withdrawing from Metz and preparation for an advance to the northeast to secure a bridgehead over the Rhine River between Oppenheim and Mannheim, and seize Darmstadt."[15]

On 9 November, the First Platoon, Battery A, was moving with the 179th Field Artillery Battalion, which was moving in support of CCB, 4th Armored Division, and was proceeding towards its new location. Second Platoon, Battery A, was attached with the 738th Field Artillery Battalion and proceeded forward section-by-section. Gun Section No. 6, supported Battery B, 738th Field Artillery Battalion, and advanced with them in the vicinity of Grémecey.

First Platoon, Battery B, was protecting the 945th Field Artillery Battalion near Vic-sur-Seille. First Platoon, Battery C, went with the 191st Field Artillery Battalion, to a new location. This unit supported the CCA, 4th Armored Division. Second Platoon, Battery C, provided AA protection for the 752nd Field Artillery Battalion. This battalion moved in support of the 6th Armored Division and they would advance later that day.

Again the platoons would move up with the unit to which they were attached and the reports of 9 and 10 November give an impression of the difficulties that the 452nd headquarters experienced in keeping track of all its platoons. A report of 9 November: "The exact locations of platoons providing AA protection for FA units moving in support of armored division can not be furnished due to the rapid movement and radio silence of supported unit."[16]

The next day it was reported:

> Command post locations above shown as "en route" are indefinite due to movement of FA battalions to which AA protection is being furnished and radio silence imposed.
>
> Second Platoon, Battery B, is furnishing AA protection to 731st FA Bn in support of the 80th Division, which is moving forward.

> The remainder of platoons shown as en route are furnishing AA protection to FA battalions moving in support of CCA and CCB, 4th and 6th Armored Divisions which are moving forward.[17]

On 11 November it noted: "Daily changes of locations of Command Post are expected as the battalions of field artillery to which AA protection is being furnished are moving forward."[18] During the next few days similar reports were filed, which indicated that the battalion headquarters were still not fully aware of the exact location of all their platoons.

On 12 November a warning went out that it was estimated that the German Air Force had some 600 light bombers in the area. Guns were to be manned with their crews being in the pit and the M-51s needed to have a man in the firing positions. Both needed to have air-guards.

Another warning went out, about an allegedly Brazilian 358th Fighter Squadron, flying P-47s. This aircraft was the same as U.S. aircraft, but the star was yellow and green, with the front part of the rudder being green and the trailing half of the rudder being yellow.

It's an example of how both the U.S. Armed Forces tried to keep the units informed, as well as how the information that was shared was incorrect. In October 1944, the 1st Brazilian Fighter Squadron arrived at the front where it was attached to the 350th Fighter Group, and indeed their insignia were as described above. However, rather than in the European Theater of Operations, this unit operated in the Mediterranean Theater. Thus, it was unlikely that the soldiers of the 452nd AAA would ever see the Brazilian pilots or their planes. Additionally, the Brazilian squadron was not the 358th Fighter Squadron. Rather, the 358th Fighter Squadron was part of the 355th Fighter Group, which had been operating in the European Theater of Operations since 14 September 1943. The unit transitioned to the P-51 Mustang in the spring of 1944.

That day, Private Sanford A. Mical, Battery C, was reported as wounded.

The field artillery battalions and their accompanying AAA platoons continued to move forward. On 14 November First Platoon, Battery B, was moving to Château-Voué, and First Platoon, Battery D, was estimated to be in the vicinity of Lesse. The next day, the Battalion Command Post moved to Vic-sur-Seille, and Second Platoon, Battery B, relocated to Vittencourt. On the 17th, Second Platoon, Battery D, moved to Hampont. It would be a busy day and the Luftwaffe, which had been rather absent the previous few days, suddenly made an appearance again. All the batteries would be in action.

Around 16:08, First Platoon, Battery D, engaged two Me 109s flying at an altitude of 3,500 ft [1,066 meters] from south to north. They were fired upon by a 40mm gun using fourteen rounds of ammunition, but there was no damage observed.

Around 16:16 two Me 109s flew from southeast to northwest in the vicinity of Arraincourt. Before approaching the area guarded by Second Platoon, Battery C, the hostile planes strafed to the south. Three M-51s and two 40mm guns engaged the planes and the aircrafts ceased firing immediately. They climbed rapidly until they were out of range. Eight rounds of 40mm were fired, as well as 368 .50 cal rounds.

The next day, the four M-51s of First Platoon, Battery C, were attached to Battery D, split equally between the two batteries. From XII Corps came a warning that all vehicles had to be moved outside of the villages and dispersed. The Army AA Section informed them that an air attack was expected later that afternoon. However, the message arrived too late. It came in at 15:50, which was ten minutes after the platoons sighted the planes.

First Platoon, Battery A, and Second Platoon, Battery A, engaged two Me 109s around 15:40 in the vicinity of Rode. They flew from east to west and then turned around to go east again. The planes committed no hostile act.

Five minutes later Second Platoon, Battery A, engaged two Me 109s, believed to be the same planes, and claimed a Cat II. Battery A expended ninety-two rounds of 40mm and 1,750 rounds of .50 cal. Second Platoon, Battery C, also fired upon them. Second Platoon, Battery C, fired thirty-five rounds of 40mm and 815 .50 cal bullets.

At 15:48, three 40mm guns and a M-51 of First Platoon, Battery D, fired thirty-nine rounds of 40mm and ninety-seven .50 cal bullets at two Me 109s flying in a straight line from southeast to northwest at 4,000 ft [1,219 meters]. The planes committed no hostile act.

At 17:35 the M-51s of Gun Sections No. 7 and No. 8 of Battery C engaged an Fw 190 flying what appeared to be a reconnaissance mission. When the plane was fired upon, it didn't take evasive action and it was hit by both guns, submitting a Cat II claim. The action took place near Arraincourt: 570 rounds were fired.

At 18:00 a Ju 88 flew over the area of Sotzeling, at 2,500 ft [762 meters]. The planes flew a straight course from south to north and did not commit a hostile act. One 40mm gun fired seven rounds at it, but no claim was submitted.

On 19 November, at around 12:45, two Me 109s approached the gun positions of both First Platoon, Battery A, and Second Platoon, Battery A, going from west to east in the vicinity of Rode. The planes were at an altitude of 4,000 ft [1,219 meters] and not committing a hostile act. They appeared to be returning to their base from a reconnaissance mission. The 40mm guns fired 129 rounds and M-51s expended 2,428 rounds. The planes were travelling at around 390 mph [627 kph]. First Platoon, Battery A, claimed a Cat III.

Ten minutes later, these same planes crossed over Battery C, flying at an altitude of 2,000 ft [610 meters]. They were fired upon and climbed higher to evade the AA guns. First Platoon, Battery C, also claimed a Cat III. They used sixty-two rounds of 40mm and 391 rounds of .50 cal.

However, an accident happened shortly afterwards. After firing on the hostile aircraft with the M-51, Private Owens of Battery C, accidentally fired a short burst. He hit Corporal Beaty of the 752nd Field Artillery Battalion, who died later.

At 13:00, near Baronville, the M-51 of Gun Section No. 4, Second Platoon, Battery B, engaged two Me 109s flying at an altitude of 1,000 ft [305 meters] from north to south. When fired upon, the planes started weaving and climbing, before disappearing to the east. A total of 280 rounds were fired.

The planes that committed hostile acts were targeting troop concentrations or field artillery units, but most of the hostile aircraft seemed to be on reconnaissance.

Second Platoon, Battery A, expected to move to Racrange, and Second Platoon, Battery C, moved to Landorff.

The next day, First Platoon, Battery C, expected to move to the vicinity of Bermering but hadn't yet done so. On 21 November, First Platoon, Battery D, was moving to new positions in Linstroff and set up the day afterwards. That same day, Private Stafford Rimes died and a slidex code was found on the road by Lieutenant Hammond. A slidex was used for encrypted messages at the front, whereby words would be encrypted by the sender and decrypted by the receiver. If the enemy got their hands on a slidex, it meant that communication was potentially compromised.

First Platoon, Battery C, went to Virming. Second Platoon, Battery B, was expected to move to Erstroff. First Platoon, Battery A, relocated to the northeast of Vergaville. Second Platoon, Battery B, moved to Linstroff. First Platoon, Battery B, moved to another position. First Platoon, Battery A, would be set up near Loudrefing. Second Platoon, Battery A, relocated to another location.

Additionally, two Polish and two French Algerian soldiers were apprehended wearing civilian clothing and turned over to Civil Affairs XII Corps.

On 23 November, Second Platoon, Battery B, and the two platoons of Battery C relocated. The next few days there would be little of significance to report. On the 25th, the M-51s that were attached from Battery C to Battery D returned to their original units. A M-51 of Battery B had to be evacuated by the order of the commanding officer of the 945th Field Artillery Battalion, although it doesn't specify why this was necessary. The 40mm of Gun Section No. 2 was taken to the 299th Ordnance Maintenance Company.

On 26 November First Platoon, Battery B, moved to the 176th Field Artillery Battalion, while First Platoon, Battery C, was attached to the 741st Field Artillery Battalion. The reason was that the maneuverability of the M-51 .50 cal MG mount was too low in a highly mobile situation.

Soldiers of the 457th Anti-Aircraft Artillery Battalion, which was an automatic weapons battalion which also fought with XII Corps, give an impression of the period:

> Everywhere the vehicles struggled through the rain and the mud to reach positions – mud which came above the hubcaps and mired down vehicles the minute they left the roads. Gun crews moved their 40mm guns into proper locations only by sheer physical exertion, and gun pits became a morass of mud and water as soon as they were dug. Usually, moreover, since the battery missions were close to the front, nearly all personnel were subjected frequently to enemy artillery fire in addition to the mud.[19]

In this environment, the M-51 trailers were unsuitable, since frequent movement would leave them stuck in the mud.

All guns of Battery B were in action and the Battalion Command Post moved to Haboudange. First Platoon, Battery C, moved to new positions in the vicinity of Pontpierre, which would be occupied the next day.

On the 27th, First Platoon, Battery C, relocated to Tetingen. The headquarters of Battery A went from First Platoon to Second

Platoon. First Platoon, Battery B, set up in Insviller. First Platoon, Battery D, moved to Leyviller.

On 28 November, the front axle of the 40mm of Gun Section No. 7, Battery A, broke. The entire gun needed to be replaced and the platoon moved to another location. Second Platoon, Battery B, moved to Petit Tenquin. Second Platoon, Battery C, moved to Petit Rohrbach.

The next day new orders arrived. "Big Ben" and "Diver" needed to be used as code words for V-2 and V-1 respectively. The *Vergeltungswaffe* 1 and *Vergeltungswaffe* 2, often abbreviated to V-1 and V-2, were two advances in German technology towards the end of the war. The V-1 was a flying bomb, while the V-2 was a ballistic missile. The V-1 had a range of around 160 miles [250 kilometers] and the V-2 had an increased range of around 220 miles [354 kilometers]. Most of these weapons were fired at London, and the port of Antwerp, Belgium.

First Platoon, Battery A, moved to Saarburg. First Platoon, Battery D, moved to Hazembourg and guns are on the highway east of Vittersbourg. Second Platoon, Battery C, moved to Nelling. Second Platoon, Battery A, relocated to St Jean Rohrbach.

On 30 November, First Platoon, Battery C, moved to Marientnal. Around 16:00, Private George Clark, of Battery C, apprehended a German soldier wearing a civilian overcoat near Lachambre. The prisoner was delivered to the 80th Infantry Division Prisoner of War enclosure. The soldier was unarmed and had no papers.

During the retreat, the Germans used everything at their disposal to delay the Allied advance. They used artillery to fire on troops, lay minefields or other booby traps. They also used time bombs, left behind in buildings in the area in which the 452nd AAA operated. As recounted by the 457th AAA:

> One device he began to use with frequency, which deserves a special word or two of comment, was the J-Feder 504, a

> time bomb. More of a psychological weapon than an effective defense weapon, this bomb usually with enough explosive in it to make match-wood of even a very large building, had a clock mechanism attached to it which could be set to ignite the charge at any time between three and twenty-one days from the time it was set. As large as they were, the enemy concealed these bombs with great cunning in likely places where they might cause the greatest damage – in coal pits in basements of buildings likely to be used for command posts or troop shelters, under the concrete of the basement itself, in the walls of buildings, under doorways, or on the outside in culverts under roads, or even in likely bivouac areas in fields. Whenever the Battalion Headquarters or a Battery moved into a new area, valuable time had to be consumed in making a painstakingly thorough search of it and even then, sometimes with specially trained engineers assisting, it was nearly impossible to be certain that the area was free of the devilish devices.[20]

As XII Corps' history recounted:

> A "captured German agent," [...] had warned of time bombs left by the retreating enemy. [...] This led to a widespread search throughout the town by engineers and enthusiastic amateurs who, by reason of their being billeted in suspected houses, had a peculiar interest in the matter. No more such infernal machines were found, but in the hour between 1730 and 1830, on the evening of Saturday, 3 Dec 44, heavy time bombs went off in five buildings of St Avold. They had been buried so deeply and skillfully as to defy detection. The toll of dead was four officers and 18 soldiers, all members of the 633d AAA AW Bn, attached to the 80th Infantry Division. Some 30 others were injured to a degree requiring evacuation.[21]

However these were not the only ones, because the 457th AAA history recounted several more incidents and how this weapon impacted their soldiers:

> At Baronville, [...] another building occupied for more than ten days was blown to pieces. A third one exploded under a road culvert just outside Morhange, and other instances were common. It became somewhat humorous but thoroughly understandable to see with what suspicion members of the [457th AAA] Battalion began to regard discolorations on the walls, or concrete patches in the basement, or any spot that looked somewhat peculiar.[22]

On 1 December, XII Corps was in contact with XX Corps, Third Army, in the northwest and XV Corps, Seventh Army, in the southeast. The corps has the 26th, 35th and 80th Infantry Divisions, the 2nd Cavalry Group, and the 4th and 6th Armored Divisions attached. The 80th Infantry Division continued with their attack, started on 8 November, and kept pressing eastwards beyond the Maginot Line, while the 4th Armored Division operated in XV Corps' zone of action. The 35th Infantry Division and the 2nd Cavalry Group were held in reserve. The 26th Infantry Division and the 4th Armored Division attacked across the Sarre river, while the 6th Armored Division attacked fortifications. To support these units during their attacks, several field artillery battalions were employed. These battalions had been bolstered with platoons of the 452nd AAA Battalion to provide local anti-aircraft protection.

On 1 December, at 05:00 hours a loud explosion was heard at the 452nd AAA Battalion headquarters, which turned out to be a time bomb at Baronville. First Platoon, Battery B, went to Diedendorf, while Second Platoon of that battery went to Cappel. At 13:25 hours, a flying bomb was spotted traveling at about 250 mph [402 kph] over First Platoon, Battery C, and going north-northwest to south-southeast at 2,000 ft [609 meters] altitude.

Gun Section No. 2 of Battery D was subjected to enemy artillery for forty-five minutes. Although they weren't hit, a cow 20 yards [18 meters] from the 40mm was killed.

The next day, another inquiry was made about a loud explosion. It turned out to be a time bomb at Morhange. The battalion informed all batteries and platoons that they would have to check the buildings for potential bombs with an SCR-625 Mine Detector.

Around 09:40 a P-47 dropped a bomb near a gun of Second Platoon, Battery A. The plane was in a level flight and made a turn, during which the bomb fell off and exploded on the ground. Since the plane didn't appear to be committing a hostile act, it was most likely an accident.

The rapid marches had left guns and equipment damaged. Three trucks were out of action, while two 40mm guns of Battery B were sent to Ordnance for repairs. The motor of a M-51 from Battery D was also at Ordnance for repairs.

The 731st Field Artillery Battalion was shelled by hostile artillery around 14:00 hours. As recounted by the 731st Field Artillery history: "On December 2nd Charlie [Battery] received heavy counterbattery fire, with about 18 rounds landing in the battery area. Four men were killed and eighteen wounded. [...] An ammunition dump behind a barn was hit and burned all through the night, with 75 rounds lost."[23] A soldier of Second Platoon, Battery B, Private John Williams, was wounded in his hand by shrapnel.

The command post of Battery C had moved to Biding and the Battery A command post would be relocated to Altwiller. Second Platoon, Battery B, was set up in the vicinity of Barst.

On 3 December, Second Platoon, Battery C, moved to St Jean Rohrbach and the password of the day was compromised by the field artillery.

That day Baker Battery of the 731st Field Artillery Battalion was shelled by enemy artillery, starting around 11:45. While this happened, Private First Class Willie Jackson, Private Edward Swindell, Private Samuel Johnson, all of Second Platoon, Battery B, rushed to aid in the evacuation of wounded soldiers, thus allowing the gun crew to continue to carry out their mission. They were commended by the battery commander of Battery B, 731st Field Artillery Battalion, for actions "above and beyond the call of duty" in providing assistance.[24] Four soldiers were killed and fourteen or seventeen wounded. This didn't include Private Eugene Morgan, of Second Platoon, Battery B, who was wounded in his hip and evacuated. The three soldiers would each receive the Silver Star Medal for their actions, although the citations erroneously report their action as 4 December.

Swindell and Jackson were also active on 4 December. They assisted in the capture of an SS trooper. A 40mm gun of Gun Section No. 4, Battery B, was sent to Ordnance for repair and a M-51 .50 cal MG motor was still in Ordnance for repair.

On 4 December Ordnance was ready to try putting sled skids on the M-51s. It was an idea of Lieutenant Pyle, Battery B, to put up with the mud. The command post of First Platoon, Battery A, moved to Burbach. Christmas cards with XII Corps insignia were allowed to be mailed.

The next day the medical team departed for a week from battalion headquarters. They would go around all the platoons to give out medical shots. The command post of First Platoon, Battery C, moved to Loupershouse and an M-51 of that platoon was out of action with a broken turret switch. Battery A reported a raid by two planes and submitted two Cat III claims. They suffered no damage. Three rounds of 40mm were used and 310 rounds of .50 cal. However, these claims were not acknowledged, since there was not enough evidence of damage inflicted. The two Me 109s were flying at low altitudes and it's unlikely that the guns could depress enough to fire upon them.

Warnings from the Anti-Aircraft Artillery Intelligence Service of raids were properly received by headquarters, but passing along the information to the platoons was difficult, due to the distance involved.

On 6 December, Second Platoon, Battery A, moved to the 738th Field Artillery Battalion northeast of Domfessel, waiting for new orders to move. Second Platoon, Battery D, moved to the north of Sarre Union. First Platoon, Battery A, moved to the vicinity of Schmittsville and First Platoon, Battery C, moved to the vicinity of Woustviller. Captain Gershkow was temporary assigned to the the 633rd Anti-Aircraft Artillery Battalion. The unit still needed to recover from the casualties of the time bomb.

On 7 December, the battalion received an ominous message from First Platoon, Battery C: "No. 4, one 40mm out of action five casualties, one killed," immediately afterwards radio silence was imposed by the 741st Field Artillery Battalion. No further details were obtained. Thirty replacement soldiers were ready at the Group Headquarters and could be picked up.

It was also around this time, that the soldiers of the 452nd AAA assisted in the capture of several deserted German soldiers. It happened because "in Metzing, one of the ackack boys noticed a picture of a German soldier in their Command Post and recognized it as a supposed civilian he had seen in the street. A search was made and the fellow found and later about thirty Wehrmacht deserters were rounded up."[25]

A meeting with all battery commanders was held the next day. Battery C reported that hostile artillery, of 150mm or larger, was shelling the positions of the 741st Field Artillery Battalion and knocked out two 40mm guns and an M-51 .50 cal MG. However, one 40mm gun could be replaced by Ordnance. The M-51 .50 cal MG has been repaired, leaving only the other 40mm gun out of action. One soldier was killed, while four others were evacuated and another was slightly wounded.

The hostile artillery has been unusual. The 741st Field Artillery Battalion had fired several missions during the previous night. The left flank of the field artillery battalion received heavy shelling starting around 15:30 and lasted fifteen minutes. Two more shells from an enemy gun or guns then struck Gun Section No. 1, First Platoon, Battery C, approximately 1,000 yards [914 meters] south of the center of impact. The German counter-battery fire jumped over the vital area and was inaccurate. Instead of hitting the 741st Field Artillery Battalion, which they were aiming at, they struck the First Platoon, Battery C, gun by chance. A wrecker was dispatched to the unit and one 40mm gun was replaced by Ordnance.

On 10 December the M-51 of Gun Section No. 4, Battery A, was out of action and taken to Ordnance. The positions of First Platoon, Battery C, were inspected by Major General Homer R. Oldfield, the Special Assistant for Anti-Aircraft to Commanding General Army Air Force, to check the morale of the remaining gun crews, which was found to be excellent.

The day after, the battalion command post relocated to Sarre Union, while it relocated to Sarreguemines on the 14th. Similarly, many platoons moved with the units to which they were attached. During the night of 13 to 14 December a soldier, Private First Class Rufus Anders, was wounded by hostile artillery.

Meanwhile, to the north of XII Corps, the German High Command had gathered a substantial force. Soon they would go on the offensive again, attacking through the Ardennes. As recounted by XII Corps' history:

> On 15 December, rain fell all day. There was no activity in the sector beyond a few scattered artillery shells from the German lines. A thick fog settled on the valley of the Moselle, along the west bank of which our men were marking time. At 6:30 on the dark Saturday morning of the 16th, the Germans opened a heavy artillery barrage all along

> the 60-mile [97-km] line. It grew in intensity and regimental commanders quickly reported back to headquarters that something must be up. They reported patrols advancing, just after nine o'clock. By noon it was evident that an enemy attack in force was in the making.
>
> General Bradley had been back at Supreme Headquarters the night before and when General Hodges of the First Army notified him, he ordered reserves thrown into the sector and flew immediately to the front. The fog and rain held for days and then snow fell and except for a few hours our planes did not leave the ground for a week. The American front crumpled. Regiments were slashed to pieces. Companies and battalions were cut off from one another and destroyed. One division fell back 30 miles [48 kilometers] and when it tried to rally found only 600 men remained with the unit; the others had been killed or captured or had escaped in small parties to other sections.
>
> It was a severe setback. The Germans stormed through the 60-mile [97-kilometer] gap. They captured towns for which we had fought long and hard, bloody hills which we had purchased at high cost.[26]

The situation became more dire and rumors filtered through to XII Corps, which learned that a major breakthrough had happened to the north. It was said that German paratroopers, who spoke English and wore American uniforms, had landed behind enemy lines. The Germans had suddenly seized the initiative again. It was a couple of tense days and it was believed that the Germans were much closer than they actually were.

On 17 December, Second Platoon, Battery D, moved to Woelfling. At 09:40 hours an Me 109 approached the position of 179th Field Artillery Battalion, defended by First Platoon, Battery A, at an altitude of 1,000 ft [305 meters], coming from the northwest and going to the southeast, going 350 mph [563 kph]. It had the intention of strafing, but when it was engaged by 40mm and .50 cal., it took sharp evasive action by swerving. It didn't help the plane to escape and a Cat I was claimed.

At 09:42, an Me 109 was engaged at 2,000 ft [610 meters] altitude when it flew over the positions of the 738th Field Artillery Battalion, which was protected by Second Platoon, Battery A. The enemy aircraft came from the north and headed south, but took evasive actions by swerving and departing to the east at an approximate speed of 350 mph [563 kph]. No claims were submitted.

At 10:16 one Fw 190 approached Second Platoon, Battery D, at 1,000 ft [305 meters] and disappeared to the east when engaged. No evasive action was taken.

At 11:30 an Me 109 approached First Platoon, Battery A, at 1,000 ft [305 meters] and took evasive action by increasing speed and swerving violently. The 40mm and .50 cal M-51s were used, but again no claims were made.

Around 13:00 an Fw 190 approached the positions of the 273rd Field Artillery Battalion, guarded by Second Platoon, Battery D, from the northeast at 1,900 ft [579 meters] and committed no hostile act. It was engaged by 40mm and M-51s. It took evasive action and swerved sharply. No hits were observed. Gun Sections No. 3 and No. 4 of Battery B engaged an Fw 190 but made no claims.

Around 14:40 hours, as the 752nd Field Artillery Battalion was moving into position near Folpersviller, and while still in a column, an Fw 190 appeared at an altitude of 700–800 ft [213–244 meters] and a slant range of 400–500 yards [366–457 meters]. The aircraft was swiftly engaged by the M-51s of Gun Section No. 5 and No. 6 of Second Platoon, Battery C, which were still coupled to the trucks and thus had a limited field of fire. The enemy aircraft started diving and smoking and disappeared behind some trees. Initially, a Cat II was claimed, but after investigating the claim was upgraded to a

Cat I. The battalion commander of the 752nd FA submitted a signed statement that he saw the plane crash and burn.

First Platoon, Battery A, engaged an Me 109 at 14:40 hours with 40mm and M-51. They suffered no damage and claimed a Cat II.

At 14:45 an Me 109 approached the area of the 179th Field Artillery Battalion, protected by First Platoon, Battery A, and was fired upon by Gun Section No. 2. It flew at a slant range to the target of approximately 500 yards [457 meters] with a speed of 400 mph [644 kph]. A Cat II was claimed.

At 14:49 hours, an Fw 190 approached the 176th Field Artillery Battalion, protected by First Platoon, Battery B, at treetop level, but committed no hostile act. It was immediately engaged by Gun Section No. 3 and No. 4 with both 40mm and M-51. The aircraft started violent evasive tactics and no claims were made.

Second Platoon, Battery D, engaged an aircraft around 16:00 hours when an Fw 190 flew over the area of the 273rd Field Artillery Battalion. It flew at 1,000 ft [305 meters] and was fired upon with six 40mm rounds. The hostile plane swerved and disappeared to the southwest.

On 18 December First Platoon, Battery A moved to Rimling, while Second Platoon, Battery A, moved to Gulderkirk. A request came in for AA protection for the 191st Field Artillery Battalion. First Platoon, Battery D, was then relieved of attachment to the 267th Field Artillery Battalion and attached to the unit that requested protection.

Around 09:35 one Me 109 was engaged by Second Platoon, Battery A, with twenty-one rounds from 40mm and 417 rounds of .50 cal ammunition. No damage and no claims were made. Around 09:40 hours First Platoon, Battery A, engaged an Me 109 with the 40mm and M-51. Seven rounds 40mm and 1,094 rounds of .50 cal were used. One Cat I was claimed by the gun sections.

First Platoon, Battery D, engaged an aircraft with three rounds from a 40mm gun around 10:16 hours. Around 11:20 another Me

109 was engaged by First Platoon, Battery A. Twenty-one 40mm and 417 .50 cal rounds were used, but no claims were submitted and no damage was suffered.

On 19 December, during an artillery shelling, a French driver tried to enter the basement where the command post was located. After proper identification, he was returned by the sentry. Private Wilburt Wrench, Battery D, was shot in the knee, potentially the result of a rifle discharging due to the heat, but still an investigation was conducted.

Due to the pressure from the Ardennes Offensive in the north, several field artillery battalions were sent to III Corps. First Platoon, Battery A, both platoons of Battery B, and Second Platoon, Battery C, all moved with their supporting units to III Corps, providing AA protection en route.

On 20 December orders finally came through. The original plans of XII Corps were discarded and instead it would move north to assist in stopping the German offensive, while XV Corps would take over most of XII Corps' sector. The next couple of days were a logistical nightmare, when the entire corps would shift direction. The headquarters of XII Corps moved from Sarralbe, France, through Metz to Luxembourg City, a distance of some 85 miles [135 kilometers]. As XII Corps' history recounted of those days:

> The offensive movement necessary to throw Third U.S. Army's striking power to the north was a gigantic and complicated operation involving a switch of the majority of Third U.S. Army's divisions and their supporting troops. Some of the most rapid troop movements in the history of warfare were required, but they had to be combined with a high degree of precise timing and coordination. Not only did the tactical units have to be faced at right angles to the Western Front but the entire supply organization had to follow in support. [...]

> In the early morning hours of 19 December, the 4th Armored Division, located at Epping-Urbach, 11 miles [18 kilometers] east of Sarreguemines, moved northward with a task force in the lead. It was followed closely by the 80th Infantry Division, located at Bining, and the 26th Infantry Division, then in training at Metz. On 20 December the 5th Infantry Division, located in the Saarlautern bridgehead, joined the procession. On 21 December 16 field artillery and six anti-aircraft battalions began to move. On 22 December the 35th Infantry Division, located at Bebelsheim, started for Metz for refitting before being committed. On 23 December a provisional task force of the 6th Armored Division, then located at Lixing started for the northern front.
>
> Spaced between these major tactical units on the road network were various regimental combat teams infiltrating toward the front, artillery, tank destroyer and engineer units, followed by the supply and service troops. Movements of varying lengths, some to positions on the north-south front of XII and XX Corps, were made by six infantry and three armored divisions, 26 battalions of field artillery and various combat teams.
>
> From 17 to 23 December 133,178 motor vehicles passed the seven traffic control points. Trucks traveled 1,254,042 miles [2,018,185 kilometers] from 18 December until the end of the month. 37 truck companies operated on virtually a full-time basis, carrying 41,935 tons of supplies of which 16,910 tons were ammunition. The equivalent of a division a day for 30 days moved during the month.[27]

Part of this tremendous shift was the 452nd AAA Battalion, which remained with XII Corps and moved along with the units they supported or were attached to new ones. In those busy days it was sometimes hard for battalion headquarters to keep track of their units, due to the coordination required for handing over protection of the units as well as the different movements.

On 20 December, Second Platoon, Battery A was at Grosrecharcing. The password was compromised and a new one was distributed. The battalion executive officer was sent as liaison officer to the 332nd AAA Group to arrange for the relief of the platoons that were now serving with III Corps.

On the 21st, Battery B was relieved of its assignment to the field artillery battalions and instead was used in anti-mechanized defense of Arlon, Belgium, where III Corps' Command Post was located, until it was relieved on 23 December and went back to XII Corps' control.

A 40mm gun needed to be replaced due to a road accident, while an M-51 was in Ordnance for repair.

New orders arrived regarding the units that needed protection. Second Platoon, Battery A, was attached to the 974th Field Artillery Battalion. First Platoon, Battery C, was attached to the 802nd Field Artillery Battalion. First Platoon, Battery D, was attached to the 191st Field Artillery Battalion. Second Platoon, Battery D, was attached to the 273rd Field Artillery Battalion. All the above attachments became active shortly after the orders were sent out and units were expected to be with their new units five hours later. Once the other platoons from the III Corps returned, they would be attached to battalions that didn't have protection yet or needed to be taken over from the 457th Anti-Aircraft Artillery Battalion.

On 22 December many units were on the move. The battalion command post was planned to relocate to Puttelange, but the destination changed when they were on the road and they went to Brounge instead. To make matters worse, heavy ground fog prevent Allied aircraft from supporting the ground units.

By the end of the day, most of the artillery units were in position. The fragment below gives an indication of the artillery support that was given to the divisions employed by Corps. As recounted by XII Corps' unit history:

> The organization for combat was: The 182d Field Artillery Group [FA Gp], with the 802d, 945th, 974th, and 273d Field Artillery Battalions [FA Bns] attached, operated in Corps general support and reinforced the 5th Infantry Division with one light and two medium battalions. The 183d FA Gp, with the 695th, 191st, 107th and 108th FA Bns attached, operated in Corps general support and reinforced the fires of the 10th Armored Division. The 177th FA Gp, with the 255th, 775th, and 215th FA Bns attached, operated in Corps general support and reinforced the 4th Infantry Division with one light and one medium battalion. The 422d FA Gp with 81st, 174th and 244th FA Bns attached, operated in Corps general support and reinforced the 4th Armored Div with one medium battalion.[28]

The underlining shows which units were protected by a platoon of the 452nd Anti-Aircraft Artillery Battalion at some point in the past, were still protected, or would be protected at some point in the future. The majority of the artillery battalions mentioned did, at some point during the Second World War, come into contact with the battalion.

On 23 December the battalion command post arrived at Huncherange. A M-51 of First Platoon, Battery C, was out of action due to a highway accident. Ordnance was notified, while two more trucks were wrecked in other accidents.

On the 24th, the movements continued. First Platoon, Battery A, was detached from the 244th FA and attached to the 108th Field Artillery Battalion. An M-51 was damaged in a traffic accident en route to the battlefield. All platoons were moving with the field artillery battalions to new positions, providing AA protection along the way and at the destination. Second Platoon, Battery B, was attached to the 215th Field Artillery Battalion. First Platoon, Battery B, was attached to the 81st Field Artillery Battalion. Second Platoon, Battery C, was attached to the 255th Field Artillery Battalion.

That same day, the administrative net frequency was changed. It interfered with the radar of a gun battalion. Second Platoon, Battery A, reported a flying bomb flying east to west at 1,000 ft [305 meters] near Reuland. It disappeared out of sight without causing any damage. Second Platoon, Battery C, had an M-51 out of action due to a loose wire as the result of an accident.

At 14:22 hours a P-47 Thunderbolt, an American aircraft, strafed friendly installations in the vicinity of Second Platoon, Battery B, from an altitude of 300 ft [91 meters]. The plane approached from the east and fired rockets. Identification panels were shown by Gun Section No. 7 and the plane left. Luckily there was no damage.

On 25 December there were three M-51s with Ordnance for repairs and another M-51 had a frozen battery. A 40mm that had been wrecked had not yet been replaced. Later Battery A would report that an M-51 was out of action with a broken elevating shaft. They also reported that Battery B, of the 447th AAA Battalion, was providing protection for the 108th Field Artillery Battalion and they had been with that unit since 19 December. First Platoon, Battery A was then attached to the 945th Field Artillery Battalion, relieving Battery E of the 457th AAA. The 457th AAA had organized all their M16B half-tracks into a mobile battery, Battery E, a unique unit.

The next day a message went out that everyone in the forward areas needed to have a gas mask. Around 10:05 eight P-47s with orange nose and tail markings divebombed friendly sites at Hiplerouen, the location of Battery B; identification panels were displayed and the attacks ceased immediately. No damage was suffered.

To prevent a similar incident to the previous day, where a field artillery battalion would have too much anti-aircraft protection, Ratcliffe sent out the following message to all battery commanders and platoon leaders: "If a platoon gets a new assignment and finds that another organization is already performing the assignment find out who, what, when, where, and why, and report this to the command post immediately."[29] Additionally, the soldiers must not

Above: Soldiers of Battery A, 452nd AAA stand by and check their equipment while the convoy takes a break, 9 November 1944. (*Courtesy of National Archives and Records Administration*)

Below: Soldiers George Cofield and Howard J. Davis guard a newly constructed bridge site over the Rhine River, built by U.S. Ninth Army Engineers, 30 March 1945. (*Courtesy of National Archives and Records Administration*)

Above left: Bertha Stallworth, 21, shown inspecting the end of 40mm artillery cartridge case at Frankford Arsenal. Many women worked in the arms industry. (*Courtesy of National Archives and Records Administration*)

Above right: Doris Miller proudly showing the Navy Cross received for his actions at Pearl Harbor, 27 May 1942. (*Courtesy of National Archives and Records Administration*)

Below: The attack on Pearl Harbor, 7 December 1941. A torpedo has just hit the USS *West Virginia*, which can be clearly seen in the centre of the photograph. (*Courtesy of Naval History and Heritage Command*)

A 40mm Bofors gun of the 452nd AAA watches over the construction of a ponton bridge over the Rhine, Germany. (*Courtesy of National Archives and Records Administration*)

Above left: Battery D, 484th AAA Battalion, at the Lashio Airstrip in Burma (now Myanmar). They were filmed by the Signal Corps on 8 May 1945. Here, an air sentry watches the sky. (*Courtesy of National Archives and Records Administration*)

Above right: A soldier of the 484th AAA keeps the telescope of the M5 director on target. (*Courtesy of National Archives and Records Administration*)

Above, below left and below right: Major General Manton S. Eddy decorates soldiers of the 452nd AAA Battalion, 5 January 1945. (*Courtesy of National Archives and Records Administration*)

Above left: A Black soldier of an AAA unit watches over the water during the Rhine crossing. (*Courtesy of National Archives and Records Administration*)

Above right: A soldier from 484th AAA tracks a target with the Bofors gun sights. (*Courtesy of National Archives and Records Administration*)

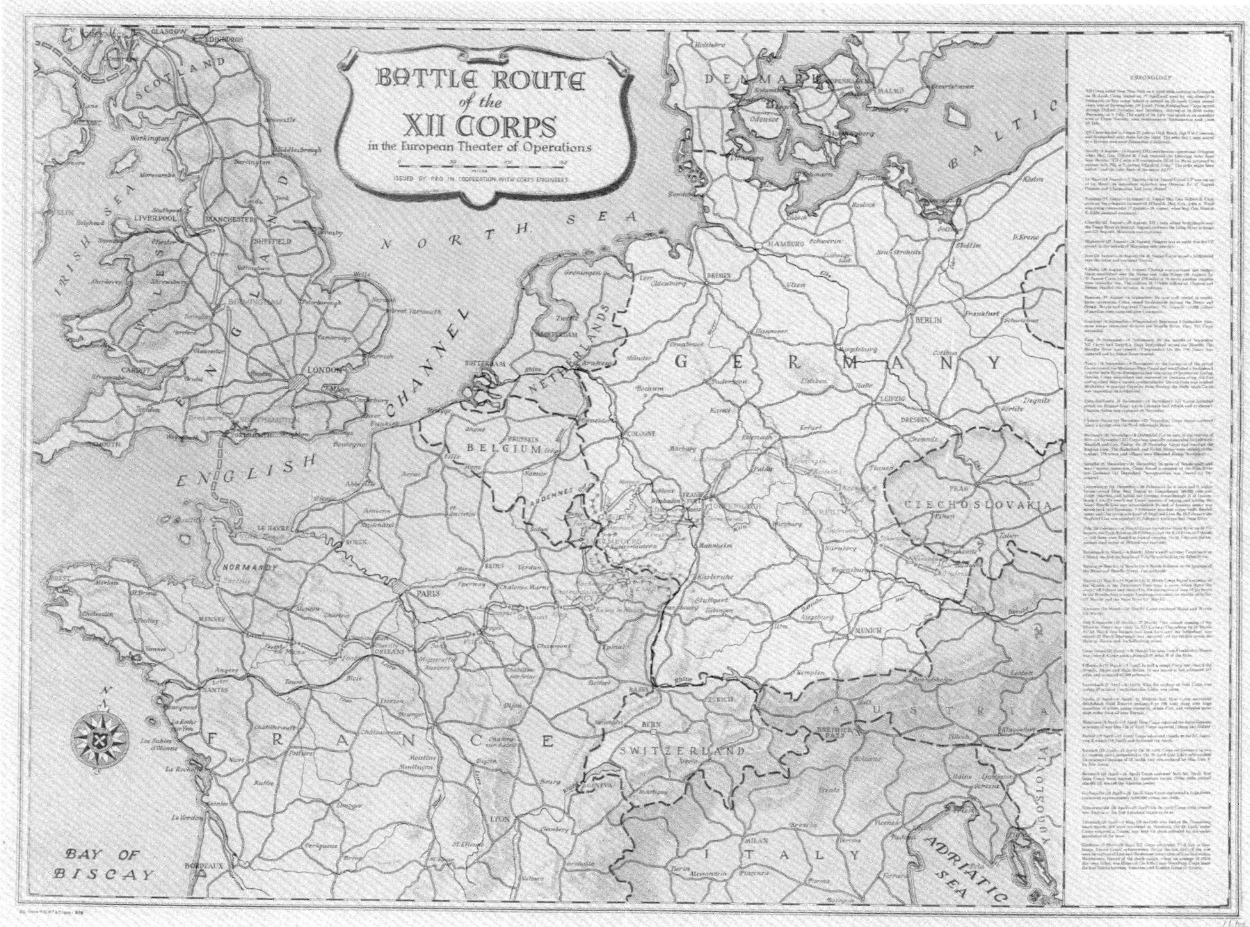

The advance of XII Corps across Europe during the Second World War. (*Courtesy of Yale University Library*)

Above left: Private Stafford Rimes, here in the uniform of Technician Fourth Grade, was killed in action on 21 November 1944. (*Courtesy of Stafford Rimes family*)

Above right: A soldier of an unidentified US AAA battalion looks through the gun sights of the 40mm Bofors gun. The image is taken from the movie *The Negro Soldier*. (*Courtesy of National Archives and Records Administration*)

A towed 40mm Bofors anti-aircraft artillery gun drives past a Third Army tank on 23 November 1944. The gun crew consists of Black American soldiers. (*Courtesy of National Archives and Records Administration*)

mention in their letters that they are in Luxembourg, that they left France, and must not write anything about the move north. Money from Luxembourg or Belgium was not allowed to be sent home.

Meanwhile, the group headquarters ordered the battalion to guard all wrecked enemy aircraft of a recent crash until headquarters was notified and the guard could be properly relieved. Nothing was to be removed from the wreckage. Friendly C-47s would fly over to drop supplies on the 101st Airborne Division between 15:15 and 15:30, however, this message was received too late, since it arrived at 15:35 hours. At 16:30 First Platoon, Battery A, fired on hostile aircraft, and at 18:00 Second Platoon, Battery A, fired on hostile aircraft.

The duty officer would check each day at 18:00 hours to ensure that all vehicles were 25 yards [23 meters] apart. A V-1 passed over the Battalion Command Post from north to south at 21:41. It was heard, but not seen, and at 22:48 flares were dropped by a plane 500 yards [457 meters] east of the battalion command post.

The battalion reported that day that one 40mm gun, two M-51 MGs, four $\frac{1}{4}$ ton trucks (which would become known as Jeeps), a $\frac{3}{4}$ ton truck (also known as Dodge WC), and five $2\frac{1}{2}$ ton trucks (also known as deuce-and-a-half), were out of action.

On 27 December a quick warning went out. A hundred hostile planes would enter the area. Second Platoon, Battery C, was to proceed to the 752nd Field Artillery Battalion to provide AA protection. Additionally, another message arrived later from the 27th AAA Group that if Allied aircraft bore hostile markings or committed a hostile act, the names of eyewitnesses and locations where they could be found for questioning would be submitted to Group Headquarters. Headquarters would then be notified of the time, place, number, and description of the plane as well as the action it committed.

A report went out that the battalion should be watching for "Divers" and "Big Bens". These would need to be reported immediately. Two field artillery battalions, 81st and 174th, were leaving the corps sector, and the AA detachments were instructed to remain with their respective units.

The M-51 of Gun Section No. 4, Battery A, was out of action. Second Platoon Battery C was in action at 18:30.

On 28 December, at 16:15 hours, civilians reported to the headquarters battery commander that three Germans shot at them. They were dressed in civilian clothing and wore long capes with black hats. They were armed with rifles and revolvers.

The 457th AAA was informed and one officer, one warrant officer, and five enlisted men made a search of the vicinity with the Luxembourg police but didn't find them.

That same day the battalion S-3, Major Kimble, went missing, as well as the Operations Sergeant, Sergeant Major, and a Jeep driver, Private Garner. They had left the battalion command post at 09:00 and checked on Headquarters, Battery B, as well as Second Platoon, Battery B. They left at 15:30 to check on First Platoon, Battery B, but never arrived. Several days later it was discovered that they had been in an accident and were evacuated.

Since the 452nd AAA was one of the few Black combat units involved in action in Europe, they garnered a lot of attention. Articles about them and their exploits appeared in newspapers, including the *Stars and Stripes*, which published the following article on 28 December:

> WITH THIRD U.S. ARMY, Dec. 27.—Negro ack-ack gunners with General Patton's forces have bagged their share of German planes, and when the Luftwaffe became scarce they turned their 40mm Bofors guns on ground targets.
>
> Over a one-month period the Section credited the 452nd AAA battalion with the highest "batting average" percentage of planes knocked down of total aircraft engaged—of all non-self-propelled outfits in Third Army.

Mainly assigned to protecting artillery areas of the Fourth Armored Division, these ack-ackers have operated closer to the front than the average AA man normally expects to get.

Took Nazi Prisoners

When Fourth Armored elements smashed across the Moselle River into Arracourt, one battery helped turn back a German counter-attack. The ack-ack men depressed their guns and, using small arms, killed and captured 30 Germans.

Led by Lieutenant Angelo Briego, of Sommerville, N.J., the crew included: 1/Sgt. William Harris, Chicago; T/5 Isaac Gabriel, Miami; T/5 Shirly Reed, St Louis, and S/Sgt. M.M. Malone, Rochdale, Tex.

During another fight in the Moselle Valley one gun crew was attacked by a patrol. They captured 42 Nazis. Crew members included: Sgt. Verge Riley, Malden, Mo.; Cpl. John Smith, Richmond, Va.; Pvt. Calvin Jamison, Houston; Cpl. Huston Hill, Kansas City, Mo., and Pvt. Benjamin Harrison, New Orleans. The crew later brought down three Me 109s.

Fought All Night

Then there's the story of the all-night battle near Arracourt by Cpl. George Cary, Houston, and Pvt. Arthur Newsome. It was highlighted by their capturing of a Nazi colonel.

One gun section, directed by Cpl. Warren Barker, Mermentau, La., brought down one Me 109 with four rounds.

> In another skirmish, a JU 52 transport was brought down by machine gunners. The crew surrounded the crippled plane as it crash-landed nearby and flushed out 17 German soldiers and nine Nazi nurses.[30]

The article highlights some of the experiences of the 452nd AAA during 1944, although it mentions seventeen airmen captured and nine nurses, whereas the unit documents list seventeen nurses captured and nine airmen captured.

On 29 December the search for the Battalion S-3 continued and a V-2 flew over the Battalion Command Post, which was heard but not seen at 14:10 hours. First Platoon, Battery B, was attached to the 736th Field Artillery Battalion, a 240mm unit, while First Platoon, Battery C, protected the 277th Field Artillery Battalion, which operated 8-inch howitzers. The platoon was in in action at 16:40 hours.

A ¾ ton truck of Battery B was damaged by a road accident in a bend on an icy road and two enlisted men were injured in the accident. S.B. Davidson received a broken hip, while S.G. Gather received a cut knee. The men were taken to the 624th Clearing Company, while the vehicle went to the 3526th Ordnance Company.

Battery C reported that three P-47s strafed a friendly convoy at 11:00 and did not engage them. Members of the 305th Engineers Company were witness to it. A B-24 bombed friendly positions at 12:45 hours and again Battery C did not engage it. Witness to it were members of Gun Section No. 1, First Platoon, Battery C.

Three M-51s were in Ordnance for repairs, while another was at Battery Headquarters for repair. A 40mm gun has returned from Ordnance. Second Platoon, Battery D, had been shelled for thirty minutes by enemy artillery of a large caliber, such as 150mm. Later, at 22:00 hours an enlisted man of Battery D was killed by hostile artillery: Porter Jeremy.

On 30 December four M-51s were with Ordnance for repairs, meaning that the one which Battery Headquarters couldn't fix was passed further up the chain.

On 31 December, the close of the year 1944, the battalion was witness to a unique kind of fireworks. At 11:50 hours several P-47s were circling in the area and dropped two 500 lb [226 kg] bombs near the highway. There were no casualties or damages. Lieutenant Edelstein, and Gun Section No. 7, Battery B, saw it happen.

At 12:50 unseen planes, thought to be medium bombers, dropped twenty-five to fifty incendiary bombs in the area. No damage or casualties. There were some P-47s in the area. Lieutenant Deming of Battery B and his driver Private First Class Elmo Howard were witness to it.

That evening friendly B-25s, P-47s, and P-51s were expected to be in the area. While the next day the M-51 of Battery B could be picked up by a 2½ ton truck.

At 15:40 six P-47s were in the area and one of these planes attacked. They were circling in the area and dropped two bombs on a section of the 945th Field Artillery Battalion. A howitzer and a tent were hit, resulting in nine dead and one badly wounded. It was the worst day in the history of the 945th Field Artillery, both because they lost so many soldiers and because it was the result of friendly fire. The soldiers of the 452nd AAA claimed to not have fired at the aircraft.

First Platoon, Battery B, and Second Platoon, Battery C, M-51s were back from Ordnance and ready to go the next day. A warning went out that hostile aircraft was expected to attack between darkness and daylight, at an altitude of 500 to 1,500 ft [152–457 meters].

Near the end of the month, the 452nd AAA was featured in a news article, which summarized the unit's history as well as how the fighting helped the relations between the Black and white soldiers. The article, titled "Fox Holes Kill All Racial Feeling", contains interesting anecdotes:

> Mutual diving for foxholes when bullets and shrapnel fly may not be a practical antidote for any racial friction on a nationwide scale but it worked wonders for the 452nd Anti-Aircraft Artillery, one of the best negro combat units.
>
> "We had our share of differences with white soldiers when sitting around," said Sergeant Leo G. Edwards of Battery A, "but since we have all been over here getting shot at together we have gotten along fine."
>
> […]
>
> The standard army formula of hard work and strict discipline used by Lieutenant Colonel Lamar Ratcliffe, a firm-jawed professional soldier, is shaping his battalion into one which frequently has won the praise of white units it has been assigned to protect from air attacks. All battalion commissioned officers are white and the remainder of the personnel is negro. Summing up battlefront racial relations as they have found them since they have been a fighting unit, Sergeant Edwards said: "We get along very well, particularly with the field artillerymen whose batteries we now are assigned to. Now that nights are getting cold we sit around campfires with them and talk about home and getting on with the war so we can get back there.
>
> When we start diving for cover no one ever looks to see what color the other fellow's skin is when two of us pile in at once as the shells come over."[31]

As December ended, the battalion had supported infantry and armored divisions, mostly of XII Corps, Third Army, during its drive northeast from Nancy, France, and then to the north during the Battle of the Bulge. The enemy attempted several raids, being more active than the previous month. Flying weather was better and enemy aircraft had been more numerous after the move to the north.

Chapter 4

Towards Victory

The start of 1945 provided XII Corps a brief moment to assess the situation and prepare for what was to come. As recounted by the corps history:

> The Corps had closed 1944 by meeting the Luxembourg shoulder of the German penetration and thrusting it back to the line of the Sauer and Moselle Rivers. At the opening of the new year, the Corps had its three infantry divisions and reinforced cavalry group on the line in active defense. The dispositions were: 80th Infantry Division on the left (northwest) flank on the high ground south of the Sure River, in contact with the 26th Infantry Division, III Corps; 5th Infantry Division on the south bank of the Sauer River; 4th Infantry Division from the south bank of the Sauer to the west bank of the Moselle River; and the 2d Cavalry Group, reinforced, on the right (southeast) flank on the west bank of the Moselle to contact with the cavalry of XX Corps.
>
> For the first part of January, the Corps continued a series of limited objective attacks, swinging its left on the stream junctions at Ettelbruck as a hinge, thrusting into the south flank of the German penetration, and keeping contact with the advance of the III Corps. Active patrolling was kept up on the other parts of the front.[1]

For the 452nd AAA, the Battalion Command Post was still housed at Huncherange, Luxembourg, while the platoons occupied positions with the field artillery battalions to which they were attached. The

Battalion and Battery Command Posts were housed in buildings, while the gun sections were quartered in pyramidal tents. Eight men slept together in a tent. Each section was also given twenty gasoline cookers, which they could use to prepare their own meals. Every gun section also made its own garbage pits and straddle trench latrines, while water came from engineer water points brought to each gun section in 5-gallon water cans. At the command posts, there were often regular flush latrines. If this was inadequate, straddle trench latrines were used.

For the men themselves, they were brought to shower points periodically and they received a change of clothing. The medical section was also authorized their own Jeep, which allowed them to move more rapidly. As the medical section summed up: "Sanitation throughout was excellent."[2]

Being a soldier in the Anti-Aircraft Artillery had a few benefits compared to other services. Most importantly, the unit had less direct contact with the enemy. An AAA battalion supports the combat units, but is not necessarily in the thick of the fighting, unlike the infantry or armored units. The 452nd AAA often didn't have to evict the Germans from the positions they were occupying.

Additionally, since 452nd AAA was a towed outfit, they were less mobile and thus often assigned missions more suitable for their this type of employment than self-propelled units. Battery E of the 457th AAA, operating with the .50 quad mount on a halftrack, was highly mobile and often in direct contact with the Germans. This comes with all the associated risks involved in combat.

Another benefit for the 452nd AAA, is that the soldiers and the artillery they supported sometimes spent longer times in the same position. On a basic level, if the unit remained in the same position for a longer time, this greatly facilitated the distribution of food and mail. It also allowed the soldiers to improve their surroundings and thus spend their time in more comfortable positions than the infantry or the armor. For example, a private wouldn't spend much time improving his foxhole if he had to leave it again in a few days.

However, with the start of the new year, the Luftwaffe became more active again. The Luftwaffe launched Operation *Bodenplatte*, intended to neutralize the Allied air superiority. Several airfields in the Netherlands, Belgium and two in Northern France were attacked by more than 1,000 Luftwaffe fighters and dive bombers. They surprised the Allied airfields and destroyed approximately 305 Allied aircraft and damaged 190 more. However, the operation was a failure.

Most Allied airplanes had been destroyed on the ground, thus casualties to aircrew were relatively light. Only the aircraft would need to be replaced. Meanwhile, the Germans had lost 143 pilots killed and missing, seventy more captured and twenty-one were wounded.[3] Among these pilots were several valuable veterans. In the last months of the war, these losses, both in pilots and airplanes, were much harder to replace for the Germans than the Allies.

The new year had started with attacks by the German Luftwaffe. The 452nd AAA was deployed in and around Luxembourg, out of the way of the flight routes that the Luftwaffe took to attack the Allied airfields. Thus, they noticed less of the operation than the AAA soldiers deployed further north. In January their raids would become more numerous. The improved weather also aided these bombing and strafing attacks, as well as reconnaissance flights.

Starting at 08:00 and lasting until 08:45 six platoons of the unit engaged two enemy aircraft identified as either two Ju 88s or two Me 410s. At first, only one aircraft flew from east to west on a level flight, and a minute later it was accompanied by the other plane and both then flew from northeast to southwest on a level flight. Both planes flew at an altitude of 2,000 ft [609 meters] and about 250 mph [402 kph]. No hostile acts were committed by the planes and both were engaged with 40mm and M-51s. When fired upon, the planes swerved slightly and climbed up into the clouds.

These were not the only planes, because at 08:45 Second Platoon, Battery D, engaged an Me 410 with an M-51 .50 cal. A few minutes later another Me 410 was engaged with both 40mm gun and M-51 gun mounts using .50 caliber machine guns. There were no claims.

On 2 January, group headquarters informed the battalion that a gold star flare would be fired from a Very pistol when German planes flew over German positions, and that "Goldregen" was the code word for low-flying planes. The underside of wings would bear wavy yellow lines on low-flying German aircraft. It's shared as an additional means of recognition. Most likely this information had been derived from captured air personnel.

At 11:15, an Me 163 flew over at a height of 2,000 ft [609 meters] and about 250 mph [402 kph]. Second Platoon, Battery A, fired on it with 40mm guns. The aircraft was seen at about 2,000 ft [609 meters] slant range and it was first seen at an azimuth of 875 yards [800 meters].

Immediately upon being engaged, the aircraft increased its speed to around 500 mph [805 kph]. No hostile acts were committed.

At 11:25 a V-1 was flying northeast to southwest and was engaged by a 40mm gun of First Platoon, Battery C, at a slant range of 1,500 yards [1,372 meters]. The altitude was approximately 2,000 ft [609 meters]. The pilotless aircraft, as the unit referred to it, was not hit and it was not seen to crash. First Platoon, Battery B, engaged the same V-1 with eight rounds of 40mm.

It was the first time that the 452nd AAA actively engaged the flying rockets. Although previously a launch site had been protected and a V-1 was seen or heard, this is the first time that the bomb was fired upon. Most of the V-1s were used on targets well to the north of the 452nd AAA, against the port of Antwerp, Liege, or targets in the UK. The V-1s were launched usually from positions east and north of their targets and the 452nd AAA had little contact with them.

On 3 January, Second Platoon, Battery B, was supporting the 215th FA and on the road to Vaux-lez-Rosières. The fluid situation at the front also reached the 452nd AAA, because a message came in that all planes committing a hostile act should be engaged. An enlisted man was selected out of all the soldiers in the battalion to go home for leave in the U.S. The person selected was chosen based on his time overseas, his awards, and his wounds.

A truck of the battalion, complete with a gun and gun section, was found broken down in Mensdorf. No guards were at the vehicle or equipment as reported by the 802nd Tank Destroyer Battalion. Ratcliffe would drop by their command post the next morning to hear the details.

On 4 January, two M-51s were in Ordnance for repair, leaving them out of action. On the 5th, two more M-51s were sent to Ordnance for repairs, leaving four of them out of action. The Second Platoon, Battery B, was attached to the 512th Field Artillery Battalion. Explicit orders came through not to fire upon P-38s flying south along Moselle River. They would be there around 14:30 and were on a photo reconnaissance mission. Second Platoon, Battery B, was in action at 19:30 hours.

Enemy counter-battery fire was heavy during this period which caused one slightly wounded battle casualty in Battery D. Counter-attacks were frequent and this with nightly patrols resulted in the gun sections deploying their guns, in many instances, as field pieces.

On 5 January, several soldiers of 27th AAA Group, which included the 457th AAA and 452nd AAA, were awarded for their bravery in action, receiving decorations such as the Silver Star Medal or the Bronze Star Medal. Major General Manton Eddy presented the medals himself and also awarded several of them to soldiers of the 452nd AAA. When awarding the medals to Technician Fifth Grade Zeno Ellis and Staff Sergeant William Campbell, who had evacuated wounded of a field artillery battalion while under fire, something remarkable happened.

Major General Eddy was personally awarding the medals. Sometimes he "was so impressed with the citation that he said the recipient should get a Silver Star for the action, and proceeded to award the higher decoration on the spot. Thus a general order of XII Corps was rescinded by another."[4]

General Eddy must have been impressed by the bravery of both men and deemed the Bronze Star Medal not enough for them. Thus, he gave both of them the Silver Star Medal. A little over a week later, on 13 January 1945, a general order went out acknowledging that both men had received the Silver Star Medal and rescinding the Bronze Star Medal.[5] It is praiseworthy that General Eddy made no distinction between the skin color of his soldiers in this regard.

On 6 January, nine Jeeps were delivered to the battalion. It was reported that friendly bombers would be over the area that night. The next day, one M-51 was still out of action and two M-51 .50 cal generators were sent over to Ordnance. Each from a platoon of Battery D. The wiring on the power charger of M-51 of Gun Section No. 1, Battery A, burned through and the M-51 was brought to Battalion Headquarters for repairs. Friendly bombers would be over the area tonight.

On 8 January, one V-1, referred to as a Diver, passed from southeast to northwest, going over Second Platoon, Battery B, at 00:30 hours. Around 09:30 hours Privates First Class Birel Fisher and Roger A. Pegram, Battery D, were slightly wounded by shell fragments from counter-battery fire. They were evacuated to the 80th Division Clearing Station.

Piper Cubs would be flying, with or without white streamers from wings or fuselage, and were not to be engaged. These light aircrafts could be used as spotters for the field artillery battalions, as messengers, or to transport essential personnel.

Neither should French aircraft be engaged. These Free French pilots would fly French aircraft, or aircraft with French stripes, blue, white, and red. The following aircraft could be seen, including P-47s, P-39s, Spitfires, B-26s, Marylands, Ju 88s, Do 24s, Potez, Lemoines and Maranes.[6] In general, if the markings could be seen, then planes may be regarded as friendly. There were no changes in the rules of engagement. It seems it had not yet been determined which aircraft the Free French Air Forces would employ, because the list included airplanes in service with the U.S. Air Force, the British Royal Air Force, the Luftwaffe, as well as old French aircraft which had been used during the invasion of France in 1940 and were again be pressed into active service.

On 7 January a German Fw 190 was shot down with three 10–12 inch [25–30 cm] stripes, yellow, white, yellow around the fuselage over the First U.S. Army. This aircraft belonged to the *Jagdgeschwader* 2 and the information was shared to keep the 452nd AAA updated on recent developments. The Fw 190 subtypes had inline engines and long noses, which were observed operating over the same area. The battalion was also informed that all pigeon lofts, or any locations where pigeons are seen flying or circling, had to be reported to the headquarters, as these birds might be used by German agents or spies to send messages across the frontlines.

Lastly, the three missing soldiers, Major Kimble, Sergeant Major, and Private Garner were located. They had been wounded and evacuated to a hospital.

Besides the previously mentioned equipment, also a Jeep, two 2½ ton "deuce-and-a-halfs", were in Ordnance for repair. One Dodge truck needed to be replaced, as well as another deuce-and-a-half truck. The battalion was also sixteen SCR-543s short. Six would eventually arrive, but the remaining ten still hadn't arrived by the time the war ended. Additionally, another Jeep and eight trailers for the Jeeps were needed.

On 10 January an M-51 .50 cal generator was repaired and returned to Battery D. Allied bombers would operate that night. The Battery A mess truck had left Sedan, France, on the 9th and was on its way to Luxembourg.

On the 11th, a wrecker was requested by Battery C. A deuce-and-a-half threw a rod and needed to be picked up. A large raid of hostile aircraft was reported, thirty planes going south on the eastern border of the corps area. No Allied bombers would be in the area that night.

The next day, another ¼ ton truck was sent to Ordnance for repair, as well as a deuce-and-a-half truck. The M-51 was repaired. Allied bombers would operate that night. An officer and three enlisted men of the 457th AAA were at the Group Headquarters with a wrecked Jeep and they needed a wrecker, which they requested from the 452nd AAA. Ratcliffe was requested to attend a meeting that day at the 80th Infantry Division's command post that day. The battalion was also informed that the next day another battery of 155mm howitzers would arrive at the front and Allied bombers would be over the area that night.

On 13 January, a 40mm gun was sent back to Ordnance for its semi-annual check from Battery A. A deuce-and-a-half truck was repaired. That left only an M-51 .50 cal generator, two Jeeps, and two deuce-and-a-half trucks in Ordnance for repairs. If paratroopers were seen, then the time and place and the names of the persons seeing the paratroopers must be reported by radio to higher headquarters. Allied bombers would once again fly over that night.

On the 14th, Second Platoon, Battery B, was relieved of the 512th Field Artillery Battalion and attached to the 215th Field Artillery Battalion. They would set up in the vicinity of Berbourg.

At 14:20 six Me 109s were engaged by First Platoon, Battery B, while First Platoon, Battery C, fired on a mixed flight of planes. There were twelve Spitfires, as well as four Me 109s. The entire action was very confusing since planes came from all directions. At 14:30 two planes from a flight of four were engaged by Second Platoon, Battery A, and the First Platoons of the three other batteries. These planes were identified as Spitfires, flying from northeast to southeast. The planes were strafing the units and altitude varied between 50 and 4,000 ft [15-1,219 meters]. They were engaged with 40mm and M-51s. No damage was reported and two Cat II were claimed. Signals were set off and panels displayed, but it made no difference.

Witnesses from both First Platoon, Battery B, and First Platoon, Battery C, say that the flights were mixed. Spitfires and Me 109s were strafing the area. An auxiliary tank, 75-gallon gasoline, made by Tappan Stove Co, serial number 4029, was dropped by the planes near Gun Section No. 1, First Platoon, Battery B.

The uncertainty of the identification is an indication of the rapidity of anti-aircraft combat, where split-second decisions need to be made and choices can have fatal consequences. Furthermore, the pilots might have made a navigational error and assumed they had spotted a German battery. Even though the Allied air forces attempted to prevent friendly fire, it's an example of the chaotic situation at the front and how fratricide could never be entirely eliminated.

At 16:40 two planes from a flight of four were engaged by the same platoons as earlier. They were identified as P-51s with U.S. markings. The planes came in flying from north to south strafing at an altitude of approximately 500 ft [152 meters]. They were engaged by both 40mm and M-51 .50 cal. Identification panels were displayed, but the attack didn't cease. One Cat III was claimed. First Platoon, Battery D, claimed two Cat II, and First Platoon, Battery B, claimed a Cat I.

Another deuce-and-a-half truck went out of action and was sent to Ordnance, while a Briggs Stratton generator was needed for the M-51.

On 16 January, one 40mm gun returned from the semi-annual check. In addition to the previous one, another Briggs Stratton generator was needed. An M-51 of First Platoon, Battery D, was damaged. Two Jeeps and five deuce-and-a-half trucks were in Ordnance. Allied bombers operated that night.

At 15:45 a loose formation of P-47s flew over the area of Second Platoon, Battery C, flying north to south. A plane left the formation and dropped a bomb from approximately 3,000 ft [914 meters] altitude, causing three casualties to the 752nd Field Artillery Battalion. This same plane then turned and passed over the area again, being engaged by both 40mm and M-51 .50 cal. Panels were displayed correctly by ground units, but they went unnoticed by the strafing plane.

At 16:00 Second Platoon, Battery D, engaged, what they initially thought was an Fw 190, but later was identified as a P-47. From certain angles, the planes could appear similar. Both were also equipped with a radial-engine.

The plane was flying from east to west at approximately 800 ft [244 meters]. It bombed and strafed nearby units. It was engaged by both 40mm and M-51 .50 cal guns. A Cat III was claimed but later dropped for insufficient evidence.

On 17 January, First Platoon, Battery B, was en route to Ettelbruck, while another 40mm was on its way to Ordnance for repairs. Two Briggs Stratton generators were needed for the unit, as well as the two Jeeps and the five deuce-and-a-half trucks. The battalion command post and headquarters battery moved to Buschdorf, Luxembourg, on 15 January occupying a school building as a command post and mess. The troops were quartered in evacuated buildings. That same day an extra 40mm gun was sent to Ordnance for a semi-annual check and one more deuce-and-a-half truck was sent over to them. Allied bombers would operate that night.

The weather had been quite severe, while the snow and wind hindered the exposed AA sites a lot. The Battery Aid Men were made trench-foot-control non-commissioned officers and due to their frequent lectures and informal talks on care and protection of feet along with demonstrations, the incidents of trench foot and frostbite were kept at a remarkably low level.

The next day:

> On 18 January the [XII] Corps made a coordinated attack on the left flank with the 80th, 5th, and 4th Infantry Divisions crossing the Sure and Sauer Rivers, while the newly joined 87th Infantry Division and the 2d Cavalry

> Group, reinforced, made demonstrations on the east flank along the Sauer and Moselle Rivers.[7]

Although the corps continued to attack over the next few days, it doesn't seem to have affected the 452nd AAA much. A deuce-and-a-half truck returned to the battalion, but a Jeep needed to be repaired. Another message went out that Allied bombers would operate that night.

On 19 January, one 40mm gun, a Briggs Stratton generation, and a deuce-and-a-half truck were returned to the unit. Only one 40mm gun, one Briggs Stratton generator for the M51 gun mount, two Jeep trucks, and three 2½-ton trucks remained in Ordnance. Allied bombers would once more operate that night.

The next day another 40mm gun went out of action. Allied bombers would operate that night. A gun section moved to the vicinity of Bech.

On 21 January, the familiar "Allied friendly bombers over the area tonight" was forwarded to the battalion.[8] In addition to the equipment still with Ordnance, there were also several other items the battalion needed, which were difficult to obtain. This included "trousers, wool, o.d. waist size 34 and larger," oil, and light preservatives. A deuce-and-a-half truck was returned to the unit.

On the 22nd it turned out that one 40mm gun could not be repaired and was written off. Another one could be repaired, as well as a deuce-and-a-half truck. There were only two Jeeps, a Dodge, and two deuce-and-a-halfs left with Ordnance. Group Headquarters sent out a reminder that not all jet-propelled aircraft were hostile; the Gloster Meteor was in service with the British Royal Air Force and had been used for defense against the V-1 flying bomb. Two days previously, on 20 January 1945, four of these aircraft had been moved to an airfield in Belgium. Friendly B-26s would fly over late that afternoon.

For the next few days, until the end of January, there was little to report, other than Allied aircraft flying over: "Expect friendly bombers over the area between the time 11:45 and 14:00 today," or, "Friendly bombers expected over the area between the time 11:15 and 13:30 this date."[9] It's an indication of the Allied material superiority that almost every day or night Allied bombers would fly over the frontlines to deliver their deadly payload on targets in Germany, while few German bombers attacked targets in the Allied rear.

During those days, equipment that had been out of action trickled back into service, as well as additionally requested material, such as six SCR 543s of sixteen necessary. By the end of the war, the ten missing SCR 543s still hadn't arrived.

In February the battalion continued to protect field artillery battalions, while hostile air activity was light. On 1 February, Second Platoon, Battery C, was attached to the 255th Field Artillery Battery, while Second Platoon, Battery B, was attached to the 512th Field Artillery Battalion. A deuce-and-a-half truck returned to the unit. Ninety friendly bombers would be over the area that night.

The next day a deuce-and-a-half truck was sent to Ordnance for repairs. One SCR 543 was at the signal depot for repairs. Second Platoon, Battery B, was set up in the vicinity of Eppeldorf.

On 3 February, First Platoon, Battery C, was attached to the 243rd Field Artillery Battalion. Also that night, friendly bombers would fly over the target area.

On the 4th, a deuce-and-a-half truck returned to the unit, while high above them friendly bombers would bomb targets in Germany.

The next day, two more deuce-and-a-half trucks needed serious repairs and were sent to Ordnance. A Jeep was fixed and returned to the unit. In total, at Ordnance, were two Jeeps and seven deuce-and-a-half trucks, as well as a 40mm gun. One SCR 543 was at the signal depot. Second Platoon, Battery A, moved to Belfort, while First Platoon, Battery B, moved near Waldbillig. Friendly bombers would fly over the units that night.

On 6 February, Headquarters, Battery D, and First Platoon, Battery D, were en route to the vicinity of Consdorf. Two deuce-and-a-half trucks and a 40mm gun returned to the unit, while one

Jeep was sent to Ordnance. One enlisted man of Battery B was wounded by hostile artillery. That night there would be no friendly bombers flying over the platoons.

The next day the engineers employed by XII Corps would force their away across the Our and Sauer rivers, allowing the infantry divisions to cross. However, despite the attack, the Luftwaffe didn't respond. That same day, First Platoon, Battery D, was en route to Berdorf. Three vehicles, a Jeep and two deuce-and-a-half trucks, were sent to Ordnance for repairs. The Battalion Command Post moved to Beringen, while a soldier of Battery B, Corporal Jessie J. Preston, was wounded in an enemy shelling and sent to the hospital. British bombers would be over the area that night.

On 8 February, a Jeep and a deuce-and-a-half truck returned to the unit. Two 40mm guns were sent to Ordnance for semi-annual checks. Heavy bombers would be over the area that night. David Blakeley, Technician Fifth Grade in Battery A, was wounded in a heavy artillery shelling and the Command Post of Battery D was hit by one round of medium caliber artillery.

On the 9th, there was a lot of equipment with Ordnance, representing the difficult circumstances in which the Allied armies had to operate. In total, at Ordnance, were four Jeeps, seven deuce-and-a-half trucks, and three M-51s, all for repairs, while two 40mm guns received semi-annual checks. The battalion was still eight Jeep trailers short. One soldier of Battery B was evacuated to a hospital, wounded by hostile artillery.

The next day, one Jeep returned to the unit, while Allied bombers would fly over the unit that night.

On 11 February, a Dodge truck was sent for repairs to Ordnance and once more Allied bombers would cross the frontlines at night.

On the 12th, at 08:00 hours, a deuce-and-a-half truck and a Jeep of First Platoon, Battery A, which had deployed in the vicinity of Echternach, were damaged by hostile artillery. The unit had been under fire since their arrival and even the Battery Command Post was hit, but there were no casualties. One 40mm and one M-51 returned to the unit. Friendly bombers flew over that night. Also on the 12th, First Platoon, Battery B, was deployed in the vicinity of Consdorf. The platoon was attached to the 945th Field Artillery Battalion and while in this position a German soldier was taken prisoner.

George A. Buck, of the 945th FA, told the following story about their time there:

> My battalion was assigned to Third United States Army under General George C. Patton Jr. the Commander of Third Army in Europe in World War II. I was assigned to the 945th Field Artillery Battalion which was a 155mm howitzer M-1 battalion and we were somewhere in Luxembourg near the town of Consdorf when the following incident occurred. I was assigned to A battery as the Reconnaissance Officer and I was spending a rare night with my battery from not being up front as a forward observer with an infantry company.
>
> Attached to our battery was part of the 1st Platoon, Battery B, 452nd Anti-Aircraft Artillery (AAA). One of the sections had a Bofors 40mm which was a double-barreled automatic anti-aircraft gun, and the other section had a multiple-barreled 50 caliber anti-aircraft machine gun. The gun had four 50-caliber barrels and was operated electrically by a soldier who sat on the gun carriage. An electric motor charged by a generator powered the guns. The guns had a very distinctive sound and one could not fail to recognize them when they were fired. The soldiers assigned to the anti-aircraft sections were all Negroes, and they called the multiple 50 caliber guns "four barrels".

The nomenclature of the gun was as follows. Machine Gun, Multiple, Caliber 50 M45 mount. Thc purpose was for AA (anti-aircraft) fire while mounted on a vehicle, ground, or fixed base. Weight is approximately 2,400 pounds [1,089 kg], width 6 feet 9.5 inches [1.94 meters], height with guns level 4 feet 7 inches [1.40 meters], the traverse is 360 degrees, and elevates to 90 degrees and depresses to -10 degrees. The guns were fired electrically by solenoids. There was a self-contained power unit that drove the armored mount; the mount movement and gunfire were controlled from hand grips in front of the gunner's seat within the mount. The gun mounted 4 MG (Machine Gun), caliber 50, HB (Heavy Barreled), M2, turret type (with barrel support) mounted outboard on R (Right) and L (Left) trunnions.

I had not been in my sleeping bag very long the night of the incident when I heard the "four barrels" firing at ground level. The reason I knew the guns were firing at ground level was that we could hear the projectiles striking the ground or some of the small bush-like growth in front of our battery. It was possible to fire the guns at ground level by moving a bracket that tilted the guns up skyward. When we heard the machine guns from the anti-aircraft artillery fire at night we never approached the gun sections as it was not safe, as it was possible they might rotate the guns and fire at us. In fact, if I was to make an inspection of the anti-aircraft gun sections after dark we always made a lot of noise, whistled or in some way let them know we were approaching their area. The Negro or Black soldiers never halted one and ask for the password, they only watched you and kept their guns on you ready to shoot. One could walk up to their gun section and right up to the guns and all you would see would be two big white eyeballs, but no challenge from the operator of the guns. I must say that they sat at those guns 24 hours every day, and one could never see the gun but a soldier would be sitting on the carriage, no matter what happened.

As the night wore on, no longer would one doze off to sleep than another burst of firing could be heard from the machine guns. This went on all night until it became light in the morning. Needless to say, no one approached the gun section all night long. After we had breakfast my battery commander, Captain George R. Mitchell, ask me if I would check the anti-aircraft gun section and try to determine what was the difficulty and find out why so much firing was taking place.

I selected one individual and the two of us proceeded to the multiple 50 caliber gun section, and there faithfully sitting on the carriage was a soldier with the guns pointing out to the front and he intently looking out in the field. I asked the soldier if he was the one firing the machine guns and he responded "Yes, Sir," this was like asking if he was a U.S. soldier, as we knew by the sound that it was he doing the firing. I asked him what was the trouble and he said, "Sir, I was sitting here on this four barrels last night when I look out in front and I see this bush coming up the hill at right shoulder arms, so I done give him a burst on the four barrels." I ask him if he challenged the bush and he said "No, Sir". I then queried him if the bush was still out there and he said "Yes, Sir, and if it moves again, I give it another burst on the four barrels." I told him to lock the guns so they could not be fired, and we would go out and see what was there. He said, "No Sir, I done ain't going out there for nothing." I explained for him not to worry and that the soldier that came with me and I would go out front and check.

> We proceeded and walked out in front of the guns, and the ground, grass, and a few bushes were riddled and all torn up by the bullets from the 50 caliber. However, there was one spot that was literally torn to shreds with no vegetation and only churned-up soil showing where most of the firing had taken place or the bullets had been hitting. Just on the other side of this torn-up area in a slight depression was a German soldier covered with dirt and scared to death that he would be shot and killed. I had him stand up and he was shaking and nervous from lying under a barrage that had lasted the entire night. He told me that he had become lost in the dark from his unit and had wandered into our lines only to be met with a hail of machine gun fire. He was so glad to give himself up and to learn and be assured that he would not be killed – he offered no opposition.
>
> So ends the saga of "the burst from the four barrels". As we walked back with the prisoner to our unit we checked about the activities of the night. However, we were not surprised by the action of the unit of the anti-aircraft section as this was their rather normal and standard procedure when they would detect anything from the normal. I often think about the expression I heard from the soldier about that bush coming up the hill at right-shoulder-arms.[10]

It's an example of the power of the guns that the 452nd AAA Battalion had at its disposal, which were not only used against hostile aircraft but could also effectively be deployed in a ground role, as an unlucky German got to experience that night.

On 13 February, at 09:52 an Fw 190 flew over the area of First Platoon, Battery B, at an altitude of 1,500 ft [457 meters]. The plane was flying from the north and when fired upon flew to the southeast. Second Platoon, Battery A, engaged that same Fw 190 as it went from east to west at 1,000 ft [305 meters]. However, they fired only one round of 40mm. In total, both platoons fired eighteen rounds of 40mm ammunition and 494 rounds of .50 caliber ammunition.

At 10:00 Second Platoon, Battery D, engaged an Me 109 flying from northwest to southeast at 1,500 ft [457 meters]. Four rounds of 40mm were fired and 288 rounds of .50 cal.

At 10:00 First Platoon, Battery D, engaged two planes of a mixed flight of three Me 109s and one Fw 190. The planes came flying low from north to south and sixteen rounds of 40mm and 116 rounds of .50 cal were fired at them.

That same day, hostile artillery damaged an M-51 gun mount of First Platoon, Battery B. At that point, there were still three Jeeps, four deuce-and-a-half trucks, two 40mm guns, two M-51 gun mounts, and two Dodge trucks with Ordnance. The damaged M-51 was swiftly replaced, and Allied bombers flew over that night.

The next day, another warning went out that between darkness and daylight, heavy bombers would fly over the platoons. Additional instructions went out for the gun sections stating the lateral gun pointer should remain in his seat at all times and observe. The vertical gun pointer should observe in the opposite direction but should not remain in his seat and the M-51 gunner should keep his feet in his seat at all times.

On the 15th, a Dodge was repaired and two more deuce-and-a-half were turned in to Ordnance for repairs. Another 40mm gun was delivered to them as well for its semi-annual check. One M-51 was repaired and returned to the unit. Once more heavy bombers would fly over the frontlines on their mission to Germany.

On 16 February, a Dodge truck was turned in for repair and a Jeep was damaged by shrapnel from hostile artillery at 15:15, so it needed a new radiator. Later that day, at 17:15, two soldiers of Second Platoon, Battery D, were wounded by enemy artillery: Private First Class C. Johnson, and Private Harold Jones.

The next day, the battalion finally received six trailers for their Jeeps. The Second Platoon of Battery D, which was stationed at Echternach, was receiving a considerable amount of enemy fire. This included direct fire from pillboxes on the other side of the river and later from self-propelled artillery. Corporal Nezmer Johnson, Second Platoon, Battery D, was killed by enemy artillery at 04:15 by a direct hit on his foxhole. At 09:45 Second Platoon, Battery D, was shelled again and two more soldiers were wounded: Corporal Travis and Private First Class Lawrence Beckwith, who died of his wounds later that day. At 14:45 a deuce-and-a-half of the same platoon was totally demolished by enemy artillery. Lost with the vehicle were also 200 rounds of 40mm.

In total three Jeeps, six deuce-and-a-half trucks, two Dodge trucks, and one M-51 were in Ordnance for repairs. Three 40mm guns were still turned in for semi-annual checks. Lastly, British heavy bombers would fly over the platoons that night.

On the 18th, several platoons were on the move again. Second Platoon, Battery A, went to Reisdorf, while the First Platoons of Battery B and D moved to Ferschweiler. One Jeep and a 40mm gun returned to the unit.

On 19 February First Platoon, Battery B, was en route to XX Corps with the 736th Field Artillery Battalion. One M-51 returned to the unit after it had been repaired; British bombers would be over that night. Both platoons of Battery B crossed the German border that day, being the first of the battalion to set up in Germany, erecting their command posts around Ferschweiler.

The next day, after returning from XX Corps, First Platoon, Battery B, would be attached to the 738th Field Artillery Battalion. One M-51 was turned in for repairs. That night there were no big formations in the sky, but single friendly bombers flying through the area.

On the 21st, another 40mm gun was turned in for its semi-annual check and once more bombers would fly over the area that night.

The day afterwards a deuce-and-a-half truck returned to the unit, while two more M-51s were turned in. Everything together, two Jeeps, one Dodge, two deuce-and-a-half, two 40mm guns, and three M-51s were with Ordnance for repairs. As usual, the platoons were warned that Allied bombers would be over that night.

On 23 February, a Jeep returned to the unit, while one 40mm gun was turned in for its semi-annual check and one M-51 was turned in for repairs. Once more Allied bombers would bomb targets in Germany that night.

The next day, the 452nd AAA had luck! Three M-51s returned to the unit, while a deuce-and-a-half needed to be repaired. Allied bombers would fly over the frontline that night. Meanwhile, Lieutenant Colonel Ratcliffe was temporarily absent from the battalion and replaced by Milton D. Lederman.

On 25 February, three deuce-and-a-half trucks returned to the unit, and another 40mm gun turned in for its annual check.

On 26 February several batteries were relieved from their previous attachments and attached to new units: Second Platoon, Battery B, was attached to the 179th Field Artillery Battalion and would join them the next day. First Platoon, Battery C, provided anti-aircraft protection for the 740th Field Artillery Battalion, while Second Platoon, Battery C, protected the 752nd Field Artillery Battalion.

Meanwhile, Second Platoon, Battery A, moved to the vicinity of Bettingen and a new deuce-and-a-half truck was delivered to the unit, although the battalion still needed two more. Additionally, a Jeep required repairs, as well as one deuce-and-a-half. Three 40mm guns returned to the unit after completing their semi-annual checks.

Enemy aircraft with Allied markings would be over the area that afternoon; they looked similar to the Piper Cub and must not be engaged. This was probably a Fieseler Fi 156 "Storch"; this aircraft had been employed by the Luftwaffe and performed a similar role as the Piper Cub in the U.S. Army Air Force. The French aircraft manufacturer Morane-Saulnier had been converted to build German aircraft, which included the Fieseler Fi 156. After the liberation of France, they continued to build these airplanes, which were used by the Free French Air Force.

Later that night bombers flew over the platoons on their way to targets in Germany.

On 27 February one deuce-and-a-half truck broke down and a new 40mm gun was brought in for its semi-annual check. Lamar C. Ratcliffe returned to the battalion and assumed command again. Bombers were over the area that night.

On the last day of February, one more 40mm gun got its semi-annual checkup and two deuce-and-a-half trucks returned to the unit. Furthermore, two trailers for the Jeeps were delivered and the battalion command post moved to Echternach. As on many nights before, friendly bombers would fly over that night.

The first days of March were relatively uneventful. The usual warnings went out about friendly bombers flying over at night, while equipment broke down and was repaired. On 2 March one man of Gun Section No. 8, Battery C, was wounded by enemy artillery and a deuce-and-a-half truck and a 40mm gun were damaged. First Platoon, Battery B, moved to Bitburg.

On 4 March, Second Platoon, Battery B, and Second Platoon, Battery A, crossed the Kyll River at Metterich around 10:00 hours.

Things changed on 5 March, when the 4th Armored Division attacked to the northeast. They would have to reach the Rhine River above Koblenz, some 65 miles [105 kilometers] beyond where they started. The two combat commands of this unit went on the attack. Combat Command A (CCA) was supported by the 974th Field Artillery Battalion, which had Second Platoon, Battery A, attached. Combat Command B was supported by the 179th Field Artillery Battalion, which had Second Platoon, Battery B, attached.

As XII Corps' history recounted:

> And it was something of a nightmare to certain other corps elements which acted in close support of the drive. The medium and heavy artillery battalions sweated their hearts out along the few poor highways,— roads never built for modern warfare in the first place, and now, after being churned up by the armor, rendered even less capable of supporting an American army in the fashion to which it had become accustomed.[11]

That same day, the battalion noticed that a deuce-and-a-half truck was evacuated and requisitioned through the 281st Ordnance Maintenance Company on 3 February, but had still not been delivered.

On 7 March, Second Platoon, Battery A, moved with the 974th Field Artillery Battalion, which was part of CCA of the 4th Armored Division, while Second Platoon, Battery B, moved with the 179th Field Artillery Battalion, which had been attached to CCB of the 4th Armored Division. That day the 4th Armored Division reached the Rhine, some fifty-eight hours after they started their attack.

First Platoon, Battery D, moved with the 191st Field Artillery Battalion, which supported the 5th Infantry Division. The next day the battalion relocated to Badem, Germany.

It was not until 10 March that the Luftwaffe was seen again. On that day, many platoons were on the move. This included the Second Platoons of Battery A and C and the First Platoons of Battery B and D.

At 16:59 Second Platoon, Battery B, engaged an Me 210 flying at 1,500 ft [457 meters]. It was fired upon with sixteen rounds of 40mm and 1,655 rounds of .50 cal, resulting in a claim for a Cat III.

At 17:08, a Ju 87 flew over the area occupied by First Platoon, Battery B. It flew at an altitude of 1,000 ft [305 meters] and the plane was clearly on reconnaissance. Two rounds of 40mm and sixty-five rounds of .50 cal were expended.

At 17:39, a Ju 87 was flying over First Platoon, Battery B, at 1,000 ft [305 meters] altitude. The platoon engaged it and fired sixty-seven rounds of 40mm and 1,065 rounds of .50 cal, claiming a Cat III.

Later that evening friendly British bombers would fly over the platoons.

On 11 March, Second Platoon, Battery D, was off the net, because it moved with the unit to which it was attached.

The next day the platoons continued to move up. Two Me 262s flew over Second Platoon, Battery B, and were engaged at 18:15 hours. The planes were apparently on a recce mission, flying at 1,000 ft [305 meters]. There were no claims and just two rounds of 40mm and 404 rounds of .50 cal were expended.

On 13 March, the Battalion Command Post left Badem and set up at Polch. Second Platoon, Battery A, set up near Pilling. At 13:50 hours First Platoon, Battery B, claimed an Me 109. The plane came from the northwest, diving and strafing in the area. Thirteen rounds of 40mm and 380 rounds of .50 cal were used, resulting in the plane crashing down northwest of Münstermaifeld.

The day afterwards, Second Platoon, Battery C, was detached from the 752nd FA and added to the 771st Field Artillery B attalion.

There were busy days ahead for the 452nd Anti-Aircraft Artillery Battalion. The 4th Armored Division would go on the offensive again and this time, the Luftwaffe resisted fiercely. As described by XII Corps' history:

> While the Eifel area was being cleared down to the Rhine and Moselle Rivers, and the city of Koblenz at their confluence was pocketed, the Corps regrouped for a change of direction to the southeast to make a surprise crossing of the Moselle. On the early morning of 14 March, with the 90th Infantry Division on the left and the 5th Infantry Division on the right, assault crossings were made in the

> Hatzenport-Treis area. Surprise was achieved over the enemy, who was engaged with moving in troops to establish a defensive line along the right bank. By noon of 15 March, the 4th Armored Division had crossed the river with one combat command in each infantry division bridgehead, and was making good progress into the high undulating ridge of the Hunsruck. The favorable weather, the improved road net, and the large expanse of rolling high plateau permitted full exploitation of the power of the armor-infantry team over an enemy who sought to disengage himself from XX Corps and Seventh Army troops farther south and flee over the Rhine. On 16 March, while the 5th and 90th Infantry Divisions swept southwest, the 4th Armored Division broke out and reached Bad Kreuznach, 35 miles [56 kilometers] southeast of the Moselle. On the same day the 89th Infantry Division crossed the Moselle near Bullay, and the 11th Armored Division, which had just been transferred from the VIII Corps, moved to cross in the 89th Infantry Division bridgehead.[12]

It would mark the beginning of another busy period for the 452nd AAA Battalion, because while XII Corps divisions moved forward, the Luftwaffe tried to halt the Allied advance. They were mostly ineffective in their attempts.

On 16 March, at 16:40 hours, First Platoon, Battery D, engaged two Me 109s from a flight of four, which resulted in claims for two Cat IIs. Eleven rounds of 40mm and 560 rounds of .50 cal were used as they flew over their area. However, these claims were later corrected to just one Cat II, which was eventually also dropped.

The next day was busy! At 08:25 hours Second Platoon, Battery B, engaged two Me 109s flying over their area from the southwest, circling above them and then going to the northeast. They expended twenty-two rounds of 40mm and 855 rounds of 50 cal, submitting two Cat II claims. However, this claim was later dropped due to insufficient evidence.

At 08:50 First Platoon, Battery D, engaged five Me 109s flying at 2,000 ft [610 meters] from west to east. The platoon used fifty-six rounds of 40mm and 880 rounds of .50 cal ammo and in exchange they claimed one Cat I and three Cat IIs, even going so far as to say: "Approximate coordinates of wreckage are M030373."[13]

At 09:54 Second Platoon, Battery B, engaged two Me 109s that circled the area at 1,000 ft [305 meters]. Unusual was that according to the soldiers, these fighters wore green crosses. In total thirty-five rounds of 40mm and 650 rounds of .50 cal were fired.

At 10:00 First Platoon, Battery D, fired forty-eight rounds of 40mm and 1,080 rounds of .50 cal at four Me 109s at 1,000 ft [305 meters].

At 10:03 hours First Platoon, Battery D, tried to shoot down three Me 109s, flying southwards at an altitude of 1,000 ft [305 meters] with twenty-four rounds of 40mm and 846 rounds of .50 cal.

At 10:30 six Me 109s flew from north to south and dove on Allied positions from an altitude of 1,000 ft [305 meters]. Second Platoon, Battery B, opened fire, expending eighty-four rounds of 40mm and 1,850 rounds of .50 cal. They submitted two Cat IIs.

Two hours later First Platoon, Battery B, engaged an Fw 190 at 12:30 hours. It flew at 4,000 ft [1,219 meters] from northwest to southeast. The soldiers used 187 rounds of .50 cal.

At 15:00 Second Platoon, Battery B, engaged an Me 109 from a flight of four. The planes circled the area at 1,300 ft [396 meters] and then flew to the southwest. A Cat I was claimed and eighty-seven rounds of 40mm and 896 rounds of .50 cal were expended.

At 15:20 Second Platoon, Battery B, engaged two Me 109s from a flight of five that were strafing and bombing in the area. The platoon claimed a Cat I and a Cat II, using forty-three rounds of 40mm and 200 rounds of .50 cal.

Thirty minutes later Second Platoon, Battery B, fired at three Me 109s from a flight of four, which were circling the area at 2,000 ft [610 meters] with ten rounds of 40mm and 100 rounds of .50 cal.

At 16:06 two Me 109s flew over Second Platoon, Battery B, at an altitude of 3,000 ft [914 meters] and one of them engaged one Me 109 with three rounds of 40mm.

At 16:15 five Fw 190s dove into the area defended by First Platoon, Battery D. The platoon returned fire and shot down two of the attackers with twenty-six rounds of 40mm and 617 rounds of .50 cal. "Coordinates of wreckage are in the vicinity of M065370."[14]

At 17:10 Second Platoon, Battery B, engaged an Me 109 from a flight of five that were flying at 1,500 ft [457 meters] to the northwest with thirty-four rounds of 40mm and 596 rounds of .50 cal.

As that day was summarized by a report in the *Anti-Aircraft Artillery Notes*, published to inform other anti-aircraft artillery officers of the latest developments, technologies, and trends in their branch of service:

> On 17 March two combat commands of the 4th Armored Division, spearheading the advance toward the Nahe River, were attacked by numerous Fw 190s and Me 109s. The planes made a number of attacks throughout the day in groups of two to five, dive bombing and strafing elements and installations of the two combat commands from an altitude of about 1,000 feet [305 meters]. They were engaged by the 489th AAA AW Bn (SP), attached to the 4th Armored Division, and twelve were destroyed. The 452nd AAA AW Bn (M), providing AAA protection for the corps artillery further to the rear, engaged more Me 109s and Fw 190s that were strafing the defended artillery positions, destroying four and probably destroying an additional four. Of a total of fifty-three planes reported over the corps area on this date, sixteen were destroyed and four probably destroyed.[15]

On 18 March, the Luftwaffe seemed equally determined to stop the Allied armies from advancing. At 14:45 a flight of six Mc 109s flew from north to south at 1,500 ft [457 meters] in the vicinity of Second Platoon, Battery B, which engaged two of them and claimed two Cat Is. They expended 201 rounds of 40mm and 1,502 rounds of .50 cal.

At 15:00 First Platoon, Battery C, engaged two Me 109s from a flight of eight strafing in the area. The planes came in from the northeast at 2,000 ft [610 meters] and disappeared to the northwest. The platoon used eighty rounds of 40mm and 263 rounds of .50 cal and claimed two Cat IIs, which were later corrected to two Cat Is.

Twenty minutes later, the same platoon engaged three planes from a mixed flight of eight Me 109s and Fw 190s with thirty-seven rounds of 40mm and 250 rounds of .50 cal. These planes flew over the area from north to south at 2,000–3,000 ft [610–914 meters].

At 15:39 Second Platoon, Battery B, engaged an Me 109 from a flight of two. The planes were flying from north to south at an altitude of 2,000 ft [610 meters]. The platoon used thirty-three rounds of 40mm and 608 rounds of .50 cal.

At 15:53 First Platoon, Battery B, engaged a plane from a mixed flight of ten, Fw 190s and Me 109s, which flew at an altitude of 1,500 ft [457 meters]. In total twelve rounds of 40mm and 250 rounds of .50 cal were expended.

Two minutes later First Platoon, Battery C, fired twenty rounds of 40mm at an Me 109, which flew from north to south at 4,000 ft [1,219 meters] over their area.

At 16:30 an Me 109, flying at 1,500 ft [457 meters] circled the area over Second Platoon, Battery D. They opened fire, using 1,573 rounds of .50 cal ammo.

Fifteen minutes later First Platoon, Battery B, engaged an Fw 190 flying over their area with 750 rounds of .50 cal.

At 16:55 an Me 109 was flying from the southwest to the northeast at 3,000 ft [914 meters] over Second Platoon, Battery C, which promptly opened fire and expended 180 rounds of .50 cal.

At the same time, nine Me 109s, flying north to south at an altitude of 1,200 ft [366 meters] were spotted by Second Platoon, Battery B. They were bombing in the area and three of the planes were engaged with eighty-four rounds of 40mm and 1,500 rounds of .50 cal.

The day had been summarized as follows in the *Anti-Aircraft Artillery Notes*:

> A bridgehead was established across the Nahe River, at Bad Kreuznach on 18 March, and the ensuing 48-hour period saw sporadic attempts by the German Air Force to knock out the bridges and to strafe adjacent installations. Peculiar tactics were exhibited by the German planes during this period. One attack was made by 28 Fw 190s that came over the bridgehead in three groups of six, ten, and twelve planes per group; the planes came over the area at medium altitude and peeled off one by one, dive bombing and strafing. In the first group, one plane dropped an ordinary log, another an empty gas tank, and a third following close behind dropped a cluster bomb. The remaining planes came in and strafed the general area. Three Me 262s approached from the east at 7,000 feet [2,134 meters] altitude and suddenly dove on the bridges, releasing their bombs at about 1,000 feet [305 meters] altitude. Another Me 262 made three separate strafing passes from 1,000 feet [305 meters]. Throughout the period, the bridges suffered no damage and AAA units destroyed eleven of the enemy aircraft and probably destroyed three. Of this total the 452nd AAA AW Bn (M) accounted for 6 of the Cat Is and 2 Cat IIs.[16]

As the 452nd remarked in one of their reports: "Enemy air activity at this time was the heaviest that we had yet encountered and claims for aircraft destroyed came in faster than they could be written up and forwarded to our headquarters."[17]

The next day, late in the evening, the Luftwaffe made another determined attack. At 18:27 First Platoon, Battery B, fired on an Me 109, which circled and bombed the area at 4,500 ft [1,372 meters], with seventy rounds of 40mm and 1,900 rounds of .50 cal.

Three minutes later, Second Platoon, Battery A, engaged two Arado Ar 234s. These airplanes were German jet bombers and reconnaissance aircraft. It was the first time they were engaged by the 452nd AAA when they were bombing in the vicinity from an altitude of 500 to 1,000 ft [152-305 meters]. They fired 100 rounds of 40mm and 804 rounds of .50 cal, submitting a Cat II claim.

Shortly afterwards, at 18:35 First Platoon, Battery B, fired upon an Me 210 flying at 2,000 ft [610 meters] altitude with two others, using forty-six rounds of 40mm and 825 rounds of .50 cal. At the same time, another gun of First Platoon, Battery B, engaged an Me 210, flying at 5,000 ft [1,524 meters] and bombing in the area. They fired sixty-two rounds of 40mm and 1,914 rounds of .50 cal ammunition at the aircraft.

At 18:40 First Platoon, Battery C, fired upon an Me 262 with fifty-seven rounds of 40mm and 400 rounds of .50 cal. The airplane was on a reconnaissance flight over their area at an altitude of 2,000 ft, going from west to east.

At 19:00 First Platoon, Battery D, engaged an Me 262, which circled the area at 2,000 ft altitude [610 meters]. They expended forty-nine rounds of 40mm and 1,050 rounds of .50 cal. At the same time First Platoon, Battery C, engaged an Me 262. This plane flew from west to east at 3,000 ft [914 meters] with fifty-four rounds of 40mm and 415 rounds of .50 cal. Meanwhile, Second Platoon, Battery A, shot at two Fw 190s. The planes were bombing, flying from southwest to northeast at an altitude of 4,000 ft [1,219 meters]. A Cat I was claimed, using 110 rounds of 40mm and 880 rounds of .50 cal.

A minute later Second Platoon, Battery B, engaged an Me 109 from a flight of two, expending thirty-five rounds of .50 cal. The planes were flying north to south and strafed in the vicinity.

At 19:10 First Platoon, Battery D, engaged two Fw 190s with forty-one rounds of 40mm and 802 rounds of .50 cal. They were going over their area at 1,000 ft [305 meters] altitude.

At 19:15 Second Platoon, Battery C, fired at one Me 109 from a flight of two, while the planes circled the area at 1,500 ft [457 meters], claiming a Cat II. They expended sixty-two rounds of 40mm and 1,165 rounds of .50 cal.

Thirty minutes later First Platoon, Battery C, used forty rounds of 40mm and 430 rounds of .50 cal to fire at an Me 262 that came in bombing from an altitude of 2,000 ft [610 meters].

That day Battalion Command Post relocated to Tiefenbach.

On 20 March, the soldiers of the 452nd AAA were ready. In fact, they greeted the appearance of German aircraft with great enthusiasm. Second Platoon, Battery A, was the first in action! At 09:00 a flight of sixteen hostile aircraft came in from the northwest and bombed and strafed from an altitude of 3,000 ft [914 meters], before disappearing to the southwest. The platoon fired on three Fw 190s, claiming two Cat Is and a Cat II. They used 154 rounds of 40mm and 1,330 rounds of .50 cal.

At 09:10 First Platoon, Battery C, engaged four Me 109s from a flight of five. These planes came in strafing the area at an altitude of approximately 1,500 ft [457 meters] from the northeast, circled the area, and disappeared to the northeast. A Cat I was claimed, using twenty-eight rounds of 40mm and 500 rounds of .50 cal.

Two minutes later Second Platoon, Battery B, turned their guns skywards and opened fire. They engaged three Me 109s from a flight of fourteen. The plane came in from the east at an altitude of 2,000 ft [610 meters]. They expended 104 rounds of 40mm and 1,150 rounds of .50 cal.

At 09:30 First Platoon, Battery C, engaged three planes from a mixed flight of eight, consisting of Me 109s and Fw 190s. The planes came in bombing the area at approximately 3,000 ft [914 meters] from the southwest and disappeared to the northeast. They went through twenty-three rounds of 40mm.

At 09:30 First Platoon, Battery D, fired at an Me 109, circling over the area at 1,500 ft [457 meters] altitude with eighteen rounds of 40mm.

A minute later a flight of twelve planes, coming from the northwest and bombing the area from an altitude of approximately 1,000 ft [305 meters], went over First Platoon, Battery B, which attempted to shoot down two Fw 190s with twenty-five rounds of 40mm and 880 rounds of .50 cal. The planes departed to the southeast.

At 09:33 First Platoon, Battery B, engaged two Me 109s with sixty-eight rounds of 40mm and 1,234 rounds of .50 cal. These planes came in from the southwest, strafed, and then swiftly disappeared to the northeast.

At 10:00 Second Platoon, Battery A, fired at four Fw 190s. They were in a flight of eleven at 4,000 ft [1,219 meters], flying from south to north, bombing, and strafing in the area as they went by. A Cat I and two Cat IIs were claimed at the expense of 194 rounds of 40mm and 2,327 rounds of .50 cal.

At the same time, First Platoon, Battery D, engaged an Me 262 circling over their area at approximately 2,000 ft [610 meters] altitude. They fired thirty-one rounds of 40mm and 500 rounds of .50 cal but didn't appear to hit their target.

At noon twelve Me 109s were strafing the area defended by Second Platoon, Battery A, from 4,000 ft [1,219 meters]. The planes went from south to north and the platoon shot at six of this flight. Two Cat Is and two Cat IIs were claimed and 142 rounds of 40mm and 800 rounds of .50 cal were used.

At 12:10 Second Platoon, Battery C, engaged four Fw 190s. The planes circled and bombed the area from an altitude of 1,500 ft [457 meters]. While the platoon used fifty-eight rounds of 40mm and 895 rounds of .50 cal, the 452nd AAA could claim three more Cat Is.

At the same time, two Fw 190s flew from south to north and bombed the area from approximately 5,000 ft [1,524 meters]. First Platoon, Battery B, fired at these two planes with eight rounds of 40mm and sixty-two rounds of .50 cal.

At 13:00 Second Platoon, Battery A, engaged six Me 109s from a flight of eleven, which were strafing in the area from south to north at an altitude of 4,000 ft [1,219 meters]. A Cat I and two Cat IIs were claimed and 105 rounds of 40mm and 601 rounds of .50 cal were expended.

Forty-five minutes later Second Platoon, Battery C, fired at two Me 210s with eight rounds of 40mm and 1,000 rounds of .50 cal. These two bombers were circling the area at an altitude of approximately 2,000 ft [610 meters].

At 13:50 Second Platoon, Battery B, engaged an Me 262 with twenty-six rounds of 40mm and 202 rounds of .50 cal. The plane flew over the platoon, going from southwest to northeast at an altitude of approximately 2,000 ft [610 meters].

At 14:15 First Platoon, Battery B, shot at two planes from a mixed group of eight Me 109s and Fw 190s. These airplanes were circling the area, bombing the area from 5,000 ft [1,524 meters] altitude; 103 rounds of 40mm and 1,070 rounds of .50 cal were used.

There was some respite, although a few hours later, at 17:45 Second Platoon, Battery A, engaged five Ar 234s from a flight of eight at approximately 8,000 ft [2,438 meters] altitude. These planes flew from south to west and the platoon fired upon them with 220 rounds of 40mm and 2,100 rounds of .50 cal.

At 17:50 Second Platoon, Battery C, fired at two Me 109s from a flight of four. These airplanes were circling the area at 1,700 ft [518 meters] altitude but didn't attack. The platoon shot 205 rounds of 40mm and 1,000 rounds of .50 cal, and also claimed a Cat I.

Thirty minutes later Second Platoon, Battery C, engaged four Me 262s in a low bombing attack. The planes flew at 1,600 ft [488 meters] altitude. The platoon claimed two Cat Is and used 244 rounds of 40mm and 2,850 rounds of .50 cal.

At the same time First Platoon, Battery B, engaged an Ar 234 with 133 rounds of 40mm and 1,593 rounds of .50 cal. The aircraft flew 2,000 ft [610 meters] altitude, going south to north.

The Ar 234s were tempting targets. The planes came in from an eastern direction varying from 2,000 to 6,000 ft [610–1,829 meters] altitude, evidently on a reconnaissance mission. At 18:30 Second Platoon, Battery A, and Second Platoon, Battery B, both engaged four Ar 234s. The planes flew over the areas that the platoons were protecting. Second Platoon, Battery A, used 185 rounds of 40mm and 2,400 rounds of .50 cal. Second Platoon, Battery B, expended eighty rounds of 40mm and 900 rounds of .50 cal.

At 19:10 First Platoon, Battery B, engaged an Ar 234 that flew at 3,000 ft [914 meters] altitude, which flew from south to north. The platoon fired eight rounds of 40mm and 350 rounds of .50 cal.

At 20:00 First Platoon, Battery D, returned fire on two enemy vehicles and an unknown number of enemy foot troops that were firing small arms into the 191st Field Artillery Battalion area. They shot nineteen rounds of 40mm and fifty rounds of .50 cal were used. Later it was revealed that a horse and three carts were knocked out.

It had been a busy day and the 452nd AAA was also featured in the *Stars and Stripes* of 25 March 1945, recounting the events to a reporter:

> "We're leading the league again," said Pvt. Chickie Johnson, of New York, of the 452nd AA, an all-Negro AA outfit with a fine reputation. "We just hit another home run."
>
> The runners squatted in the pit around the 40mm and looked at the moon-dappled Rhine flowing under the bridge, their slender-barreled piece protected. "Seems like they've been coming in every minute," said Pfc Sullivan Washington, of Chicago. "We just got an Me 109 a half hour ago."
>
> "Five of them come in at the bridge," said Cpl. Dan Haynes, of St Louis. "Real low and going like hell. This

> gun got one of them. It caught on fire and fell in the woods over there."
>
> * * *
>
> They came again, one at a time, snarling down the valley of the Rhine. But the ack-ack went up and the plane turned around and went back to the mystery beyond the enemy lines. The gunners listened to it until the motor faded to a snarling whisper. They watched the Rhine and smoked and waited for the planes to come again.[18]

Similarly, 20 March was summarized as follows in the *Anti-Aircraft Artillery Notes*:

> A total of 248 enemy aircraft attacked the area during the day and night of 20 March. The type of planes employed were Fw 190s, Me 109s, and Me 262s. Most of the attacks were made during daylight hours and in groups of four or more planes. The Fw 190s and Me 109s exhibited the usual tactics of dive bombing and strafing, operating at altitudes of 1,200 to 4,500 feet [366-1,372 meters]. The Me 262s exhibited slightly different tactics by approaching in groups of six at 6,000 feet [1,829 meters] and diving singly to 4,000 feet [1,219 meters] before releasing their bombs. One Me 262 made a direct attack on the position of Battery A of the 129th AAA Gun Bn (M), dropping two AP bombs from about 5,000 feet [1,524 meters]. The bridge area was also subjected to shell fire by German 88mm positions across the Rhine River to the north during this period. Of the 248 enemy aircraft attacking the area, 36 were definitely destroyed by AAA fire and 14 probably destroyed. High scorers for the period were the

> 452nd AAA AW Bn (M) with 12 Cat Is and 4 Cat IIs, and the 489th AAA AW Bn (SP) with 11 Cat Is. No damage was caused to the bridges.[19]

On 21 March, the Luftwaffe attacked early in the morning, just after sunrise. At 06:35 two Ar 234s appeared in the sights of Second Platoon, Battery A. The planes flew from east to west at 2,000 ft [610 meters] and bombed in the vicinity. The platoon fired sixty rounds of 40mm and 430 rounds of .50 cal.

At 06:40 First Platoon, Battery C, engaged an Me 109 and two Me 262s with 298 rounds of 40mm and 1,200 rounds of .50 cal. The planes circled in the area and dropped bombs from approximately 1,000 ft [305 meters] altitude. The other platoon of Battery C fired upon the same planes. They used 228 rounds of 40mm and 3,000 rounds of .50 cal, while the planes flew at an altitude of 1,500 to 2,000 ft [457-610 meters].

At the same time, First Platoon, Battery B, engaged an Ar 234 with twenty-one rounds of 40mm and 1,125 rounds of .50 cal. The plane flew southwards at 6,000 ft [1,829 meters] altitude.

Fifteen minutes later, Second Platoon, Battery B, shot at four Ar 234s from a flight of six. The planes were bombing in the area from 2,500 ft [762 meters] and flew off to the northeast. They expended thirty-seven rounds of 40mm and 1,200 rounds of .50 cal.

At 07:00 a flight of twelve Me 109s was strafing from an altitude of 2,000 ft [610 meters] near Second Platoon, Battery B. They opened fire on three of them, using twenty-nine rounds of 40mm and 800 rounds of .50 cal.

The same platoon was back in action ten minutes later when they engaged a He 111 flying and bombing at 1,000 ft [305 meters] with forty-seven rounds of 40mm and 1,400 rounds of .50 cal.

At the same time, First Platoon, Battery B, fired at one Ar 234 with thirty-six rounds of 40mm. The plane flew southwards at 6,000 ft [1,829 meters] altitude.

At 07:13 First Platoon, Battery D, engaged a mixed flight of eight Me 109s and Fw 190s with 247 rounds of 40mm and 1,620 rounds of .50 cal. In total fifteen planes circled above them at an altitude of 500 to 2,000 ft [152-610 meters].

At 07:20 Second Platoon, Battery B, shot at nine Me 109s from a flight of fifteen. The planes circled the area, dived, and strafed from an altitude of 2,400 ft [732 meters]. The platoon fired 103 rounds of 40mm and 1,100 rounds of .50 cal back at them.

At 08:20 a mixed flight of eight German planes, consisting of Me 109s and Fw 190s appeared within the sights of First Platoon, Battery D. The planes circled at an altitude of 500 to 2,000 ft [152–610 meters] and the platoon expended 169 rounds of 40mm and 1,084 rounds of .50 cal.

Forty minutes later First Platoon, Battery A, engaged five Me 109s with 140 rounds of 40mm and 170 rounds of .50 cal. In total eighteen planes were flying southwest to northeast, diving from an altitude of 3,000 to 5,400 ft [914-1,646 meters].

At 09:10 the same platoon fired at an Me 109 strafing in the area with thirty-two rounds of 40mm and 530 rounds of .50 cal. There were two planes and they made a low strafing attack, coming in from the southwest at approximately 800 ft [244 meters] and disappearing to the northeast.

Twenty minutes later, once more First Platoon, Battery A, was in action. They shot at four Me 109s, coming in from the southwest and going to the northeast, strafing in the area with fifty-two rounds of 40mm and seventy rounds of .50 cal. The planes were strafing from 3,600 ft [1,097 meters].

At 10:50 hours First Platoon, Battery D, engaged an Me 262, which flew over their area at 2,000 ft [610 meters] altitude with two rounds of 40mm and 110 rounds of .50 cal.

A few hours later, at 14:04 hours, First Platoon, Battery D, was back in action. Three Me 262s going west to east and the platoon fired six rounds of 40mm and 150 rounds of .50 cal at two of them.

The next day, 22 March, was relatively calm for the 452nd AAA. Second Platoon, Battery A, provided AA protection for the Third Army Engineer Dump. They would continue to do so until an AAA unit from Third Army could take over.

Second Platoon, Battery D, provided AA protection for engineer construction material and personnel during assembly and construction across the Rhine River. Another warning went out that many P-51s and P-47s would be over the bridgehead during the daylight hours and night fighters would be present during the hours of darkness. The fighters would be operating from minimum altitudes and careful identification and fire control were stressed to prevent friendly-fire accidents.

Meanwhile, the Battalion Command Post relocated to Gau-Bickelheim.

However, that evening, the 5th Infantry Division would launch an assault across the Rhine. Supporting this unit in its crossing were several corps artillery battalions, as taken from XII Corps' history:

> The Division Artillery had been assigned two groups of reinforcing artillery which were in turn assigned to the 19th (FA Bn) with instructions that when the 11th (Infantry Regiment) crossed, the 182d FA Gp was then to reinforce the 46th FA Bn. Thus the line-up of artillery for the 11th Inf's crossing was the 19th, reinforced by the 21st FA Bn, 177th and 182d Gps. The composition of the groups is listed below:
>
> *182d FA Gp*
> 512th FA Bn (105 Howitzer)
> 771st FA Bn (155 Howitzer)
> 945th FA Bn (155 Howitzer)
> 740th FA Bn (8" Howitzer)

177th FA Gp
276th FA Bn (Armored 18 105s)
758th FA Bn (8" Howitzer)
179th FA Bn (155 Howitzer)
191st FA Bn (155 Howitzer)[20]

At that time, the underlined units were protected by platoons of the 452nd AAA Battalion. Two other platoons protected the engineers and their material.

The Rhine River had been the last major river that the Allies would have to cross in Germany and both sides were fully aware of its significance. The Third Army was advancing to get across it as soon as possible, while the German forces tried to stay ahead of them. The area around Oppenheim had already been studied as a possible crossing site in November 1944, before the Ardennes Offensive disrupted the Allied planning. A benefit of the site was that the western side of the river was higher than the eastern plain, thus favoring an attack from that direction. Another benefit for XII Corps was that the German High Command deemed Mainz, further to the north, as the most likely area of crossing. Thus, there were fewer defenders opposing them.

On 23 March, the Luftwaffe again attacked early in the morning and several platoons fought battles against aerial attackers around the bridgehead. At 06:28 Second Platoon, Battery D, engaged two Me 109s strafing the Rhine bridgehead area with fourteen rounds of 40mm and 825 rounds of .50 cal. There were eight planes in the flight, coming from the south and strafing the Rhine bridgehead from 500 to 800 ft [152–244 meters], and at least one was shot down because the platoon claimed a Cat I.

At 06:30 First Platoon, Battery C, saw ten Me 109s at 500 ft [152 meters] altitude and fired at three of them, claiming a Cat I. The platoon expended eleven rounds of 40mm and 100 rounds of .50 cal.

Five minutes later Second Platoon, Battery B, had five Me 109s in their vicinity, diving from 400 ft [122 meters]. The platoon engaged an Me 109 with nine rounds of 40mm and 200 rounds of .50 cal.

At 07:00 hours six Me 109s appeared over Second Platoon, Battery D, and proceeded to strafe the bridgehead, going west to east at 800 ft [244 meters]. The platoon fired at an Me 109 with twelve rounds of 40mm and 417 rounds of .50 cal, claiming a Cat I, although this claim was later dropped.

At 07:35 First Platoon, Battery C, shot at two Fw 190s. The planes were going west to east at 1,500 ft [457 meters] altitude and the platoon expended five rounds of 40mm and thirty-one rounds of .50 cal.

Three minutes later, four Me 109s were going from the northwest to the southeast over First Platoon, Battery D, which fired at three of them with twenty rounds of 40mm and 174 rounds of .50 cal.

At 07:45 Second Platoon, Battery B, engaged an Fw 190 that was dive bombing their area from the north to the south. Ten rounds of 40mm and fifty rounds of .50 cal were expended.

That afternoon P-51s arrived to take over the aerial patrol. They would take care of any hostile aircraft. The Allied fighters were much more mobile and offered additional protection. Later that night, friendly bombers would be flying over the platoons. In the afternoon the German forces launched a coordinated attack against the bridgehead, but this attack faltered under American artillery. Further hampering the mounting of a proper German defense was the fatally wounding of their commander: *Generalmajor* Siegfried Runge. He had been wounded by shrapnel and died shortly afterwards. This left the resistance uncoordinated and allowed the American forces to expand their bridgehead.

However, the day was not without casualties. Corporal Vance, Second Platoon, Battery D, was wounded by enemy artillery.

Later that day the Luftwaffe attacked again. At 18:30 hours Second Platoon, Battery A, engaged two Me 109s from a flight of three strafing the bridgehead area at 1,500 ft [457 meters]. They flew from the northwest to the southeast and the platoon claimed a Cat I.

At the same time, Second Platoon, Battery D, saw twelve Me 109s from the northeast to the southwest at 1,500 to 2,000 ft [457-610 meters]. The platoon engaged six Me 109s with thirteen rounds of 40mm and 725 rounds of .50 cal and claimed a Cat I. However, this claim was later dropped and assigned to Second Platoon, Battery A.

Second Platoon, Battery A, was relieved of its previous mission and attached as AA protection for the engineer bridge construction material and personnel during assembly and construction across the Rhine.

At 18:33 hours two platoons: First Platoon, Battery C, and Second Platoon, Battery B, both fired at a flight of twelve Me 109s and Fw 190s that strafed in the area. First Platoon, Battery C, shot at four Me 109s with thirty-nine rounds of 40mm and 610 rounds of .50 cal, claiming three Cat Is. Second Platoon, Battery B, engaged four Me 109s and Fw 190s with twenty-seven rounds of 40mm and 400 rounds of .50 cal and submitted two Cat I claims.

At 18:35 Second Platoon, Battery C, engaged three Fw 190s from a formation of eight, which strafed the field artillery battalion. The planes went from north to south at 1,500 ft [457 meters] and the platoon shot back thirty-eight rounds of 40mm and 930 rounds of .50 cal expended, resulting in two Cat I claims.

At 18:43 Second Platoon, Battery A, engaged two Fw 190s from a flight of three, which bombed the area. The planes were going from the northwest to the southeast at 1,800 ft [549 meters] altitude. The platoon expended eighty-one rounds of 40mm and 1,600 rounds of .50 cal, but also submitted a Cat II claim.

Two minutes later, First Platoon, Battery D, shot at two Me 109s strafing the field artillery battalion area. They dove and came from the southeast, while the platoon fired forty-five rounds of 40mm and 875 rounds of .50 cal.

At 20:30 a flight of four Me 109s was going from the northeast to the southwest at an altitude between 1,500 and 2,000 ft [457–610 meters]. Second Platoon, Battery D, had two of them in their sights and expended 400 rounds of .50 cal.

The Luftwaffe tried to make the most use of the sunrise on 24 March. Five Me 109s were in action early that day. However, the planes were engaged by First Platoon, Battery B, both platoons of Battery C, and First Platoon, Battery D. First Platoon, Battery B, engaged one Me 109 at 5,000 ft [1,524 meters] strafing the field artillery battalion area. They used forty rounds of 40mm and 567 rounds of .50 cal.

First Platoon, Battery C, fired at two Me 109s at 1,500 ft [457 meters] with twenty rounds of 40mm and 329 rounds of .50 cal. Second Platoon, Battery C, shot at three Me 109s at 1,500 to 2,000 ft [457–610 meters] with fifty-four rounds of 40mm and 681 rounds of .50 cal ammo. First Platoon, Battery D, engaged the entire flight with fifty-three rounds of 40mm and 899 rounds of .50 cal.

At 06:20 hours Second Platoon, Battery B, had two Me 109s in their sights out of a formation of ten planes, which flew from the southeast to northwest at 1,000 ft [305 meters] altitude. They fired ten rounds of 40mm and 375 rounds of .50 cal.

Ten minutes later Second Platoon, Battery D, fired 220 rounds of .50 cal at two Me 109s, which went east to west at 2,000 ft [610 meters] altitude.

At 07:00 hours two platoons tracked two Me 109s. First Platoon, Battery A, engaged two Me 109s with sixty-four rounds of 40mm and 1,200 rounds of .50 cal as they went from the north to the east at 600 to 1,000 ft [183-305 meters] altitude, while Second Platoon, Battery D, engaged these two Me 109s with 284 rounds of .50 cal as they flew from the east to west at 1,500 ft [457 meters].

At 18:25 Second Platoon, Battery D, First Platoon, Battery C, and Second Platoon, Battery C, all fired on a flight of six Me 109s that flew over the area. Second Platoon, Battery D, fired at two with thirteen rounds of 40mm and 625 rounds of .50 cal as they flew from the west to the east. The planes bombed and strafed from 500 to 1,500 ft [152-457 meters] altitude. Second Platoon, Battery C, shot at one with seventy-seven rounds of 40mm and 360 rounds of .50 cal, which flew at 2,500 ft [762 meters] altitude and bombed in the area. First Platoon, Battery C, also engaged one with twenty-two rounds of 40mm and 575 rounds of .50 cal as the plane flew from west to east at 1,500 ft [457 meters] altitude.

First Platoon, Battery A, engaged two Me 109s at 18:45. The planes flew in a flight of four, going from the north to the east at altitudes between 400 to 1,000 ft [122-305 meters], bombing and strafing as they went. The platoon expended forty-three rounds of 40mm and 300 rounds of .50 cal.

That same day, Lieutenant Colonel Ratcliffe checked in with Second Platoon, Battery A, and Second Platoon, Battery D. Both of them were ordered to provide AA protection on the far side of the bridge. Allied bombers would be over that night. Second Platoon, Battery B, with the 179th Field Artillery, and First Platoon, Battery D, attached to the 191st Field Artillery, were moving across the Rhine River. That day a deuce-and-a-half truck and an M-51 were damaged by enemy artillery.

Two soldiers were reported as wounded that day, Alvin A. Johnson of the medical detachment, and Joseph B. Moses, Battery D.

The day was summarized by the AAA Section of XII Corps as follows:

> On 22 March the 5th Infantry Division reached the Rhine River in the vicinity of Oppenheim, and elements of the Division crossed in assault boats that night. All bridges crossing the Rhine on the Third Army sector had been blown, and it was decided to construct a pontoon bridge in the 5th Division sector at Oppenheim. Work was commenced immediately, and a concentrated AAA defense

> was set up around the area; most of the AAA units that had been employed at Bad Kreuznach were moved to the Oppenheim area. The first AAA unit of the Third Army across the Rhine was Battery C of the 457th AAA AW Bn (M), which ferried across in assault boats at about 1500 hours on the afternoon of 23 March. Although the first bridge was not completed until the morning of 24 March, heavy enemy air activity began during the daylight hours of the 23rd and continued sporadically throughout the night. The daylight attacks were made by Fw 190s, Me 109s, Me 262s, and one He 111. The planes made shallow strafing dives on the troops crossing the river and on artillery and AAA positions. Heavy enemy shelling of the bridgehead area was experienced during the afternoon of the 23rd. A total of 58 enemy planes operated over the area during this period of which 19 were destroyed and 8 probably destroyed by AAA units. 10 of the Cat Is were registered by the 452nd AAA AW Bn (M).[21]

On 25 March Second Platoon, Battery C, was detached from the 771st Field Artillery Battalion and attached to the 974th FA Battalion.

As usual, the Luftwaffe was back in action early in the morning. At 06:00 hours three Me 109s bombed areas defended by First Platoon, Battery B, and Second Platoon, Battery D. They were circling the area at altitudes between 800 to 1,000 ft [244–305 meters] altitude. First Platoon, Battery B, engaged one of these planes with fifteen rounds of 40mm and 416 rounds of .50 cal. Second Platoon, Battery D, shot at two of these planes with fifty-three rounds of 40mm and 630 rounds of .50 cal.

Ten minutes later four Me 109s flew over bombing and strafing the area of First Platoon, Battery A, and First Platoon, Battery C. All four planes, flying between 50 and 400 ft [15–122 meters] were engaged by First Platoon, Battery A, as the planes went from the southeast to northwest. The platoon claimed one Cat I, expending forty-three rounds of 40mm and 900 rounds of .50 cal. First Platoon, Battery C, also shot at these planes, while they flew at 1,500 ft [457 meters] and circled over the area. They used seventy-three rounds of 40mm and 500 rounds of .50 cal.

At 06:15 First Platoon, Battery D, engaged one Me 109, which flew at 500 ft [152 meters] to the east. They claimed a Cat I at the expense of 250 rounds of .50 cal ammo.

From 06:17 to 06:33 eight Me 109s bombed and strafed the area of Second Platoons, Battery C, and Battery D. Second Platoon, Battery C, shot at three of these planes flying at altitudes between 50 to 2,000 ft [15-610 meters]. They used 126 rounds of 40mm and 2,377 rounds of .50 cal. Second Platoon, Battery D, engaged two of these planes flying from the west to the northeast at approximately 20 ft [6 meters]. They claimed one Cat I and one Cat II, expending forty-eight rounds of 40mm and 903 rounds of .50 cal ammo in the process. Second Platoon, Battery A, also engaged three of these planes flying from east to west at approximately 500 ft [152 meters]. The platoon claimed two Cat Is, having fired 216 rounds of 40mm and 1,420 rounds of .50 cal.

At 06:35 Second Platoon, Battery D, shot two Me 109s circling their area at approximately 1,000 ft [305 meters] altitude. In total, they fired thirty rounds of 40mm and 311 rounds of .50 cal.

At 06:35 Second Platoon, Battery B, got two Me 109s from a flight of four in their sights. The planes were flying at an altitude of 1,500 ft [457 meters]. The platoon used thirty-three rounds of 40mm and 400 rounds of .50 cal.

At 06:45 Second Platoon, Battery B, engaged two Me 109s from a flight of four. The planes went from east to west at approximately 1,500 ft [457 meters] altitude. They fired eighteen rounds of 40mm and 347 rounds of .50 cal, resulting in a Cat II claim. This claim was later dropped.

At 06:55 hours Second Platoon, Battery B, shot at two Me 109s from a formation of four. These airplanes were flying to the east at 1,500 ft [457 meters] altitude. The platoon expended thirty-five rounds of 40mm and 374 rounds of .50 cal.

At 09:00 First Platoon, Battery D, engaged two Me 109s dive bombing in the area from a low altitude. They used twenty rounds of 40mm and 390 rounds of .50 cal.

At 18:30 hours Second Platoon, Battery B, shot at one Me 109 from a flight of four flying east at 2,700 ft [823 meters] altitude, using thirty-three rounds of 40mm and 500 rounds of .50 cal.

At 19:30 Second Platoon, Battery D, engaged a plane at approximately 1,500 ft [457 meters]. However, they used just five rounds of 40mm.

At 20:50 a Ju 88 strafed and bombed from an altitude of 1,500 ft [457 meters] in the vicinity of First Platoon, Battery D. The platoon fired at the plane with five rounds of 40mm and 697 rounds of .50 cal.

Battalion Command Post relocated to a new destination, leaving Gau-Bickelheim. That day there were four casualties. Two soldiers were wounded by shrapnel from enemy artillery. One soldier was wounded by rifle fire and another man suffered the amputation of a finger.

The next day, 26 March, at 06:30 hours First Platoon, Battery D, engaged two Me 109s that were dive bombing their area. The planes came in low and flew westwards. The platoon shot nineteen rounds of 40mm and 375 rounds of .50 cal at the hostile aircrafts.

At 07:00 four Me 109s were seen by Second Platoon, Battery B, which fired at three of them. The planes were strafing in the area at around 1,500 ft [457 meters] flying towards the northwest. The platoon used thirty-three rounds of 40mm and 370 rounds of .50 cal.

At 07:15 First Platoon, Battery D, engaged one He 111 flying over their area at a very low altitude as it flew to the southeast. They claimed one Cat II, expending twenty rounds of 40mm and 553 rounds of .50 cal.

Thirty minutes later four Me 109s were fired upon by First Platoon, Battery D. The planes flew to the north at 1,000 ft [457 meters] altitude. The platoon used thirty-one rounds of 40mm and 410 rounds of .50 cal.

At 08:00 the same platoon engaged four Me 109s as they flew over their area at 1,000 ft [305 meters] to the south. The platoon fired twenty-five rounds of 40mm and 440 rounds of .50 cal.

At 09:35 Second Platoon, Battery B, shot at an Me 109 flying over their area to the northeast at 2,000 ft [610 meters] approximately. The platoon expended seventeen rounds of 40mm and 225 rounds of .50 cal.

At 12:15 one Me 109 flew over the area protected by First Platoon, Battery A, and First Platoon, Battery B. First Platoon, Battery A, engaged the plane at 3,000 ft [914 meters], flying southeast to northwest. They fired twenty-nine rounds of 40mm and fifty rounds of .50 cal. First Platoon, Battery B, shot at this plane when it flew at 4,500 ft [1,372 meters], flying northwest. The platoon used eleven rounds of 40mm and 1,033 rounds of .50 cal.

The fighting over the previous couple of days had been the fiercest experienced by the battalion so far. The spearhead of XII Corps was advancing rapidly and the enemy was incapable of offering organized resistance. The Luftwaffe had stepped in to blunt the Allied assault but paid a heavy price for their feeble attacks.

Between 17 and 26 March, the Luftwaffe attempted to stop the Nahe and Rhine crossings. According to an early tally, Allied units submitted 146 claims for aircraft destroyed and forty-five claims for a probable, while 851 aircraft had been over the corps area.[22] However, as the report mentions, "it is desired to point out that the claims as cited do not have final Army confirmation, but have been carefully screened and duplications eliminated."

On 27 March, at 02:00 two enemy soldiers were captured by Gun Section No. 1, Battery B. The platoon had stopped and subdued the fleeing men with five rounds of .30 cal M1 ammo. That day, First

Platoon, Battery C, provided anti-aircraft protection for the 740th Field Artillery Battalion (FA Bn), which was in general support of the corps artillery, and the battalion moved in support of the 5th Infantry Division.

First Platoon, Battery B, delivered one enemy officer and twenty-one enemy soldiers to the prisoner of war enclosure. These soldiers had surrendered to the platoon.

The next day, First Lieutenant Harold G. Loesch was wounded by the enemy, while Private First Class William L. Brown, was wounded by shrapnel from anti-aircraft fire. Both men served in Battery C.

On 29 March, the Luftwaffe made a single showing that day. At 18:10 First Platoon, Battery D, engaged one Fw 190 at 2,000 ft [610 meters] flying to the east. They fired two rounds of 40mm and 205 rounds of .50 cal.

On 30 March many of the platoons were on the move and later that night bombers would fly over the platoons.

First Platoon, Battery A, was attached to the 945th FA, which moved with the 11th Armored Division.

First Platoon, Battery B, supported the 738th Field Artillery Battalion.

Second Platoon, Battery B, provided AA protection for the 179th FA, which was part of CCA, 4th Armored Division. First Platoon, Battery D, moved with the 191st Field Artillery, which had been attached to CCB, 4th Armored Division.

First Platoon, Battery C, supported the 740th FA, and Second Platoon, Battery C, was attached to the 974th Field Artillery Battalion, which went along with the 6th Armored Division.

The other two platoons remained at the bridge, protecting them from any aerial attackers.

At 07:00 hours, Second Platoon, Battery B, engaged an Me 109, expending 300 rounds of .50 cal ammo as it flew northeastwards at 1,000 ft [305 meters].

At 07:50 First Platoon, Battery D, shot at an Fw 190. The plane flew at 750 ft [229 meters] going eastwards. They used twenty-two rounds of 40mm and 804 rounds of .50 cal.

At 09:40 hours the same platoon engaged one Fw 190, using twenty-one rounds of 40mm and 398 rounds of .50 cal ammo. The plane flew westwards at a very low altitude.

At 15:10 hours, Second Platoon, Battery B, engaged an Fw 190, which was dive bombing in the area. The platoon claimed a Cat II, expending 156 rounds of 40mm and 1,590 rounds of .50 cal.

On 31 March, at 06:30 hours First Platoon, Battery D, shot at two Me 109s, firing fifty rounds of 40mm and 550 rounds of .50 cal. The planes made a reconnaissance flight over their area.

Thirty minutes later the same platoon fired at two Me 109s from a flight of three with seventy-six rounds of 40mm and 536 rounds of .50 cal ammunition. The planes came in flying at a low altitude.

At 14:50 an Me 262 flew at 1,000 ft [305 meters], going south to north, and was fired upon by First Platoon, Battery C, which used sixteen rounds of 40mm ammo.

At 17:45 First Platoon, Battery D, engaged one of the two Me 109s flying over their area at medium altitude. The platoon expended 150 rounds of .50 cal ammo.

Five minutes later Second Platoon, Battery B, shot at two Me 109s and used eight rounds of 40mm and 1,555 rounds of .50 cal as the planes flew southwestwards at 3,000 ft [914 meters].

At 18:02 two Me 109s flew southeastwards at 2,500 ft [762 meters] when they got in the sights of Second Platoon, Battery B. The platoon swiftly opened fire and expended twenty-seven rounds of 40mm and 1,726 rounds of .50 cal. That night, there would be friendly bombers flying over.

To summarize the month, in March the AA battalion continued to protect the field artillery battalions supporting infantry and armored divisions in XII Corps, Third U.S. Army, during its drive south and across the Rhine River and to the northeast. Two platoons were initial AA protection for the assembly and construction of the Third Army bridge across the Rhine River at Oppenheim. The weather was good and the enemy also noticed this, being more active in the air. The unit experienced more action at this time than since its arrival on the Continent. During the Rhine River crossing, the platoons defending the bridge site received heavy artillery fire. Platoons defending the field artillery battalions in the vicinity of Frankfort were also under heavy artillery fire. Seven enlisted men were wounded by shrapnel fire. Two 2½ ton trucks, a 40mm gun, and an M-51 were materially damaged.

Additionally, "a careful estimate indicated that between 24 Mar 45, when the first bridge opened, and 31 Mar 45, about 60,000 vehicles had crossed over XII Corps' bridges. These included approximately 10,000 vehicles of XX Corps."[23] XII Corps continued its advance and with them went the 452nd AAA Battalion.

XII Corps would launch its final assault into the Third Reich. As explained by Lieutenant General Walter B. Smith:

> From the day our invasion broke over the beaches of Normandy, the goal of every Allied soldier had been Berlin. The Supreme Commander, the staff and all the troops shared driving ambition to seal the defeat of Nazi Germany by seizing the capital of the Reich itself. During our planning days in England, there seemed every reason to believe that after the Ruhr was encircled and its troops destroyed, we could end the war by taking Germany's political heart—Berlin.
>
> By the end of January 1945, the German Government was evacuating the capital, fleeing to temporary safety in the Thuringian Forest and south to Hitler's own retreat in mountainous Berchtesgaden. Deserted by its Nazi masters, ruined by our air bombardments, the city was becoming a shell—an empty symbol of the Nazi's brutal grandeur. It was losing all meaning as a military objective.

> Our task was to end the war swiftly and conclusively. Berlin was no longer a major factor in reaching that end. Every plan, decision and purpose of the Allied command was determined always by one inflexible rule—"Destroy the German forces, speedily and completely." By 2 April, when the ring snapped shut around the Ruhr, we were convinced that there would be no general surrender as long as Hitler remained in command. The war would be finished now by only one means; we must root out and destroy every remnant of military strength until no organized force remained in Germany to carry on the fight. [...]
>
> In the south, Gen. Devers' forces and perhaps the Third Army, would drive through Nuremberg and Regensburg, following the Danube Valley into Austria. There we should meet the southern wing of the Red Army coming in from the Balkans. Besides destroying considerable German forces east of Munich, this drive would also cut off the Alpine area containing the mysterious National Redoubt, where we had every reason to believe the Nazis intended to make their last stand among the crags. Around Berchtesgaden and Salzburg, we should run down the principal government departments fled from Berlin. Beating through the tortuous terrain of the Austrian Alps, our forces would destroy the safety of this promised Nazi refuge.[24]

Thus the remaining territory that the enemy still held would be separated from each other. While XII Corps' history remarked:

> XII Corps' destiny, then, was to be the force that cut Germany in two by entering Czechoslovakia along the whole southern face of the "Bohemian Bastion," and interposed itself between the German armies fighting the

> Russians on the east to block their last retreat toward the much advertised "National Redoubt."[25]

At 06:55 on the first day of April 1945, Second Platoon, Battery B, engaged two Me 109s firing thirty-nine rounds of 40mm and 550 .50 cal. The planes flew southwards at 1,000 ft [305 meters].

The Battalion Command relocated to a new position. The rapid advance also brought with it certain risks. Sniper fire had resulted in three men of the 177th Field Artillery Group being wounded. An officer of the 179th Field Artillery Battalion requested Second Platoon, Battery B, to fire at the houses nearby, which subsequently poured 1,100 rounds into them.

The 191st Field Artillery Battalion had its own encounter with the enemy, as mentioned in the unit history: "Moving out at 0630 1 April, we continued along the Autobahn. Near Wommen our batteries received 20mm and machine-gun fire from across the Werra River, which attached AA guns silenced."[26] To summarize, at around 11:30 hours, the column of the 191st Field Artillery Battalion and First Platoon, Battery D, were fired upon by an enemy 20mm gun as well as small arms fire. The anti-aircraft gunners pulled the guns out of the column, located their target, and opened fire, destroying the 20mm gun and silencing the small arms fire. They used fifty-three rounds of 40mm HE, twenty rounds of 40mm AP, and 1,200 rounds of .50 cal. However, a deuce-and-a-half truck belonging to Battery D was slightly damaged.

The battalion was still twenty-eight enlisted men short and reported two wounded of Battery B: Privates Willie M. Robinson and Samuel Johnson. It also needed ten SCR 543s. One Jeep, five deuce-and-a-half trucks, one Dodge truck, and three M-51s all needed to be repaired.

The next day First Platoon, Battery B, moved near Honebach. At 07:09 hours Second Platoon, Battery B, engaged three Fw 190s from a flight of seven that were dive bombing and strafing in the area from 300 ft [91 meters]. Ninety rounds of 40mm and 1,500 rounds of .50 cal were used.

At 07:25 the same platoon fired at two planes from a mixed flight of twenty Me 109s and Fw 190s. These planes came in, dropped armor-piercing bombs, circled above them, and then strafed, diving down to 600 ft [183 meters]. The platoon expended 116 rounds of 40mm and 2,500 rounds of .50 cal.

At 07:30 hours forty planes bombed and strafed an area defended by First Platoon, Battery D, for thirty minutes. It was a mixed flight of forty Fw 190s and Me 109s, of which twenty-five were fired upon. The planes flew at various altitudes and came in from all directions. Five Cat Is, seven Cat IIs and ten Cat IIIs were claimed; 638 rounds of 40mm and 3,429 rounds of .50 cal were used.

Fifteen minutes later Second Platoon, Battery B, engaged five planes of a mixed formation of twenty Me 109s and Fw 190s. The planes circled several times, coming down each time dropping armor-piercing bombs and strafing. The platoon submitted two Cat I claims. There was no damage to the defended area, but two 40mm guns were slightly damaged and four soldiers manning these guns were wounded. Three of them were evacuated. Among the wounded was Private First Class Sylvester Jones. In total, 205 rounds of 40mm and 3,250 rounds of .50 were fired.

At 08:17, First Platoon, Battery B, shot at two Me 109s from a flight of six that were strafing in the area. The planes were flying southeastwards, strafing from 3,000 ft [914 meters]. They used thirty-two rounds of 40mm and 612 rounds of .50 cal ammo.

Four minutes later, an M-51 that was at Battalion Headquarters for repairs was used to shoot at an Fw 190 from a flight of five airplanes. The planes came in from the north and strafed a column on the road from 100 to 1,500 ft [30-457 meters] altitude. The quad-mount expended 456 rounds of .50 cal.

At 11:10 hours, Second Platoon, Battery C, engaged seven Fw 190s from a flight of sixteen, while they were making low-level bombing attacks from 700 to 900 ft [213-274 meters]. The platoon fired 128 rounds of 40mm and 1,015 rounds of .50 cal.

Fifteen minutes later First Platoon, Battery D, shot at an Me 109 with forty-five rounds of 40mm and 327 rounds of .50 cal ammo, while the plane flew northwards at 1,000 ft [305 meters].

At 13:47 Second Platoon, Battery B, had an Me 109 in their sights and fired at it with forty-five rounds of 40mm and 1,150 rounds of .50 cal.

At 14:05 the same platoon engaged an Fw 190 strafing the area from 2,000 ft [610 meters]. They expended ten rounds of 40mm and claimed a Cat I.

Forty-five minutes later First Platoon, Battery D, shot at an Me 109 with thirty-one rounds of 40mm and 490 rounds of .50 cal, while the plane flew eastwards at 500 ft [152 meters].

At 15:03 First Platoon, Battery B, engaged an Fw 190 expending forty-eight rounds of ammunition and 1,473 of .50 cal ammo, while the plane flew to the northeast at 500 ft [152 meters].

At 18:30 Second Platoon, Battery B, fired at an Me 109 from the three that were strafing in the area. The planes circled above at 1,500 ft [457 meters]. The platoon used twenty-nine rounds of 40mm and 2,250 rounds of .50 cal.

Like many nights before, dozens of Allied bombers would be over that night.

On 3 April, at 14:05 Second Platoon, Battery B, engaged two Me 109s at 1,000 ft [305 meters]. They expended fifty rounds of .50 cal.

At 16:00, Second Platoon, Battery B, engaged one of four Me 109s that were strafing in the area at 1,000 ft [305 meters], flying towards the southeast. The platoon fired 135 rounds of .50 cal at them.

Twenty minutes later First Platoon, Battery D, shot at five Me 109s strafing the area at various altitudes, using 244 rounds of 40mm and 1,182 rounds of .50 cal.

At 19:10 the same platoon engaged two Me 109s strafing the area with fifty-five rounds of 40mm and 192 rounds of .50 cal ammo. These plans flew southwards at medium altitude.

At 19:30 hours Second Platoon, Battery B, fired at two Me 109s of a flight of five that were strafing in the area. The planes strafed the defended positions from altitudes between 500 and 1,000 ft [152-305 meters]. One Cat I was claimed, expending twenty-three rounds of 40mm and 1,575 rounds of .50 cal ammo.

At 20:10 First Platoon, Battery D, engaged four Me 109s at medium altitude with thirty-seven rounds of 40mm and 400 rounds of .50 cal ammo.

Ten minutes later, Second Platoon, Battery B, shot at an Fw 190 from a flight of three, which were bombing the area from an altitude of 1,500 ft [457 meters]. They fired thirty-two rounds of 40mm.

On 4 April, at 07:00 a flight of five planes circled the area near Second Platoon, Battery B, at 2,000 ft [610 meters]. The platoon engaged three Me 109s and expended twenty-four rounds of 40mm and 376 of .50 cal.

Three minutes later, First Platoon, Battery D, shot at two Me 109s with eighty rounds of 40mm and 616 rounds of .50 cal, while they flew west at a low altitude.

At 09:40 Second Platoon, Battery B, engaged one Fw 190 strafing in their area from 500 ft [152 meters]. The platoon claimed a Cat II, using nine rounds of 40mm and 382 rounds of .50 cal.

Twenty minutes later, First Platoon, Battery D, had two Me 109s in their sights, while the planes flew to the southwest at medium altitude. The platoon fired ninety-eight rounds of 40mm and 600 rounds of .50 cal.

First Platoon, Battery D, stayed busy, engaging two Me 109s at 10:10 with forty rounds of 40mm and seventy-five rounds of .50 cal. Five minutes later, they shot at two Me 109s, while the planes headed west at medium altitude. The platoon used fifty rounds of 40mm and seventy-five rounds of .50 cal. At 11:15 they fired at one Me 109 with 233 rounds of .50 cal ammo, while the plane flew west at low altitude.

At 11:15 Second Platoon, Battery B, engaged four Fw 190s out of nine bombing in the area. The planes flew south to north and bombed from 1,500 ft [457 meters]. Two Cat IIs were claimed, at the expense of 117 rounds of 40mm and 2,020 rounds of .50 cal.

While forming a column on the road at 12:47, First Platoon, Battery D, shot at an Me 109, which flew southeastwards at medium altitude, with 163 rounds of .50 cal ammo and claimed a Cat I.

At 12:55 Second Platoon, Battery B, engaged an Fw 190, as it flew eastwards at 1,000 ft [305 meters], and claimed a Cat I at the expense of fifty-nine rounds of 40mm and 1,262 of .50 cal. German pilots insisted on going down fighting and the 452nd AAA was only happy to oblige in this suicidal intent.

At 17:30 First Platoon, Battery D, fired at an Me 163 with thirteen rounds of 40mm. The plane flew westwards at high altitude.

At 19:05 Second Platoon, Battery B, had an Me 262 at 1,500 ft [457 meters] in their sights. They shot three rounds of 40mm and 260 rounds of .50 cal at it, but no hits were registered.

At 20:00 hours First Platoon, Battery D, engaged an Me 109 at medium altitude, while the plane flew westwards. They fired fourteen rounds of 40mm.

The same day both platoons still at the river crossing were relieved of their previous assignments and given new missions. Second Platoon, Battery A, now provided AA protection for the 771st Field Artillery Battalion, while Second Platoon, Battery D, supported the 273rd Field Artillery Battalion. The Battalion Command Post was also relocated.

On 5 April, Second Platoon, Battery B, and First Platoon, Battery D, were moving with their units, which were part of VIII Corps.

At 07:15 First Platoon, Battery D, engaged one Me 109 with twenty-nine rounds of 40mm and 400 rounds of .50 cal, while the plane flew at 750 ft [229 meters] to the east. At the same time Second Platoon, Battery B, shot at three Me 109s with sixty-three rounds of 40mm and 1,016 rounds of .50 cal ammo. The planes flew in a formation of four at 1,500 ft [457 meters] to the south.

Ten minutes later one Me 109 was fired upon by First Platoon, Battery D, with twenty rounds of 40mm and 209 rounds of .50 cal.

At 07:35 hours Second Platoon, Battery B, engaged on Me 262 with thirty-five rounds of 40mm and seventy-five rounds of .50 cal, while the plane flew at 2,500 ft [762 meters] southwards.

At 11:35 two Fw 190s, flying eastwards at 2,000 ft [610 meters], were shot at by Second Platoon, Battery B, with seventy-four rounds of 40mm and 1,740 rounds of .50 cal.

At 13:30 the same platoon engaged six Fw 190s out of a flight of fifteen, which were strafing in the area at altitudes between 1,000 and 2,000 ft [305-610 meters]. They expended 336 rounds of 40mm and 5,750 rounds of .50 cal.

At 14:45 First Platoon, Battery D, shot at six Me 109s from a formation of fifteen. The planes came in from all directions at medium height but made no attack. The platoon used 182 rounds of 40mm and 1,608 rounds of .50 cal.

At 18:30 Second Platoon, Battery B, engaged a single Fw 190 with sixteen rounds of 40mm and 600 rounds of .50 cal. The plane was flying northeastwards at 2,000 ft [610 meters].

On 6 April, things became calmer. While the Luftwaffe was still active, they made fewer attacks than in the previous days. Just twice they were engaged by platoons of the 452nd AAA. Once, at 08:45 First Platoon, Battery D, fired at three Me 109s from a flight of five with eighteen rounds of 40mm and 482 rounds of .50 cal. The second attack was at 18:50, when Second Platoon, Battery B, engaged two Fw 190s from a flight of three with thirty-two rounds of 40mm and 1,225 rounds of .50 cal. The planes circled the area at 1,500 ft [457 meters].

The next day, Warrant Officer Junior Grade Samuel D. Peters, the reconnaissance officer, was transferred out of the unit. The Battalion Command Post was relocated. At 18:20 Second Platoon,

Battery C, fired upon an Fw 190 with twenty-one rounds of 40mm and 285 rounds of .50 cal. The plane was flying southwestwards at 500 ft [152 meters]. At 19:02 Second Platoon, Battery D, shot forty-eight rounds of 40mm and 671 rounds of .50 cal at two Me 109s, while the plane was flying northeast at medium altitude.

No aerial attacks were made over the next two days. The Battalion Command Post relocated again and First Lieutenant George J. Deming was assigned to the unit. First Platoon, Battery D, was attached to the 731st Field Artillery Battalion.

On 10 April, First Platoon, Battery D, engaged a single Me 109 at 14:50 and claimed a Cat II. They used twenty rounds of 40mm and 204 rounds of .50 cal. The accidental discharge of a weapon wounded one soldier.

The next day the usual warning about bombers flying over the platoons went out again. That same day at 12:45 Second Platoon, Battery B, shot at two Me 109s out of a formation of four that were bombing the area. The planes bombed the area from 2,000 ft [610 meters] and flew to the southwest. The platoon expended five rounds of 40mm and 375 rounds of .50 cal.

On 13 April, XII Corps received news that President Roosevelt had passed away the previous day. Roosevelt's health had been in decline, but this had been kept secret from the public. Regardless of their personal feelings, the soldiers were saddened by the death of their Commander-in-Chief. At 16:20 First Platoon, Battery C, shot at two Me 109s out of a flight of three, which were strafing the area from west to east. The planes flew at an altitude of 150 to 200 ft [46-61 meters] and the platoon used thirty-three rounds of 40mm and 200 rounds of .50 cal.

At 19:45 two Fw 190s out of four strafing in the area were fired upon by Second Platoon, Battery C. The planes flew from west to east and the platoon expended fifty-one rounds of 40mm and 200 rounds of .50 cal were used.

Later that night, there would be heavy bombers in the skies over the platoon. The same warning would go out the next day. There were two deuce-and-a-half trucks that needed to be repaired.

Also on 14 April, at 12:50 First Platoon, Battery C, shot at eight Fw 190s. There was a formation of twelve planes that were strafing in the area at an altitude of 150 to 200 ft. The platoon submitted a claim for a Cat I, expending 132 rounds of 40mm and 1,150 rounds of .50 cal.

The next day another warning was issued, about Soviet aircraft operating in the area. It was a sign of how the Third Reich was crumbling from all sides. The Battalion Command Post moved to a new area and Second Lieutenant Fred G. Beattie was hospitalized with a non-battlefield injury.

At 10:15 First Platoon, Battery C, engaged two Fw 190s with twenty-six rounds of 40mm and 800 rounds of .50 cal, while the planes flew from southwest to northeast at 200 ft [61 meters].

Later that same day, at 16:30 the same platoon shot at an Me 262, which was flying from southeast to northwest at 200 ft [61 meters] with thirty-three rounds of 40mm and 404 rounds of .50 cal.

On 16 April, there would be friendly bombers in the skies above the platoons.

The next day, the area of Second Platoon, Battery D, was strafed by an unknown plane at 01:30. It didn't return fire. At 17:40 Second Platoon, Battery D, engaged an Me 109, flying from east to west at 1,500 ft [457 meters] with eight rounds of 40mm and ninety-eight rounds of .50 cal. They claimed a Cat I. There would be friendly bombers flying over the platoons that night.

On 18 April, unlike previous nights, there was no warning about Allied bombers operating above the platoons. That day, the 90th Infantry Division would be the first unit of XII Corps that crossed the Czechoslovakian border. The Third Reich had been cut in two, with troops trapped to the north and south of it.

On the 19th there would be "friendly bombers operating between hours of darkness and daylight."[27]

On 20 April, General Manton Eddy left XII Corps. He was replaced by General Stafford LeRoy Irwin, who had previously commanded the 5th Infantry Division. As for the 452nd AAA, the battalion headquarters relocated and the familiar warning about Allied bombers went out. First Lieutenant Donald W. Lange was promoted to captain and Second Lieutenants Robert E. Bassett and Edward H. Mohar were promoted to First Lieutenants.

At 23:00 Gun Section No. 7 of Battery B, expended 100 rounds of .50 cal against the enemy in a ground role. Six enemy foot troops were engaged after being spotted by the gun section and a field artillery outpost advancing uphill towards the field artillery position near Waldershof, Germany.

In the next few days the platoons and the battalion headquarters kept moving forward and during several nights, but not all, there would be Allied bombers flying over the units. The battalion also received seven additional soldiers, leaving them still twenty-one enlisted men short.

On 24 and 25 April, Second Platoon, Battery C, was requested several times, by the 974th Field Artillery Battalion, to spray wooded areas with .50 cal fire. The action occurred while on the march from Grafenwöhr to Regen and southward of Passau on the Austrian border. At one point, in the vicinity of Moosbach, forty prisoners and several enemy vehicles were captured. The vehicles were destroyed by officers of the 974th Field Artillery Battalion. The platoon used 2,000 rounds of .50 cal and there were no casualties to the 974th FA.

Also on the 24th, Second Platoon, Battery C, shot at two Me 109s at 15:25. These planes were strafing in the area from 2,000 ft [610 meters] and 525 rounds of .50 cal were used.

Twenty minutes later, the same platoon fired at two Fw 190s, as the planes flew from north to south at 2,000 ft [610 meters] expending thirty-six rounds of 40mm and 1,002 .50 cal were used.

On 25 April, First Platoon, Battery A, was near Freyung, and at 18:40 Second Platoon, Battery C, engaged an Fw 190. This plane was flying at 500 ft [152 meters] from the northeast to the southeast. The platoon claimed one Cat I and used eleven rounds of 40mm and 327 rounds of .50 cal.

At 19:20 First Platoon, Battery A, fired upon five Fw 190s, strafing near their position from an altitude of 800 ft [244 meters] and flying from north to south. Two Cat Is were claimed, expending twenty-nine rounds of 40mm and 625 rounds of .50 cal.

At 19:55 three Me 109s that strafed the area from 500 ft [152 meters] were shot at by First Platoon, Battery C. The planes were circling above the platoon and they used nine rounds of 40mm and 600 rounds of .50 cal.

Twenty minutes later, the other platoon of Battery C engaged four Me 109s with sixty-one rounds of 40mm and 1,660 rounds of .50 cal were used. The planes flew from north to south at 700 to 1,500 ft [213-457 meters].

The next day, the Luftwaffe launched several ferocious assaults, and the battalion engaged in action multiple times to fend off them off. At 06:30 Second Platoon, Battery C, engaged three Fw 190s from a flight of six while they were strafing in the area. The planes flew from east to west at 1,000 to 1,900 ft [305-579 meters] as they attacked the area. The platoon used forty-four rounds of 40mm and 950 rounds of .50 cal.

At 06:45 hours First Platoon, Battery C, fired upon one Me 109, while it strafed in their vicinity. The plane went over from northwest to southeast at 200 ft [61 meters] and the platoon claimed a Cat I. They shot forty-four rounds of 40mm and 200 rounds of .50 cal.

Five minutes later the same platoon engaged two Me 109s from a flight of three, while they were strafing. The planes flew at 500 ft [152 meters] from the southwest to the northeast. Two Cat Is were claimed, expending eleven rounds of 40mm and 300 of .50 cal.

Ten minutes later First Platoon, Battery C, was again in combat. They shot at four Fw 190s while they were circling, strafing, and bombing in the area. In total forty-five rounds of 40mm and 415 rounds of .50 cal ammo were expended.

At 09:00 six Me 109s were circling above Second Platoon, Battery C, at approximately 2,000 ft [610 meters]. The unit fired at one of them with eight rounds of 40mm and 400 rounds of .50 cal.

At 10:50 the same platoon engaged three Me 109s out of a flight of seven. The planes were bombing and strafing in their vicinity. A Cat I was claimed, expending 133 rounds of 40mm and 3,328 rounds of .50 cal.

At the same time Second Platoon, Battery C, engaged an Fw 190, which flew east to west over a column on the road and used 500 rounds of .50 cal.

Ten minutes later, again an Fw 190 flew over Second Platoon, Battery C. This time it flew from west to east. The platoon fired 500 rounds of .50 cal at it.

At 14:30 hours First Platoon, Battery A, shot at two Me 109s, which flew at 900 ft from the south to the southeast. The platoon expended 500 rounds of .50 cal and claimed a Cat I.

At 18:00 hours First Platoon, Battery A, engaged ten Me 109s, flying at various altitudes from 600 to 1,000 yards [549-914 meters]. They fired forty-six 40mm and 2,400 rounds of .50 cal.

At 19:30 hours Second Platoon, Battery C, engaged four Me 109s. A formation of six airplanes was bombing and strafing from 3,000 ft [914 meters]. One Cat I was claimed, expending sixty-nine rounds of 40mm and 1,781 rounds of .50 cal.

That day, Technician Fifth Grade Osie Layton was reported as wounded.

On 27 April, the Luftwaffe was active early in the morning but didn't show itself otherwise. At 06:00 First Platoon, Battery A, shot at two Me 109s which were strafing in the area. The planes flew at

1,500 ft [457 meters] from south to east. One Cat I was claimed, expending three rounds of 40mm and 720 rounds of .50 cal.

At 06:44 hours Second Platoon, Battery C, engaged a German observation plane as it flew over their defended area from west to east. A Cat I was claimed, expending eleven rounds of 40mm and 383 rounds of .50 cal.

The rest of April was calm, except for one incident. On 29 April, at 14:10 First Platoon, Battery A, fired at two Me 109s. The planes were strafing from 900 ft [274 meters] and flying from south to east. One Cat I was claimed, expending forty-seven rounds of 40mm and 1,075 rounds of .50 cal. The Battalion Headquarters relocated, trying to keep up with the platoons in their mad dash across Germany.

On 30 April 1945 Adolf Hitler and his wife Eva Braun committed suicide in a bunker in Berlin. Meanwhile, the Allied advance continued and the Third Army pushed deeper and deeper in to Germany.

As XII Corps looked back on their achievements of April 1945, they wrote:

> There was going to be no last-ditch fight there. XII Corps, by sealing the southwestern and southern exits from the Bohemian Bastion, had bottled up the German armies which were intended to implement the plans of Hitler, Goebbels & Co for that fanatic defense. As General Marshall says of this operation in his relevant Biennial Report: "the swift advances into the mountains of Austria and Bohemia had prevented the establishment of an inner fortress." It was XII Corps' special destiny, then, to establish the much-advertised "National Redoubt" as a myth.[28]

As the battalion summarized their month, the 452nd AAA provided AA protection to FA battalions as XII Corps proceeded to the Czechoslovakian border in the east and the Austrian border in the southeast. The weather was good, although the enemy was active. Platoons supporting armored units, especially those protecting FA units, experienced a lot of action. This month, for the first time, the unit experiencing loss due to enemy air activity. Four enlisted men were wounded and two 40mm guns were slightly damaged during an attack by twenty Me 109s and Fw 190s.

The war was approaching its last days and as the corps history recounted:

> XII Corps Hq and divisional liaison planes had been scouting boldly ahead of the ground forces for some time, hoping to sight some Russian activity. Rumors of Russian tactical aircraft deep within our lines had been running around with the usual cheerful irresponsibility of such reports; the Patton Legend picked up a new angle when it was said that the general himself had been shot at in error by a Russian plane while flying over Nurnberg in an L-5 [Piper Cub]. But few if any XII Corps personnel could be found to swear to first hand observation of a red star on the wing of a plane.[29]

This posed an additional risk for the 452nd AAA, as they might erroneously engage a Soviet aircraft, potentially causing unnecessary casualties and diplomatic tension. On 1 May there was little to report. One Jeep, one Dodge truck, three deuce-and-a-half trucks, and a 40mm gun were with Ordnance for repairs.

The next day, at 19:43, Second Platoon, Battery C, engaged a Ju 52 as it flew from the southwest to the northeast, expending 20 rounds of 40mm and 262 rounds of .50 cal.

On 3 May, late in the evening, several platoons were assigned new missions. First Platoon, Battery B, protected the bridge at Regen. First Platoon, Battery C, provided AA protection for the bridge at Deggendorf; Second Platoon, Battery C, protected a bridge at Passau; First Platoon, Battery D, protected the 974th Field Artillery Battalion; Second Platoon, Battery D, protected the Corps Command Post at Grafenau; the remaining platoons continued with their original missions.

That same day, a soldier of the battalion was killed. A group of enemy soldiers armed with machine pistols ambushed a Jeep. In this Jeep, en route to the Battalion Headquarters, were the commanding officer of Battery C, his driver, and the battery clerk.

Furthermore, the men were alerted about enemy cub planes, which would be on a sabotage mission.

On 4 May, at 06:25 hours Second Platoon, Battery C, engaged an Me 210 as it flew from south to north at 200 ft [61 meters]. A Cat I was claimed by the platoon, which expended 460 rounds of .50 cal.

Twenty-five minutes later, two Ju 88s flew from north to south at 600 ft [183 meters] over the positions of First Platoon, Battery A, and First Platoon, Battery D. These were fired upon and First Platoon, Battery A, claimed a Cat I. That platoon spent six rounds of 40mm and 763 rounds of .50 cal.

At 09:45 Second Platoon, Battery C, engaged a Ju 88, which came from the south and went north at 200 ft [61 meters].

The platoons were also notified about jet-propelled aircraft, which would be flying together with P-47s over their area; these were friendly planes and must not be engaged. Friendly bombers would be flying over the unit, and these also were not to be fired upon.

The other message clarified the warning given a day before: "Be on alert for German liaison planes and German Air Force personnel. Planes have the mission of blowing bridges, roads, etc. Planes are loaded with TNT. Fifty planes reported and only ten accounted for."[30]

The battalion received thirteen more reinforcements.

On 5 May, Deggendorf didn't need to be protected anymore. Instead, the Class III dump at Tittling needed to be protected. Thus First Platoon, Battery C, would provide AA protection for it, starting the next day.

On 6 May, the Battalion Command Post relocated and Captain Charles E. Morris was promoted to major. The next day, another warning went out about friendly bombers passing overhead as well as the announcement: "All hostilities will cease at 0001B 9 May 1945. All offensive operations will continue. All troops will remain in their present positions unless moving for occupation duties. No release to press will be made until 'Big Three' have made a joint release to the public."[31]

On 8 May, the last hours of the war in Europe, the 452nd AAA was still in the thick of it. The men must have had mixed feelings about continuing to fight so close to the end of the hostilities.

At 15:56 Second Platoon, Battery D, engaged an Fw 190 with thirteen rounds of 40mm and 300 rounds of .50 cal ammunition. The plane flew from northeast to southwest at 500 ft [152 meters].

Ten minutes later, the same platoon shot at a two-engine enemy transport plane, which was marked with black crosses. The plane was flying from northeast to southwest at 500 to 1,000 ft [152-305 meters]. They expended seven rounds of 40mm.

At 16:50 Second Platoon, Battery C, engaged an Fw 190 and an Me 109 flying from west to east at 700 ft [213 meters] altitude. The planes were strafing and the platoon fired twenty-two rounds of 40mm and seventy-five rounds of .50 cal back at them.

Fifteen minutes later Second Platoon, Battery D, engaged an Fw 190 with 200 rounds of .50 cal ammunition as it flew from northeast to southwest over their area.

At 17:35 First Platoon, Battery B, shot at an enemy observation plane with eight rounds of 40mm and eighty-three rounds of .50 cal. The plane was flying from the northeast over their area and they forced the plane to land, capturing its pilot.

At 18:10 an Me 109 was flying from northeast to southwest over Second Platoon, Battery C. The platoon then fired nineteen rounds of ammunition and 830 rounds of .50 cal ammunition at it.

The same platoon engaged two enemy observation planes from a flight of three at 19:55. They used fourteen rounds of 40mm and

890 rounds of .50 cal, claiming two Cat Is. The platoon also reported capturing a plane as well as the pilot and co-pilot. That evening an order went out that during daylight hours, no enemy aircraft would be engaged until they commit a hostile act.

On 9 May the hostilities were supposed to be over and XII Corps celebrated the end of the war, but at 06:15 Second Platoon, Battery D, engaged a Ju 88 with 100 rounds of .50 cal ammunition. That day, VE Day, platoons of the 452nd AAA were in three different countries: Germany, Austria, and Czechoslovakia. The platoons attached to the field artillery battalions were relieved of their mission and needed to prepare to move to Viechtach in the northeast sector of the district, where the unit would be used as occupational troops. Road clearance was needed for four or more vehicles in a convoy.

The next day, First Platoon, Battery B, both platoons of Battery C, and Second Platoon, Battery D, would move to the district on 11 May in the morning, where they would link up with the battalion.

On 12 May the advance detail left the Command Post for the new location and the rest of the headquarters followed a day later.

On 14 May a battery was needed to be prepared for Russian dignitaries who would visit XII Corps at Grafenau. Major Morris was in charge.

The next day a reminder went out that all enemy prisoners of war without discharge by the Allies needed to be picked up.

On 16 May, the battalion was notified that unit reports were no longer required. A provisional battery made up of two sections from each battery fired 1,662 rounds of 40mm and 30,077 rounds of .50 cal ammunition in salute to Russian dignitaries visiting XII Corps.

The next day 194 enemy soldiers were turned in at the prisoner of war enclosure.

On 18 May two enemy soldiers were halted at Arnbruck and then fled. When fired upon, one of them was wounded. They were evacuated to a German hospital at Viechtach. The battalion delivered 161 enemy soldiers to the detention center.

The next day, a British plane crashed near Battery C. It was not possible to identify several of the bodies. Group Headquarters wanted to know how many prisoners of war were turned over to the Soviets, directly or indirectly. The battalion responded that it had handed over 400 of them.

A day afterwards a message went out that prisoners of war were to be turned over to the 104th Infantry Division, starting the next day.

On 21 May at 09:15, the guard outposts of Battery A stopped a man claiming to be a civilian. However, they found a German soldbuch (a military paybook) in his boot. The man started to run and a halt was called, but he ran on and they started firing. The man was wounded and turned over to a nearby aid station.

At 11:35 a patrol of Battery C was fired upon from buildings in Drachselsreid, which they all searched.

The next day, the battalion had 254 PoWs present.

On 23 May, there were three German colonels found, dressed in civilian clothing, near Scherenben.[32] They had passes issued by the burgomeister of Drachselsreid. Otto Bruckmayer, and Rudy Kleff, his assistant burgomeister were turned over to the military government authorities of Viechtach for issuing unauthorized passes and aiding German PoWs.

The day after orders were received that the 452nd AAA would proceed to the Landau district. It would move there the next day. All PoWs were turned over to the 255th Field Artillery Battalion.

On 25 May the battalion moved to its new location. The platoons were spread out over the surrounding area. The unit was now under the command of the 115th AAA Group.

The next two days there were 26 and 27 May. On 28 May, the battalion was alerted that the next day a convoy would move Russian displaced persons from Landau to Budějovice. The battalion would supply ten trucks under the command of Lieutenant Deming.

Two other AAA battalions, the 537th and the 462nd, would also supply ten.

On the 29th, two batteries, A and D, moved to new locations, north of the Isar river. Battery D was warned that there were fifty SS soldiers reported in the area by a civilian.

On 30 May, Hungarian and Polish PoWs were also to be placed in prisoner of war enclosures.

The last day of May concluded with setting up a control post on the MSR. Civilian traffic was not allowed on the road.

During May the 452nd AAA continued to perform its operations, protecting the field artillery battalions against hostile aircraft, and providing support for XII Corps. The unit also protected bridges across the Danube and Corps Forward CP. On VE Day, the platoons of the 452nd AAA were spread out over three different countries: Germany, Austria, and Czechoslovakia. On 9 May the unit began with occupational duties. The German Luftwaffe lashed out in its death throes, but it barely achieved anything.

Following the cessation of hostilities, the ETO spent much time in a recreational program consisting of baseball, swimming, fishing, horseback riding, volunteer hikes, and ping pong. Championship games were played in baseball. The information and education program commenced upon receipt of the necessary materials.[33]

Now that the fighting in Europe was over, the 452nd AAA did not need to provide anti-aircraft protection anymore. On 18 June 1945, the 452nd AAA was relieved of attachment to XII Corps, and on 24 June the 452nd AAA was relieved of assignment to the 44th AAA Brigade and attached to the 55th AAA Brigade, where it would be attached to the 115th AAA Group.

The unit would go through several changes in command. On 1 July 1945 Major Milton D. Lederman assumed command of the battalion. He was replaced on 24 July by Major Milton S. Hoffman. He didn't stay long either, because on 8 September Lieutenant

Colonel C.W. Wilmore took over. On 15 September Major Milton S. Hoffman assumed temporary command of the unit in the absence of Lieutenant Colonel C.W. Wilmore.

The need for soldiers in Europe diminished. The U.S. Army classified units into four categories: Category I would remain in Europe as part of the occupational force. Category II was redeployed to the Pacific. Category III was reorganized, retrained, and then reclassified as either Category I or II.

Lastly, Category IV consisted of units that would be deactivated. The 452nd AAA battalion had been classed as a Category IV unit on 27 June according to Station List No. 91, Headquarters XII Corps, dated 17 June 1945.[34]

On 6 August the Japanese city of Hiroshima was bombed. Three days later an atomic bomb was dropped on Nagasaki. On 2 September 1945, the war in the Pacific came to an end when Japan surrendered. The Second World War was finally over.

Meanwhile, the 452nd AAA was rapidly diminished. Soldiers were discharged or transferred out of the unit. What remained of the battalion made the trip back on board the SS *John Sergeant*, where they disembarked in Boston in November. The battalion was disbanded on 17 November 1945 at Camp Myles Standish, Massachusetts.

The 452nd AAA experienced a brief revival. The battalion was activated again on 17 June 1946 at Kimpo Airfield, Korea, as a self-propelled battalion. On 30 June Major Ralph N. Ross assumed temporary command of the unit in the absence of Lieutenant Colonel Daniel M. Wilson. On 27 July 1946, Major Ross would again be the commanding officer.

A month later, on 27 August 1946, Major Eben L. Webber assumed temporary command of the unit until Major Ross returned on 6 September 1946. On 9 September Lieutenant Colonel Ramon C. Dougan assumed command of the unit. On 13 December the unit was deactivated once more and hasn't been reactivated since.

Several years later, on 26 July 1948, President Harry S. Truman signed Executive Order 9981. It stated that there would be no more discrimination on color, race, national origin or religion. In the years afterwards the United States Armed Forces integrated and segregated units ceased to exist.

Chapter 5

Written Out of History

In history, selections need to be made about what should be included and what should be excluded. People write about what they deem important to remember. Because the 452nd AAA was a Black American unit, there might be those who do not attach much importance to its history due to (latent) racism. However, there are also additional historical factors at play which cause certain decisions to be made. The result of all this is that the history of the 452nd AAA is relatively unknown.

There are several explanations for why this happened; as mentioned, some might be due to racial prejudice, others to the ways in which history is remembered and recorded. By failing to write about the achievements of these Black soldiers, we deny them their rightful place in history, and we diminish their efforts; to push this argument further, we also deny others their chance to learn about a particular aspect of history. Moreover, the absence of these aspects in history deprives present and future generations of a comprehensive understanding of the complexities of our shared history.

This is crucial because if we don't know that something ever happened, we cannot learn more about it or from it. While the experiences of a white AAA AW battalion can more easily be interchanged with the experiences of another white AAA AW battalion, the same does not apply to the experiences of Black American soldiers. In their service, and the judgment of it, there is a racial element which did not exist among white units.

The 452nd AAA performed excellently during the Second World War. It might not be the most vaunted anti-aircraft artillery unit, but the 452nd AAA fought well and they played an exemplary role. They were Black American soldiers in combat at a time when most Black Americans were viewed as only suitable for service units.

Yet Black soldiers were not regarded the same as their white comrades. The 457th AAA Battalion, made up of white soldiers and serving with XII Corps, just like the 452nd AAA, can in some ways be compared to them, but like a left and right hand, both were needed for the success of XII Corps. While one battalion secured bridgeheads and advanced alongside armored units, the other provided protection for the field artillery battalions, which supported the armored divisions with their firepower.

The artillery battalions protected by the 452nd AAA were usually further behind the frontline than the bridges being protected by the 457th AAA. As such, the 457th AAA was more in a position for ground combat than the 452nd AAA.

Bridges were seized by reconnaissance elements and then protected by the 457th AAA, while the record of the 457th AAA shows that they have 27 $^{7}/_{12}$ Cat I claims, 10 ½ Cat II claims, and 6 Cat III claims. However, seven of their Cat Is come from just four days ashore.[1] The 457th AAA was further bolstered with .50 cal quadmounted half-tracks, of which sixteen were delivered. These were organized in an additional battery, "E". From the records, it cannot be said whether the 452nd AAA also had these vehicles. There will be several comparisons to the 457th AAA and the intention is not to diminish the glory of the 457th, but rather to put the service and the memory of the 452nd AAA in perspective. The purpose is not to accuse the 457th of anything; rather, their history is taken as an example of how Black soldiers are often rendered invisible and their efforts during the Second World War are ignored.

Perspectives

Differing perspectives are another reason that the service of the 452nd AAA has been forgotten. Although some soldiers wrote about their experiences or interactions with the 452nd AAA, their unit histories remain silent. This is because the unit writes only about what's important for that particular unit, which might be different from what the individual soldiers would decide write about.

To start with the 457th AAA; this outfit was one of the two anti-aircraft artillery battalions of the 27th AAA Group, the other battalion in this group was the 452nd AAA. The 457th AAA makes no mention of the 452nd AAA in their entire book. However, they do mention being camped next to Hawaiian Japanese soldiers during an exercise: "On 6 April the entire unit moved out of Camp Shelby in convoy with the 85th Division, destined for the Louisiana Maneuvers. [...] The unit bivouacked next to the 100th Infantry Battalion – the Hawaiian Japanese who were later to distinguish themselves in combat in Italy."

The 457th unit history further mentions that their commanding officer contacted the 467th AAA and the 197th AAA, which were deployed beside them. Elsewhere the 480th AAA is mentioned, which takes over positions of the 457th AAA. The only vague reference to the existence of the 452nd AAA is in the following:

> On the 25th, the First Platoon of D battery was brought up to the Rhine to reinforce C battery. Part of three other automatic weapons battalions and two complete gun battalions (90mm) were in place in the Rhine crossing, and it was a veritable hornet's nest for any German plane that dared to approach.[2]

One of the "three other automatic weapon battalions" is the 452nd AAA.

During an award ceremony on 5 January 1945, members of the 452nd AAA and the 457th AAA were decorated personally by Major General Eddy, the commanding general of XII Corps. This event was held at the 27th AAA Group Command Post in Luxembourg City; the 457th AAA makes no mention of the presence of the 452nd AAA, which was also there.

In "AAA with a Corps", a study written by Lieutenant Colonel Ratcliffe after the war, details the employment of the 27th AAA Corps and uses that unit to explain how AAA battalions could be used.[3] The 27th AAA Group had two AW battalions attached, the 457th AAA and the 452nd AAA. In it, Ratcliffe wrote:

> in assigning missions to the Corps AAA Units wherever possible the same units were used on similar type missions. In the XII Corps, one battalion normally protected the corps artillery and the other battalion protected engineer activities and installations. This resulted in a minimum of confusion and a maximum of coordination and cooperation.[4]

He also mentions that AAA protection was done together, because "there were seldom enough units to satisfy all requests for AAA protection and it was considered foolish to spread the AAA so thin as to give everyone a little protection and no one adequate protection."[5]

With this in mind, the absence of the 452nd AAA in the 457th AAA unit history is remarkable. The 457th AAA isn't the only unit in history where the 452nd AAA is absent.

The same occurred in the unit history of some field artillery battalions. In the unit history of the 731st Field Artillery Battalion, there's a mention at the end of the book, once a platoon was again attached to the unit in April 1945. The 452nd AAA is not mentioned when it was first attached, although one of the "ack-ack" soldiers is credited with locating a German deserter, which he recognized from a photo he had seen.

Black soldiers are rendered invisible at other times as well. Throughout its history, the 731st FA suffered thirteen deadly casualties. From Battery B, five of them occurred on 4 December and the fighting is described as such:

> The following day Baker received the heaviest fire. A trailer, filled with 24 rounds of white phosphorus shell, was hit, and disregarding the danger, Lieutenant Chance and T/4 Jordan, of B Battery, fastened a winch cable to the burning trailer and with a tractor towed the exploding shells away from the battery area and an important crossroads, for which they were awarded the Silver Star. Under fire Cpt. [*sic*] Gabriellini manned a gun completely by himself, loaded it, rammed the shells, and laid it for direction and elevation and was ready to fire in time for the next mission. Pfc. Damm was killed while delivering protective material to the gun sites on his own initiative. Under all this shelling the three batteries continued their duties and carried out their assigned missions.[6]

It makes no mention of the soldiers of the 452nd AAA that assisted in the evacuation of the wounded. Neither does it acknowledge that by evacuating the casualties, the guns continued were able to continue firing. This can be explained by the adopted perspective because it's a unit history and the focus is on what the unit experienced. Naturally, they would give preference to their own heroes and the Silver Star Medals they won.

Even more curious is the fact that the 731st FA was bombed and strafed by enemy aircraft just a few days before the 452nd AAA became attached to it. In the early morning of 6 August, the outfit was illuminated by flares and then strafed. Three soldiers were killed and thirteen were wounded. The importance of anti-aircraft protection had been violently hammered into the consciousness of the 731st FA, yet there's just one mention of the 452nd in their history and one other reference to the unit.

This is quite a disparity with the message of the battery commander of Battery B, who messaged the 452nd AAA, to tell them of the three soldiers that went "above and beyond the call of duty" in the action, which left five killed and fourteen wounded. He even sent this message to the headquarters of the 452nd AAA Battalion, ensuring they were also aware of the courage of their soldiers.

This is contrasted with the individual soldiers. One such soldier of the 731st FA, George F. Threlfall, wrote a book, *Fighting with Patton's Third Army: World War II Memoirs of George F. Threlfall*, about his experiences during the Second World War. He wrote about the same attack, but also he didn't mention the 452nd AAA during that attack. It might be due to "weapon focus", as psychologists call it, which means that people remember the threat, but not the surrounding details of the event.

Elsewhere Threlfall did write about the 452nd AAA, where he mentions one particular soldier with whom he had a good connection:

> Duke was a real character assigned to an anti-aircraft protection outfit. His outfit was all black, except for the officers. He had us laughing all the time.
>
> One day when I was going by his gun, he asked me where I was going. I told him I was going over to that house nearby to go looting. He said he had already been there and found nothing. When I returned I handed him seven rings I had found. He named me the very best looter in the ETO (European Theatre of Operations).
>
> Another time I was with Duhowski. Duho had picked up a submachine gun on the battlefield and had it slung over his shoulder. Old Duke never missed a trick. Wanted to know if Duho could shoot that thing. "Yep," was Duho's answer, "I can shoot it." Not good enough for Duke. He challenged him. "Let's see if you can hit my helmet," he said, taking it off and throwing it up in the air. Rat-a-tat-tat-tat. When Duke's helmet finally hit the ground it was full of holes. He could shoot that thing!

> Duke kept that helmet and wore it whenever we traveled. When we entered a town, he would play like he had head wounds. Civilians used to look at him with amazement. Couldn't understand how he was still alive.[7]

Also in *Fighting with Patton's Third Army*, Threlfall writes about the less glamorous aspects of war. As mentioned above, the soldiers looted and sometimes appeared more concerned about their next meal than their next mission. Since Threlfall wrote about his personal experiences, in other words, how he and not his unit experienced the war, he is in the position to decide what is included and what is omitted. Furthermore, since he writes about his own experiences, he can also write about actions that others might have frowned upon, such as stealing a case of C-rations, which would not be featured in the unit's history.

To make matters even worse for the 452nd AAA, it also depended on the assignment. If an AAA battalion was attached to a division for a long time, it was sometimes considered an organic part of the division. If the division moved from one corps to another, the AAA battalion moved with them. The AAA battalion operated within the divisional area. For an AAA battalion attached to a corps, the scope increased. The distances between the AAA platoons were bigger and often several divisions were supported at the same time. Their assignments might be vastly different since the corps area was much greater than that of a division. Thus, an AAA battalion attached to a corps has a substantially different perspective than a divisional AAA unit.

In the case of the 452nd AAA Battalion, they were stretched over a large area. The fact that at the end of the war in Europe, the battalion had detachments in three different countries, Czechoslovakia, Germany, and Austria, is an indication of this. The 452nd AAA had been attached to XII Corps, one of the many units attached to it. However, since the 452nd was just a battalion that operated within this corps' zone of influence, it could easily get lost among the larger units, such as regiments or divisions. They weren't an organic part of the unit, they didn't fight as a collective, they didn't liberate any towns, and assisted others when needed.

As for why this matters, it's due to the adopted perspectives. The unit histories, as the name implies, focus on the history of that particular unit and no other units. However, because every unit adopted this framework, the 452nd AAA slipped through the cracks. The unit did not fight as a whole, but attached platoons to several field artillery battalions and thus served with them. Whereas some, such as Barrett James Whiteley, George F. Threlfall, and George A. Buck, do talk about the soldiers and acknowledge them, others remain silent on their service. Thus, the common soldiers would write about their experiences and their interactions with the battalion from their own perspective, their own war experiences, rather than the perspective of the unit.

To push the argument further, the reasons for this silence can be disinterest or (latent) racism. More reasons to speculate could be that the creators of the unit histories did not have contact with the AAA gunners or that their records were restricted by time or pages. However, in the end, the result is still the same. These units have their histories and their service records, while the service of the 452nd AAA, and by extension many other Black American units, has faded from public memory.

Echo through the ages

It is often said that written words echo through the ages, and this is another reason why so little is known about the 452nd AAA. They don't have a written unit history.

The book *XII Corps: Spearhead of Patton's Third Army*, was written by Lieutenant Colonel George Dyer and published in 1947. It narrates the history of XII Corps in meticulous detail and is an interesting document to analyze. Both the 452nd AAA and the 457th AAA are mentioned as being the best of their type.

In the history of XII Corps, Dyer acknowledged that the 457th AAA wrote a unit history and incorporated this book in the history of XII Corps. Dyer quotes several passages from it and drawings and photographs from the 457th AAA's unit history are featured in the book. The 457th AAA is mentioned seventeen times in the work; the 452nd AAA is mentioned just five times – a substantial difference.

From Dyer's perspective this is understandable. He needed to work with the sources at his disposal and because the 457th AAA wrote a unit history, and the 452nd AAA did not, they are featured much more prominently. In other words, the source material for the 457th AAA was much more easily accessible than for the 452nd AAA. Because of this, more people can interact with it, and from there it spreads further.

As for the reasons why the 452nd AAA didn't write their own unit history, we can only speculate. It could be lack of time or lack of skill. Once the enlisted men returned home, there might have been more immediate concerns based on their economic and social situation. Families had to be taken care of and bills had to be paid. Some enlisted men lost contact with the soldiers they had served alongside. Several veterans of the unit put out contact messages to get in touch with men they served alongside or by relatives to request more information about their service.

As for their officers, there are some additional factors to take into account. Whatever their relationship with the soldiers under their command, the white officers returned to a segregated society. As mentioned by Ulysses Lee, in *The Employment of Negro Troops*:

> Prejudice was even applied to white officers serving with Negro troops, as though they had become tainted. One of the very first questions asked by a civilian on meeting

> an Army officer was, "What type of troops do you have?" The officer with Negro troops was often made to feel that his was a secondary role and that, as an officer, he was not contributing as fully and seriously to the conduct of the war as those men who were assigned to white units. At times, officers assigned to Negro troops felt that they were being penalized or that they were not considered fully competent.[8]

Taking these factors into account, it's understandable that some of the white officers might not have felt comfortable writing about, let alone publishing, their own experiences or those of their unit during the Second World War. Even if they had wanted to, would anyone in the segregated society of the time be willing to read it? They had to consider how such a publication might affect them and their career in the future.

In the end, the result is the same: less is known about the history of the 452nd AAA than the 457th AAA, and so it is harder to learn more about the 452nd AAA. To make matters worse, this lack of recorded unit history might have led to the 452nd being rendered invisible in the work of some historians. Whether or not this was done intentionally is a different discussion.

Reactionary force

Of course, the AAA is a reactionary service, meaning that it reacts to hostile aircraft, and when no hostile aircraft appears, it is rendered passive. Although the 452nd AAA performed its service well, the AAA is a less glamorous service than some others. The 40mm Bofors guns don't capture people's attention in the same way as rumbling tanks or roaring airplanes do. It might explain why there's more interest in the Tuskegee Airmen or the 761st Tank Battalion, both then and now.

One claim about the battalion, that no unit they protected suffered materiel damages or personnel killed, must be used with caution. The keyword in this phrase is "killed". As Ulysses Lee mentions in his book *The Employment of Negro Troops*: "No installation defended by the 452d suffered materiel damage or personnel killed by enemy aircraft, although the battalion and the field artillery battalions which it protected suffered personnel losses from other types of enemy action."[9] This statement is derived from the reports that the 452nd AAA produced, but this doesn't mean that the installations or units didn't suffer wounded soldiers. Earlier, on 31 December 1944, nine soldiers of the 945th Field Artillery died when accidentally bombed by a P-47. One more was wounded.

However, this is not the only incident, because in the history of the 191st Field Artillery Battalion, there's the following encounter:

> The next morning our positions were attacked by enemy fighter bombers in considerable strength, one flight of 50 Fw 190s was particularly aggressive, but we received only one light casualty. [...] On 3 April Combat Command B attacked Gotha, the Battalion arriving in area 1 mile North of the town at 1310. Again fighter bombers were active in the area; we received 1 casualty from bombs.[10]

In both encounters, soldiers were wounded but not killed. In the unit report, however, the following was written: "No casualties and no damage to defended area was reported."[11] This suggests that the statement by Lee must be treated with caution.

Indeed, the AA gunners provided good protection and many artillery soldiers will have been grateful for the protection that the 452nd AAA offered. However, to aggrandize the actions of the 452nd AAA Battalion is neither appropriate nor fair to them.

On the opposite side of the spectrum, the 452nd AAA has also received insincere praise from certain commanders. The commanding officers of the 452nd AAA AW Battalion received a commendation from E.W. Timberlake, Brigadier General, U.S. Army:

> As a representative of the Brigade as a whole, I am gratified and proud to transmit this commendation to the officers and men of the 452d AAA AW Battalion, who earned it on the field of battle. Your command served as a part of the 49th AAA Brigade from: 24 June 1944 to 1 August 1944.[12]

This is incorrect because the dates are wrong. The 452nd AAA was attached to the 49th AAA Brigade on 30 April and relieved again on 20 July 1944. The first units of the battalion landed on 23 June 1944 in Normandy and the unit didn't experience serious combat, until it was attached to XII Corps. So this praise, however well-meant it might be, doesn't do credit to the combat record of the 452nd AAA and reads like a standard message sent out to all units.

However, the 452nd AAA fulfilled an essential role in the war. The installations and the units the 452nd AAA protected were essential for the Allied victory. The 452nd AAA was attached to the 27th AAA Group, together with the 457th AAA. Both units were needed for the success of XII Corps. Measured in claims Cat I and Cat II, the 452nd AAA has substantially more kills. As mentioned previously, the record of the 457th AAA shows that they have 27 $^{7}/_{12}$ Cat I claims, 10½ Cat II claims and 6 Cat III claims, while the 452nd has 67 $^{11}/_{12}$ Cat Is, 19 Cat IIs and 11 Cat IIIs. Now, these claims are an arbitrary method of measurement because in the chaos of combat mistakes can easily be made, yet some things can be deduced from them. The differences are so large, that it can safely be claimed that the 452nd AAA didn't just "do its job", it did it very well. Each of those hostile airplanes formed a threat and was neutralized. Rounded up, the 452nd shot down sixty-eight aircraft, which is equivalent to almost two Luftwaffe *gruppe* (between thirty and thirty-five aircraft, although some *gruppen* had up to forty planes). The Luftwaffe *gruppe* is the equivalent of the United States Army Air Force Group. Each of these planes, ranging from observation planes to jet bombers, ceased to be a threat. In doing so, the 452nd AAA didn't just defend the units or installations they were protecting, but actively contributed to the destruction of the German Air Force and ultimately the Allied victory over Nazi Germany.

Furthermore, by fighting bravely alongside white soldiers, they earned their respect and changed their perceptions about Black Americans. In doing so, the battalion not only contributed to destroying the Luftwaffe, but also Jim Crow. Thus, the 452nd Anti-Aircraft Artillery Battalion fought and contributed to the war on both fronts, rightfully earning their place in the proud traditions of the U.S. Armed Forces.

The 452nd AAA AW Battalion is credited with the following campaigns:

Ground Combat, EAME Theater: 7 December 1941 – 2 September 1945

Normandy: 6 June – 24 July 1944

Northern France: 25 July – 14 September 1944

Rhineland: 15 September 1944 – 21 March 1945

Ardennes-Alsace: 16 December 1944 – 25 January 1945

Central Europe: 22 March – 11 May 1945

Total ammunition expended by the 452nd AAA.

Ammunition expended						
Caliber	Type	Fuze		AA fire	Ground fire	Total
40mm	Cart HE-T (SD) Mk II	W/PD		13,611	74	13,685
40mm	AP			0	20	20
.50	AP I & T (2-2-1)			198,677	4,450	203,127
.30	Carbine			0	0	0
.30	M-1			0	109	109
.45				0	3	3

Appendix

Units and installations protected by the 452nd Anti-Aircraft Artillery Battalion, starting from 17 August 1944 until 9 May 1945

	Protected	From
Battery A		
First Platoon		
	179th Field Artillery Battalion	17 August – 22 December 1944
	244th Field Artillery Battalion	23 December – 23 December 1944
	108th Field Artillery Battalion	24 December – 26 December 1944
	945th Field Artillery Battalion	27 December 1944 – 9 May 1945
Second Platoon		
	558th Field Artillery Battalion	17 August – 23 August 1944
	Bridge Souppes	24 August – 25 August 1944
	SP at X645681	26 August – 27 August 1944
	Bridge Arcis-sur-Aube	28 August – 2 September 1944
	738th Field Artillery Battalion	2 September – 20 December 1944
	974th Field Artillery Battalion	21 December 1944 – 22 March 1945
	Third Army Engineer Dump	22 March – 22 March 1945
	Engineer Bridge Construction	23 March – 3 April 1945
	771st Field Artillery Battalion	4 April – 9 May 1945
Battery B		
First Platoon		
	945th Field Artillery Battalion	17 August – 25 November 1944
	176th Field Artillery Battalion	26 November – 23 December 1944
	81st Field Artillery Battalion	24 December – 29 December 1944
	736th Field Artillery Battalion	30 December 1944 – 21 February 1945
	738th Field Artillery Battalion	22 February 1945 – 2 May 1945
	Regen Bridge	3 May – 9 May 1945

Second Platoon

731st Field Artillery Battalion	17 August – 23 December 1944
215th Field Artillery Battalion	24 December 1944 – 4 January 1945
512th Field Artillery Battalion	5 January – 11 January 1945
215th Field Artillery Battalion	12 January – 31 January 1945
512th Field Artillery Battalion	1 February – 26 February 1945
179th Field Artillery Battalion	27 February – 9 May 1945

Battery C

First Platoon

191st Field Artillery Battalion	17 August – 17 August 1944
Bridge Fréteval	18 August – 19 August 1944
Captured Enemy Flying Bomb Depot	20 August – 21 August 1944
191st Field Artillery Battalion	22 August – 25 November 1944
741st Field Artillery Battalion	26 November – 20 December 1944
802nd Field Artillery Battalion	21 December – 29 December 1944
277th Field Artillery Battalion	30 December 1944 – 2 February 1945
243rd Field Artillery Battalion	3 February – 4 February 1945
775th Field Artillery Battalion	5 February – 25 February 1945
740th Field Artillery Battalion	26 February – 1 May 1945
Deggendorf Bridge	2 May – 4 May 1945
Class III Dump Tittling	5 May – 9 May 1945

Second Platoon

802nd Field Artillery Battalion	17 August – 17 August 1944
Bridge Fréteval	18 August – 20 August 1944
802nd Field Artillery Battalion	21 August – 3 September 1944
253rd Field Artillery Battalion	4 September – 24 September 1944
Bridges Dombasle	25 September – 26 September 1944
752nd Field Artillery Battalion	27 September – 23 December 1944
255th Field Artillery Battalion	24 December – 26 December 1944
752nd Field Artillery Battalion	27 December 1944 – 31 January 1945
255th Field Artillery Battalion	1 February – 25 February 1945
752nd Field Artillery Battalion	26 February – 13 March 1945
771st Field Artillery Battalion	14 March – 24 March 1945
974th Field Artillery Battalion	25 March – 1 May 1945
Passau Bridge	2 May – 9 May 1945

Battery D

First Platoon

Corps Forward Echelon Command Post	17 August – 23 August 1944
POL Dump (X219585)	24 August – 25 August 1944
Bridges and Creeks Sens	26 August – 28 August 1944
176th Field Artillery Battalion	29 August – 24 September 1944
Bridges St Nicholas Du Port	25 September – 27 September 1944
176th Field Artillery Battalion	28 September – 28 October 1944
267th Field Artillery Battalion	29 October – 18 December 1944
191st Field Artillery Battalion	19 December 1944 – 8 April 1945
731st Field Artillery Battalion	9 April – 1 May 1945
974th Field Artillery Battalion	2 May – 9 May 1945

Second Platoon

Corps Rear Echelon Command Post	17 August – 17 August 1944
Bridge – Cloyes	18 August – 21 August 1944
24th Ordnance Battalion	22 August – 22 August 1944
POL Dump (X219585)	23 August – 24 August 1944
Bridges and Creeks Sens	25 August – 28 August 1944
974th Field Artillery Battalion	29 August – 30 August 1944
775th Field Artillery Battalion	31 August – 24 September 1944
Bridges St Nicholas Du Port	25 September – 27 September 1944
278th Field Artillery Battalion	27 September – 20 December 1944
273rd Field Artillery Battalion	21 December 1944 – 21 March 1945
Engineer Construction Site	22 March – 3 April 1945
273rd Field Artillery Battalion	4 April – 13 April 1945
244th Field Artillery Battalion	14 April – 1 May 1945
Corps Command Post at Grafenau	2 May – 9 May 1945

Literature and Sources

'Across the Rhine', *Stars and Stripes*, 25 March 1945.

'Crack Negro Ack-Ack Unit Awaits Jerry', *The Michigan Chronicle*, 18 March 1944.

'Fox Holes Kill All Racial Feeling', *The Daily American*, 1 January 1945.

'Negro Ack-Ack Men Keep 'Em Falling for 3rd', *Stars and Stripes*, 28 December 1944.

191st Field Artillery Battalion, Combat Operations 1945, accessed through: https://donl702.tripod.com/191st/Combat_Operations-1945.html.

Anderson, James B., 'Comments', 6 April 1944, 452nd AAA AW Battalion, Dwight D. Eisenhower Library, Box 296.

Anti-Aircraft Artillery Notes, Headquarters European Theater of Operations, United States Army, Number 6, 28 November 1944.

Anti-Aircraft Notes, Headquarters European Theater of Operations, United States Army, Number 26, 18 April 1945.

Buck, George A., 'Four Barrels', 945th Field Artillery Battalion.

Byers, Jean, *A study of the Negro in Military Service*, June 1947.

Cibula, Alvin M., Anti-Aircraft Command and Center, Army Ground Forces, Study No. 26, 1946.

Converse, Elliott, et al., *The Exclusion of Black Soldiers from the Medal of Honor in World War II*, 2008.

Douglas, Helen Gahagan, 'The Negro Soldier: A partial record of Negro devotion and heroism in the cause of freedom gathered from the files of the War and Navy Departments,' House of Representatives, January 22, 1946.

Dyer, George, *XII Corps: Spearhead of Patton's Third Army*, 1947.

Field Manual 44-2, Employment of Anti-Aircraft Artillery Automatic Weapons, December 1944.

From Texas to Teisnach with the 457 AAA AW Battalion, 1945.

Headquarters 49th AAA Brigade, APO 758, U.S. Army, 25 June 1945, National Archives and Records Administration: CABN-452.

Headquarters 55th Anti-Aircraft Artillery Brigade, 27 June 1945, categorization of units, National Archives and Records Administration: CABN-452.

Headquarters XII Corps, General Orders 4, 13 January 1945, National Archives and Records Administration: CABN-452-1.13, General Orders.

Kirkpatrick, Charles E., *Archie in the AEF*, 1984.

Lee, Ulysses, *The Employment of Negro Troops*, 1963.

Manrho, John, and Ron Pütz, *Bodenplatte: The Luftwaffe's Last Hope*, 2010.

Medical Detachment, 452nd AAA Auto WPNS BL (MBL), 30 June 1945, semi-annual report, Dwight D. Eisenhower Library, Box 296.

Memorandum, 30 October 1943, 452nd AAA AW Bn (MBL), National Archives and Records Administration: CABN-452-0.1, History – 452nd AAA AW Bn, Year 43.

National Archives and Records Administration, Prologue, 2001, vol. 33, No. 4, 'FDR's "Day of Infamy" Speech'.

Ratcliffe, Lamar C., 'AAA With A Corps (Based On AAA Activities In XII Corps, Third U.S. Army, 1 August 1944 to 8 May 1945)', 1946-1947.

Report After Action Against Enemy, April 1945, 452nd AAA AW Bn (MBL), National Archives and Records Administration: CABN-452-0.3, A/A Reports.

Report After Action Against Enemy, December 1944, 452nd AAA AW Bn (MBL), National Archives and Records Administration: CABN-452-0.3, A/A Reports.

Report After Action Against Enemy, January 1945, 1944, 452nd AAA AW Bn (MBL), National Archives and Records Administration: CABN-452-0.3, A/A Reports.

Report After Action Against Enemy, May 1945, 1944, 452nd AAA AW Bn (MBL), National Archives and Records Administration: CABN-452-0.3, A/A Reports.

Report of Inspection, 28 December 1943, 452nd AAA AW Battalion, Dwight D. Eisenhower Library, Box 296.

Semmens, Paul E., *Hammer of Hell*, 1990.

Smith, Walter Bedell, 'Eisenhower's Six Great Decisions: The Only Way It Could End', *The Saturday Evening Post*, volume 219, 13 July 1946.

The Combat History of the 731st Field Artillery Battalion: Never Forget, n.d.

Threlfall, John E., *Fighting with Patton's Third Army: World War II Memoirs of George F. Threlfall*, 2010.

Unit Report No. 224, 18 March 1945, 452nd AAA AW Bn (MBL), National Archives and Records Administration: CABN-452-0.9, Unit Reports 1945.

Unit Report No. 241, 4 April 1945, 452nd AAA AW Bn (MBL), National Archives and Records Administration: CABN-452-0.9, Unit Reports 1945.

Unit Report No. 97, 452nd AAA AW Bn (MBL), 10 November 1944, National Archives and Records Administration: CABN-452-0.9, Unit Reports 1944.

Unit Report No. 98, 452nd AAA AW Bn (MBL), 11 November 1944, National Archives and Records Administration: CABN-452-0.9, Unit Reports 1944.

Unit Report No. 99, 452nd AAA AW Bn (MBL), 12 November 1944, National Archives and Records Administration: CABN-452-0.9, Unit Reports 1944.

Unit Report, 22 August 1944, 452nd AAA AW Bn (MBL), National Archives and Records Administration: CABN-452-0.9, Unit Reports 1944.

Unit Report, 23 August 1944, 452nd AAA AW Bn (MBL), National Archives and Records Administration: CABN-452-0.9, Unit Reports 1944.

Werrell, Kenneth P., *Archie to Sam*, 2005.

Whiteley, Barrett James, 'On the Way!' Memoirs of an Artilleryman in WWII, accessed through: https://donl702.tripod.com/191st/index.htm#ontheway.

Wiley, Bell I., 'Training of Negro Troops', Army Ground Forces, Study No. 36, 1946.

Endnotes

Introduction

1. National Archives and Records Administration, Prologue, 2001, vol. 33, No. 4, 'FDR's "Day of Infamy" Speech'.

Chapter 1

1. Alvin M. Cibula, Anti-Aircraft Command and Center, Army Ground Forces, Study No. 26, 1946, 1.
2. Charles E. Kirkpatrick, *Archie in the AEF*, 1984, 10.
3. Ibid, 35-36.
4. Ibid, 58.
5. Ibid, 58.
6. Ibid, 63-64.
7. Ibid, 64.
8. Kenneth P. Werrell, *Archie to Sam*, 2005, 3.
9. Kirkpatrick, *Archie in the AEF*, 74.
10. Ibid, 123.
11. Paul E. Semmens, *Hammer of Hell*, 1990, 4.
12. Cibula, Anti-Aircraft Command and Center, 2.
13. Semmens, *Hammer of Hell*, 8.
14. Ibid, 8.
15. Ibid, 8.
16. *Archie to Sam*, Kenneth P. Werrell, 2005, 50-51.
17. Semmens, *Hammer of Hell*, 10.
18. Cibula, Anti-Aircraft Command and Center, 6.
19. Ibid, 3.
20. Ibid, 18.
21. Ibid, 18.

Chapter 2

1. Ibid, 28-29.
2. Semmens, *Hammer of Hell*, 16.
3. Ibid, 18.
4. Ibid, 41.
5. Werrell, *Archie to Sam*, 7.
6. Ibid, 47.
7. Ibid, 48.
8. Ibid, 48-49.
9. John Manrho, Ron Pütz, *Bodenplatte: The Luftwaffe's Last Hope*, 2010, 463.
10. *Field Manual 44-2, Employment of Anti-Aircraft Artillery Automatic Weapons*, December 1944, 9.
11. Ibid, 11.
12. Cibula, Anti-Aircraft Command and Center, 209.
13. *Field Manual 44-2, Employment of Anti-Aircraft Artillery Automatic Weapons*, 5.
14. Ibid, 1.
15. Ibid, 16-17.
16. Ibid, 13.
17. Ibid, 14-16.
18. Ibid, 6.
19. Barrett James Whiteley, 'On the Way!' Memoirs of an Artilleryman in WWII, Part 2, accessed through: https://donl702.tripod.com/191st/index.htm#ontheway.
20. *Field Manual 44-2, Employment of Anti-Aircraft Artillery Automatic Weapons*, 23.
21. Ulysses Lee, *The Employment of Negro Troops*, 1963, 241, 245.
22. Bell I. Wiley, 'Training of Negro Troops', Army Ground Forces, Study No. 36, 1946, ii.
23. Ibid, 3.
24. Ibid, iii.
25. Ibid, 1.
26. Ibid, 10.

27. Ibid, 10.
28. Ibid, 12.
29. Ibid, 15.
30. Ibid, 15.
31. Ibid, 13.
32. Ibid, 17.
33. Ibid, 17.
34. Ibid, 17.
35. Lee, *The Employment of Negro Troops*, 183.
36. Wiley, 'Training of Negro Troops', 25.
37. Ibid, 25.
38. Ibid, 26.
39. Ibid, 30.
40. Ibid.
41. Ibid, 37.
42. Ibid, 38.
43. Ibid.
44. Ibid, 31.
45. Ibid.
46. Ibid, 37.
47. Cibula, Anti-Aircraft Command and Center, 48.
48. Wiley, 'Training of Negro Troops', 50-51.
49. Ibid, 52.
50. Ibid, 53.
51. Ibid.
52. Ibid.
53. Ibid.
54. Ibid, 54.
55. Ibid.
56. Ibid.
57. Cibula, Anti-Aircraft Command and Center, 50.
58. Ibid, 48.
59. Ibid.
60. Helen Gahagan Douglas, 'The Negro Soldier: A partial record of Negro devotion and heroism in the cause of freedom gathered from

the files of the War and Navy Departments,' House of Representatives, January 22, 1946.

Chapter 3

1. Memorandum, 30 October 1943, 452nd AAA AW Bn (MBL), National Archives and Records Administration: CABN-452-0.1, History – 452nd AAA AW Bn, Year 43.
2. Report of Inspection, 28 December 1943, 452nd AAA AW Battalion, Dwight D. Eisenhower Library, Box 296.
3. 'Crack Negro Ack-Ack Unit Awaits Jerry', *The Michigan Chronicle*, 18 March 1944.
4. James B. Anderson, "Comments", 6 April 1944, 452nd AAA AW Battalion, Dwight D. Eisenhower Library, Box 296.
5. The unit history refers to LST-1164 and LST-1165. These two ships were actually constructed after the Second World War.
6. Unit Report, 22 August 1944, 452nd AAA AW Bn (MBL), National Archives and Records Administration: CABN-452-0.9, Unit Reports 1944.
7. Unit Report, 23 August 1944, 452nd AAA AW Bn (MBL), National Archives and Records Administration: CABN-452-0.9, Unit Reports 1944.
8. The unit history notes the '24th Ordnance', but there was no such unit attached to XII Corps, Unit Report, 23 August 1944, 452nd AAA AW Bn (MBL), National Archives and Records Administration: CABN-452-0.9, Unit Reports 1944.
9. Uncertain as to whom he meant since several Black soldiers might be eligible.
10. Whiteley, 'On the Way!' Part 1, accessed through: https://donl702.tripod.com/191st/index.htm#ontheway.
11. Whiteley, 'On the Way!' Part 2, accessed through: https://donl702.tripod.com/191st/index.htm#ontheway.
12. Ibid.
13. Anti-Aircraft Artillery Notes, Headquarters European Theater of Operations, United States Army, Number 6, 28 November 1944, 4.
14. Jean Byers, *A study of the Negro in Military Service*, June 1947, 158, and Elliott Converse et al., *The Exclusion of Black Soldiers from the Medal of Honor in World War II*, 2008, 79.
15. George Dyer, *XII Corps: Spearhead of Patton's Third Army*, 1947, 250.

16. Unit Report No. 97, 452nd AAA AW Bn (MBL), 10 November 1944, National Archives and Records Administration: CABN-452-0.9, Unit Reports 1944.
17. Ibid.
18. Ibid.
19. *From Texas to Teisnach with the 457 AAA AW Battalion*, 1945, 116.
20. *Ibid*, 123.
21. Dyer, *XII Corps*, 262.
22. *From Texas to Teisnach with the 457 AAA AW Battalion*, 124.
23. *The Combat History of the 731st Field Artillery Battalion: Never Forget*, n.d., 32.
24. Report After Action Against Enemy, December 1944, 452nd AAA AW Bn (MBL), National Archives and Records Administration: CABN-452-0.3, A/A Reports.
25. *The Combat History of the 731st Field Artillery Battalion*, 33.
26. Dyer, *XII Corps*, 228.
27. Ibid, 288.
28. Ibid, 294. Underlining not in original.
29. Report After Action Against Enemy, December 1944, 452nd AAA AW Bn (MBL), National Archives and Records Administration: CABN-452-0.3, A/A Reports.
30. 'Negro Ack-Ack Men Keep 'Em Falling for 3rd', *Stars and Stripes*, 28 December 1944.
31. 'Fox Holes Kill All Racial Feeling', *The Daily American*, 1 January 1945.

Chapter 4

1. Dyer, *XII Corps*, 300, 304.
2. Medical Detachment, 452nd AAA Auto WPNS BL (MBL), 30 June 1945, semi-annual report, Dwight D. Eisenhower Library, Box 296.
3. Manrho and Pütz, *Bodenplatte*, 462.
4. Dyer, *XII Corps*, 228.
5. Headquarters XII Corps, General Orders 4, 13 January 1945, National Archives and Records Administration: CABN-452-1.13, General Orders.
6. Maranes probably refers to the French Morane-Saulnier M.S.406 fighter, employed by the French forces.

7. Dyer, *XII Corps*, 304.
8. Report After Action Against Enemy, January 1945, 1944, 452nd AAA AW Bn (MBL), National Archives and Records Administration: CABN-452-0.3, A/A Reports.
9. Ibid.
10. George A. Buck, 'Four Barrels', 945th Field Artillery Battalion.
11. Dyer, *XII Corps*, 334.
12. Ibid, 338.
13. Unit Report 224, 18 March 1945, 452nd AAA AW Bn (MBL), National Archives and Records Administration: CABN-452-0.9, Unit Reports 1945.
14. Unit Report No. 224, 18 March 1945, 452nd AAA AW Bn (MBL), National Archives and Records Administration: CABN-452-0.9, Unit Reports 1945.
15. Anti-Aircraft Artillery Notes, Headquarters European Theater of Operations, United States Army, Number 26, 18 April 1945.
16. Ibid.
17. Medical Detachment, 452nd AAA Auto WPNS BL (MBL), 30 June 1945, semi-annual report, Dwight D. Eisenhower Library, Box 296.
18. 'Across the Rhine', *Stars and Stripes*, 25 March 1945.
19. Anti-Aircraft Notes, Headquarters European Theater of Operations, United States Army, Number 26, 18 April 1945.
20. Dyer, *XII Corps*, 378. Italics in original. Underlining not in original.
21. Anti-Aircraft Notes, Number 26, 18 April 1945.
22. Ibid.
23. Dyer, *XII Corps*, 378.
24. Walter Bedell Smith, 'Eisenhower's Six Great Decisions: The Only Way It Could End', *The Saturday Evening Post*, volume 219, 13 July 1946.
25. Dyer, *XII Corps*, 398, 402.
26. The 191st Field Artillery Battalion, Combat Operations 1945, accessed through: https://donl702.tripod.com/191st/Combat_Operations-1945.html.
27. Report After Action Against Enemy, April 1945, 452nd AAA AW Bn (MBL), National Archives and Records Administration: CABN-452-0.3, A/A Reports.

28. Dyer, *XII Corps*, 424.
29. Ibid, 432, 434.
30. Report After Action Against Enemy, May 1945, 1944, 452nd AAA AW Bn (MBL), National Archives and Records Administration: CABN-452-0.3, A/A Reports.
31. Ibid.
32. It's unclear which town is meant exactly, since there's no town in the area called Scherenben.
33. Medical Detachment, 452nd AAA Auto WPNS BL (MBL), 30 June 1945, semi-annual report, Dwight D. Eisenhower Library, Box 296.
34. Headquarters 55th Anti-Aircraft Artillery Brigade, 27 June 1945, categorization of units, National Archives and Records Administration: CABN-452.

Chapter 5

1. *From Texas to Teisnach with the 457 AAA AW Battalion*, 51.
2. Ibid, 159.
3. Lamar C. Ratcliffe, 'AAA With A Corps (Based On AAA Activities In XII Corps, Third U.S. Army, 1 August 1944 to 8 May 1945)', 1946-1947.
4. Ratcliffe, 'AAA With A Corps', 9.
5. Ibid, 8.
6. *The Combat History of the 731st Field Artillery Battalion*, 32.
7. John E. Threlfall, *Fighting with Patton's Third Army: World War II Memoirs of George F. Threlfall*, 2010, 66-67.
8. Lee, *The Employment of Negro Troops*, 185.
9. Ibid, 659.
10. The 191st Field Artillery Battalion, Combat Operations 1945, accessed through: https://donl702.tripod.com/191st/Combat_Operations-1945.html.
11. Unit Report No. 241, 4 April 1945, 452nd AAA AW Bn (MBL), National Archives and Records Administration: CABN-452-0.9, Unit Reports 1945.
12. Headquarters 49th AAA Brigade, APO 758, U.S. Army, 25 June 1945, National Archives and Records Administration: CABN-452.

Index